Critical Human Resource Development

Critical Human Resource Development
Beyond Orthodoxy

Edited by
Dr Clare Rigg
Professor Jim Stewart
Professor Kiran Trehan

Prentice Hall
FINANCIAL TIMES

An imprint of Pearson Education
Harlow, England • London • New York • Boston • San Francisco • Toronto
Sydney • Tokyo • Singapore • Hong Kong • Seoul • Taipei • New Delhi
Cape Town • Madrid • Mexico City • Amsterdam • Munich • Paris • Milan

Pearson Education Limited

Edinburgh Gate
Harlow
Essex CM20 2JE
England

and Associated Companies throughout the world

Visit us on the World Wide Web at:
www.pearsoned.co.uk

First published 2007

ISBN-13: 978-0-273-70559-8
ISBN-10: 0-273-70559-8

British Library Cataloguing-in-Publication Data
A catalogue record for this book is available from the British Library

Library of Congress Cataloging-in-Publication Data
A catalog record for this book is available from the Library of Congress

10 9 8 7 6 5 4 3 2 1
10 09 08 07 06

Typeset in 10.5pt Sabon by 30
Printed and bound in Great Britain by Bell & Bain Ltd, Glasgow

The publisher's policy is to use paper manufactured from sustainable forests.

Contents

Contents

About the contributors

Lisa Anderson is a lecturer in HRM at the University of Liverpool Management School. Her research interests centre around social learning, particularly how language use in groups helps to create critical reflection. Other areas of interest include action learning and management and leadership development in the SME sector.

Dr Helen Francis is a Senior Lecturer and Teaching Fellow in the Business School at Napier University. Her research interests include the application of discourse theory in management research, theory development in HRM/Development, and management learning – including work on emotional intelligence training, the psychological contract, and changing roles of HR practitioners. Helen regularly presents her work at national and international conferences on HRM/Development and Critical Management Studies. She has published a wide range of articles in leading management journals and has contributed to two forthcoming textbooks on HRD.

Dr Brendon Harvey is a highly experienced action researcher, consultant and university lecturer. Formerly Senior Lecturer at two business schools, Brendon now runs his own consultancy that specializes in research and evaluation for the public and private sectors. He is also an Associate Lecturer of the Open University.

Dr Tim Hatcher spent 25 years working in international business and industry in performance improvement and quality management before coming to academia. He is currently Associate Professor and Program Coordinator of Training & Development and Adult Education, at North Carolina State University. His research interest and passion is business ethics and enhancing the social impact of organizations through HRD. He has published over 70 articles, book chapters and books.

Dr Leonard Holmes has over 28 years' experience in the training and development field, as practitioner, teacher and researcher, working in and with organizations in the private, public and not-for-profit sectors. The thesis for his PhD, awarded by the Institute of Education, London University, was a critical examination of the learning and competence movement.

Jean Kellie is a lecturer at the University of Hull Business School, particularly involved with Masters programmes and corporate management programmes. Her teaching interests are predominantly in the field of Organizational Behaviour and Human Resource Management. Her research interests lie in the area of management and organization development together with a range of associated themes – management learning, pedagogical practice, the organization and context of management learning and the social construction of management knowledge.

Dr Beverly Dawn Metcalfe is based in the University of Hull Business School, as well as being Research Associate at the Centre for Diversity and Work Psychology, Manchester Business School and Visiting Research Fellow in International Diversity at the Graduate School of Management of Australia's Griffith University. She teaches, writes and consults on equal opportunities, managing diversity and gender mainstreaming; management and leadership development; cultural change, HRD and performance management, international HRM, cross-cultural and comparative HRD. Her two main current research interests are international dimensions of human resource development and gender management and organization analysis. Within the field of HRD she is interested in unravelling the cultural and societal process that influence HRD systems in the global economy. Her interest in gender, management and organization analysis is underpinned by a critical management studies and feminist theory framework especially the post-structuralist writers Luce Irigaray and Helene Cixous.

Dr Valerie Owen-Pugh is a chartered psychologist and member of the academic staff at the Institute of Lifelong Learning, the University of Leicester, where she currently assists in the delivery of distance-learning postgraduate courses on topics including Training and Development, Human Resource Management and Researching Work and Learning. Her current research interests are in figurational sociology, group processes, the social dimensions of learning, developmental relationships in organizations, and careers in sport, counselling and psychotherapy.

Dr Christopher J. Rees is Programme Director for MSc in Organisational Change and Development at the Institute for Development Policy and Management, University of Manchester. He has research interests in organizational behaviour and human resource management and experience of research and teaching HR in Central and Eastern Europe.

Dr Clare Rigg is Senior Lecturer in the School of Business and Social Studies at the Institute of Technology, Tralee, Ireland. Her early work was in local government and the voluntary sector working on urban regeneration. For many years she has worked with practitioners from all sectors, integrating action learning and action research into issues of organization development, leadership and management development, and to improving inter-agency working. She has researched and written on action learning, critical action learning, management learning and HRD.

Dr Sally Sambrook studied and worked at Nottingham Business School for eight years and retains her links there as a Visiting Research Fellow in HRD. Sally joined the University of Wales Bangor (UWB) in 1999 and after several years as Lecturer in Human Resource Management (HRM) joined the Faculty of Health, where she is Programme Leader for the MSc in Health and Social Care Leadership. Sally leads several MSc modules, including Research Methods, Managing and Developing People, and Organizational Behaviour and Leadership, and has recently been awarded a Teaching Fellowship for excellence in teaching. With her nursing background and involvement in training other nurses, Sally's research interests include studying HRD within the health service. In addition, Sally researches the changing role of HRD professionals, managers and learners, explores the factors influencing learning in work and has recently become interested in a critical approach to the study of HRD. Sally has published numerous journal articles, edited texts and book chapters on HRD and was awarded Outstanding Paper, by the Emerald Literati Club in 2005.

Professor Jim Stewart is Professor of HRD at Nottingham Business School where he teaches and researches HRD. He is Joint Course Leader of the School's highly successful Doctorate in Business Administration and, as an active researcher and writer, is the author and co-editor of ten books as well as many journal articles and conference papers. These include special editions of the *Journal of European Industrial Training* and the *International Journal of Training and Development* which he co-edited with Clare and Kiran. Jim is also Chair of the University Forum for HRD and holds three appointed roles with the Chartered Institute of Personnel and Development, including membership of the Vice President for Learning, Training and Development's Advisory Committee.

Professor Richard Thorpe is professor of Management Development and Deputy Director of the Keyworth Institute at the University of Leeds. His research interests include: performance, entrepreneurship, management learning and management development. He has a strong commitment to process methodologies and a focus on action in all its forms; an interest in and commitment to the development of doctoral students and a commitment to collaborative working with colleagues on projects of mutual interest.

Professor Kiran Trehan is Head of Department of Management at the University of Central England where she undertakes research, teaching and consultancy with a variety of public and private sector organizations in the area of human resource/organizational development. Her fields of interest include critical approaches to HRD, management learning, power and emotions in organizational development. Her current research interests include critical thinking in HRD, critical reflection and action learning in practice with particular reference to leadership development, power relations and group dynamics.

Claire Valentin is director for MSc programmes in HRD at the University of Edinburgh. She has worked largely in the public and voluntary sectors and as a consultant. Her research interests are in the application of critical approaches to the study of organizational learning and vocational education and training, critical pedagogy in HRD education, and corporate social responsibility.

Acknowledgements

We would like to express our thanks to the contributors to this volume, for the time and patience they have put in to preparing their chapters and responding to our requests for changes in tight timescales. We all have family without whose support and forebearance this book would not have reached fruition: Jim would like to thank his wife, Pat; Clare is ever appreciative of her partner Simon, and children Róisín and Danny Cian; and Kiran thanks Aaron her nephew for his inspiration and patience. Finally we would like to thank Amanda McPartlin at Pearson for backing the project.

Publisher's Acknowledgements

We are grateful to the following for permission to reproduce copyright material:

Table 7.1 © 1983 from *Guide to the Successful Thesis and Dissertation: A Handbook for Students and Faculty* by Mauch, J.E. and Birch, J.W. Reproduced by permission of Routledge/Taylor & Francis Group, LLC; Table 7.2 reprinted by permission of Sage Publications Ltd, from Vince, R. (1996) 'Experiential Management Education as the Practice of Change' in French, R. and Grey, C. (eds) *Rethinking Management Education*.

In some instances we have been unable to trace the owners of copyright material, and we would appreciate any information that would enable us to do so.

Introduction

A critical take on a critical turn in HRD

Clare Rigg, Jim Stewart and Kiran Trehan

■ A critical turn in HRD

We first proposed a 'critical turn in HRD' in autumn 2001 as a stream for the 'Critical Management Studies' conference held at Lancaster University, UK in June 2002. Critiques of the values, purpose and approaches to HRD were only beginning to gain attention as areas of academic debate and practitioner concern. Since then interest has grown and there have been a number of related publications, with edited collections such as Monica Lee's (2003) *HRD in a Complex World*, Carole Elliott and Sharon Turnbull's (2005) *Critical Thinking in Human Resource Development*, Tim Hatcher's (2002) *Ethics and HRD*, and special journal issues dedicated to the theme of critical HRD in the *Journal of European Industrial Training* (Trehan, Rigg and Stewart, 2004) and *International Journal of Training and Development* (Trehan, Rigg and Stewart, 2006). Through these collections we see the development of a body of accounts on expediting a critical approach to HRD. However, now there is this build-up of experience it is also timely to offer critical reflections on critical HRD: to look behind and beyond at what is problematic, as well as recording the achievements.

This book adds to the debate by contributing a series of accounts from practitioners who have been practically trying to work with critical HRD, attempting to implement concepts and methods in their work as HRD practitioners. Not only does this book engage with the theoretical ideas and debates surrounding critical HRD, but it also differs from others by offering a breadth of experience in expediting those ideas. Added to this it includes examples from working with critical HRD in three different contexts: as professional development, within workplaces and within the classroom. Each of these contexts offers its own challenges such that, taken together, this collection provides an original set of insights into potentials and pitfalls, expectations and concerns of advancing a critical turn on HRD in practice. Its uniqueness lies in bridging theory and practice, offering practical ideas and examples.

The purpose of this introduction is to introduce what we mean by taking 'a critical turn in HRD', to argue why this is necessary and to outline the structure of the book. In elucidating the question, 'Why a critical turn?', we start with an examination of traditional HRD, by looking at four conventions: its purpose; the core assumptions of human behaviour and relations; underpinning representationalist organization thinking; and customary pedagogical approaches to the teaching of HRD. We go on to describe what commonly is encompassed by 'a critical turn', or being critical, before arguing why it is time to critique the critical turn in HRD, in the sense of being able to reflect now there is some experience of working with critical approaches to HRD. This introduction concludes with an overview of the structure of the book, providing an introduction to the individual chapters, the themes they are grouped into and the ways in which the book can be used as a teaching text.

■ Traditional HRD: purpose, approach and rationale

HRD has never been neatly and uncontentiously defined, not least because of its multi-disciplinary nature. In general terms, HRD has been described as being concerned with 'supporting and facilitating the learning of individuals, groups and organizations' (McGoldrick, Stewart and Watson, 2002: 396). However, whether the emphasis is put on individuals or organizations, and whether learning is supported through instruction, self-direction or some other means varies, influenced by the variety of ways in which what is now encompassed by the term HRD has evolved across the world. For example, in America there are strong roots in adult education; in Europe, the origins are more strongly rooted in work-based training activities. Internationally, a third key influence comes from organization development. Others have argued more eloquently that these multiple origins have produced a multi-disciplinary ancestry of economics, behaviourist psychology and sociology. Readers who want to familiarize themselves further with debates on what constitutes HRD are guided to the following introductory readings: Garavan *et al.*, 2000; Garavan *et al.*, 2004; Lee, 2003; McLean, 1998; Russ-Eft, 2000; Swanson, 1992; Walton, 1999; and Weinberger, 1998.

■ Why a critical turn in HRD?

From this literature it is possible to say that traditional HRD, though multi-disciplinary and multi-rooted, is nevertheless characterized by key features which define it as traditional and lacking critical perspective. And these give us our four main reasons for advocating a critical turn:

1 Whether the focus of development is individual or organizational, the purpose of HRD has been seen fundamentally to improve performance. In other words, HRD traditionally has been overwhelmingly dominated by performative values, preoccupied with improving performance of individuals and/or organizations, with performance invariably defined only in economic terms.

2 The expectations of what HRD might deliver has been disproportionately dependent on humanistic assumptions about individual identity and self.

3 Traditional HRD has typically also been informed by representationalist organization perspectives, that is, the attempt to capture and describe an organization as if it were an external reality such as an actual structure or system (see Clegg and Hardy, 1999 for further reading on this theme).

4 The HRD curriculum has traditionally been disseminated through traditional pedagogical methods, with minimal attention to issues of power and emotion in the learning process.

In the following sections we elaborate on each of these four critiques of traditional HRD.

■ Critique one – the purpose of HRD

There is a growing body of concern amongst HRD practitioners and academics over the wider consequences of our work. Whilst we might describe our interventions with people in benign terms such as enabling, developing potential, empowerment and such like, are we failing to see a bigger picture of our work? Might our work in fact have the consequence of refining individual skills and developing organizational capabilities to continue operating in ways that have serious human and ecological consequences? Corporate scandals such as Enron[1], Arthur Andersen[2], WorldCom[3], ImClone Systems[4] and mis-selling of financial products such as endowments[5], have focused attention on the ethics of managing. Events as far afield as Cancun or even the UK Hutton Inquiry have directed critical attention onto the social relations of work organizations and the impact of business on people's lives. Such events provide accumulating impetus for those who argue for management education and development to integrate consideration of social and environmental terms of business.

The traditional view of HRD has been a technocratic 'development of effective practitioners'. Invariably the rationale for development is to better pursue competitive advantage; to 'meet the changing character of market conditions' (Storey *et al.*, 1997: 207); or to fulfil the needs of business strategy – 'organizational management is a vital ingredient in securing improved business performance' (Woodall and Winstanley, 1998: 3). The performative rationale for such development conceives of people not only as resources to be developed and from whom more value can be extracted, but also as technocrats who, in becoming more resourceful, will become more effective at extracting value from other resources and delivering benefits for the customer and shareholder. There has been very little consideration of the role HRD might play in either preventing or sustaining such corporate behaviour as the scandals above exemplify. There is rarely consideration of the non-financial costs across a value chain in technicist development and where there is, it is bundled into a separate subject termed 'business ethics' or 'corporate social responsibility'. The social relations of work (Whittington, 1992), the emotional (Fineman, 2000) and psychosocial dynamics of organizations have no place and there is little space for raising questions about the environmental and international consequences of business activity. Questions of business standards or the role and moral basis of business in society receive no priority.

McGoldrick *et al.* (2002) were an early exception to the narrowly economic performative focus of HRD when they identified three main themes of HRD. They argued first that, 'HRD has a central focus on and concern with learning'; second, that HRD is likely to have a wider constituency and purpose than organizational success, which suggests that HRD practice has a broader accountability than performance, and third, that 'HRD is clearly a political activity', in that it is central to power and control processes.

Within HRD there have long been inherent tensions within competing rationales for whether the focus is developing the resourcefulness of individuals or developing the capacity of the organization's resources. But a further challenge comes from critiques of the purpose of business which question whether the world can sustain organizational practices that do not incorporate wider societal responsibilities. This line of critique leads to questions such as: Is it good enough simply to be concerned with the production of better technocrats? What is the purpose of HRD? What or whose values inform those decisions?

These are the questions that begin to define what is meant by 'critical HRD'. In the past decade, ideas of critical thinking have been increasingly related to management and HRD more widely. A key rationale for encouraging human resource developers to be critical lies in the realization of how powerful corporations are in the world now, yet how poorly traditional HRD has prepared those who run them for considering questions of power and responsibility. Hatcher and Lee (2003) have made the following challenge to HRD:

'How can a profession that espouses democratic ideals such as workplace empowerment, teamwork and the promise of ethical behaviours support systems (defined here as organizations) that are undemocratic even totalitarian; that view workers and society as mere resources or worse as objects of abuse?'

▨ Critique two – humanist assumptions about human behaviour and relations

Our second rationale for taking a critical turn in HRD is what we argue is an unbalanced reliance on humanist assumptions about identity and personhood that imbues traditional HRD. A central discourse of HRD is the value of focusing on the needs and aspirations of individuals and that the rationale for HRD interventions is to help to bring out the best in people so that all people can have the best in life or at least to cope better with the world. Of course, at one level how could anyone disagree with such aspirations of helping individuals to fulfil themselves? Key elements of HRD are self-development and personal development, which many of us use unquestioningly. However, several commentators shed light on the limitations and biases resulting from humanist perspectives on 'self' and 'identity'. Kuchinke (2005) argues that the literatures on HRD, HR and management are dominated by an instrumental view of personhood and self, to the exclusion of alternative discourses. He argues this limited insight into how the 'self' is constructed has curtailed understanding, theorizing and practical application of HRD. In a similar vein, Hughes (2005) observes how HRD as a concept tends to be assumed to be an egalitarian and gender neutral one. She argues to the contrary that HRD is predicated on Enlightenment and Cartesian rationality and that 'humanist personhood privileges a masculine, self-directed, autonomous, choosing subject'. Such criticisms problematize a core principle of HRD, the autonomous, self-directing and self-fulfilling 'I', highlighting how, far from being universal, they are culturally and temporally specific, open only to some members of society.

Others have problematized humanism's premise of the rational self. Valerie Owen-Pugh, later in this book, argues that 'underlying much HRD literature is the unstated assumption that organizations are composed of groups of individuals who will respond in predictable, logical and therefore, arguably, "rational" ways to the introduction and working through of dynamic organizational systems'. Dirkx (2005) also highlights how behavioural and humanistic perspectives have largely dominated the discourse of workplace learning. Grounded in modernist assumptions of rationality and the progressive accumulation of knowledge and skill, he argues that these perspectives oversimplify our complex relationships with work.

Our call for a critical turn in HRD derives from a conviction that whilst humanist assumptions might be good for helping people to cope with the world HRD also needs to be helping people to change the world.

5

▮ Critique three – representationalist organization perspectives

The third rationale for a critical perspective arises from the reliance of traditional HRD on representationalist perspectives on organization and the limiting consequences this has for research and practice. Although recent theorizing on HRD has broadened to encompass learning and to see HRD as integral to organizing processes, HRD research remains dominated by HRD defined as training activities and by a reification of organizations in which they are conceived of as 'things', particularly structures. This narrowly frames the possibilities for research, encouraging a quantitative approach, so only measuring the easily measurable dimensions like expenditure, training days and qualifications. The consequences for HRD have been highlighted by McGoldrick *et al.* (2002) who argue that impoverished research has a seriously detrimental impact on theory.

Going beyond representationalist perspectives in HRD has implications for research in terms of what is researched and how. For example, if HRD is framed as learning, the research focus shifts to processes through which individuals learn and onto organizational processes which promote learning. If a discourse perspective is taken where 'organizations' are conceived as 'networks of shared meaning which are created, perpetuated and modified through discursive practices', research can focus on the 'social relationship processes', the language used, the discursive resources and the practices deployed. Taking a discursive view of HRD implies therefore to research how HRD is done and talked about, and how development occurs in the course of talking and working.

Also implicit within traditional HRD research and practice has been the presumption of knowledge and practice to be objective, apolitical and value-free. Many writers have challenged this and argued the need to deconstruct the discourse of practice. Edwards and Potter (1992: 155), for example, writing on adult education, argued: ' "practice" is already informed by overt or covert discursive understandings and exercises of power'. Watson (1994: 2), writing on management: 'managers themselves, however much they tend to scorn the very idea of theory, are inevitably theorists of a sort.' And Schein (1992: 97), writing on shared assumptions about nature, reality and truth, stated:

> 'A fundamental part of every culture is a set of assumptions about what is real, how one determines or discovers what is real... how members of a group determine what is relevant information, how they interpret information, how they determine when they have enough of it to decide whether or not to act, and what action to take.'

This has important constraints on practice. For example, Ruona (2005) suggests that most modern change models are quite ill-positioned to provide HRD professionals with an authentic understanding of the change process. She argues for a more naturalistic and phenomenological understanding of change as a central feature in working towards more critical HRD perspectives of the relationship.

■ Critique four – critical pedagogy

The fourth reason we advocate for a critical turn in HRD is that traditionally the HRD curriculum has, for the most part, been disseminated through traditional pedagogical methods. However, increasing awareness of the influence of power relations in shaping pedagogical agendas has provided considerable impetus for the issue of critical HRD. There has been a growing demand in the academic literature of the past few years for HRD educators to engage more critically with their subject than has been the tradition (see, for example, Welton (1995)).

The use of the term 'critical' here is broader than the sense of constantly questioning taken-for-granted ideas and practices (Watson, 1999). 'Critical thinking' as used by critical management and critical education writers has a specific meaning, concerned with achieving a society with social justice and free from oppression (howsoever defined). Guba and Lincoln, for example, suggest the aim of critical inquiry is 'the "critique and transformation" of the social, political, cultural, economic, ethnic and gender structures that constrain and exploit humankind' (1994: 113). Likewise, Carr and Kemmis exhibit a concern for the outcome of critical thinking, 'to articulate a view of theory that has the central task of emancipating people from the "positivist domination of thought" ' (1986: 130). In allied areas such as management and management learning there are also established arguments for strengthening the critical perspective (Alvesson and Willmott, 1998) to the labour process and for a revision of management education generally (French and Grey, 1996). Critical thinking here is intertwined with the use and generation of critical theory (abbreviated by some authors as CT). As Alvesson and Willmott see it (1996: 12–13):

> 'The intent of CT (*deriving from the pre-second world war Frankfurt School and neo-Marxist thinkers such as Max Horkheimer, Theodor Adorno and Herbert Marcuse*) is to challenge the legitimacy and counter the development of oppressive institutions and practices.'

Habermas, for instance, saw critical theory as the product of applying Marx's method of critique: 'relentless criticism of all existing conditions' (as cited by Carr and Kemmis, 1986: 138). For Habermas the aim of critique is 'for the individual to be able, through his or her own transformed self-understanding to interpret herself and her situation differently and so also alter those conditions which are repressive' (Carr and Kemmis, 1986: 138). This introduced the concept of 'critical self-reflection', drawn from psychoanalytic methods, referring to a critical questioning of the content of self-understanding and constraints on freedom and autonomy.

The hopes of critical educators, such as Freire, are that criticism is the pedagogic route to conscientization, where conscientization refers to 'learning to

7

perceive social, political, and economic contradictions, and to take action against the oppressive elements of reality' (Freire, 1972: 15). Ideas of critical thinking have also been developed by feminists and post-colonial educators such as bell hooks, Patricia Collins and Heidi Mirza, also centring the idea of experiential learning, in the sense of starting from the black student's social reality. For example, for bell hooks, transformation is a struggle to work against a colonizing mind-set towards 'that historical moment when one begins to think critically about the self and identity in relation to one's political circumstances' (1993: 147).

See also Welch (1994), Gore (1993), Jackson (1997) and Weiner (1994) for an exploration of feminist educators.

■ A critical turn in practice

The critical turn on HRD urges HRD teachers to 'analyse HRD in terms of its social, moral and political significance and to challenge HRD practice rather than seek to sustain it' (Hughes, 2000). The challenges may come from different perspectives, as we have shown, from critical theory, liberationist (Freirian), feminist and post-colonialist scholarship, to Marxism and labour process analysis. While differences between these schools of thought are too significant to be overlooked, together they comprise a critical perspective, which provides a basis for rethinking HRD education.

When applying a critical approach to HRD education, however, a critical pedagogy means not only offering a challenging view of HRD interventions and management as social, political and economic practice. Critical teaching and learning also deploys methods that stimulate student participation of a kind that is rare in other forms of academic education. Reynolds (1998) describes this as a combination of content radical (subject matter that raises questions of power, social relations, environmental consequences, etc.) and process radical (pedagogical relations that are likely to include some of action learning sets, learning community and critical reflection which subvert traditional teacher/learner power relations). In this sense, critical learning goes beyond critique, in the Watson (1999) sense of thinking and arguing or questioning of convention, to also critique through practice the power dynamics of learning relationships.

In practice, the principles of a critical pedagogy in HRD are applied in different ways. Taking content first, critical perspectives might be reflected in the curriculum, drawing from the range of post-colonialist, feminist or Marxian, etc. ideas (Nord and Jermier, 1992); it could be manifest in the kinds of material used – incorporating cinema and fictional literature – for example, McGivern and Thompson (2000), and in drawing on students' work experiences as well as their experience of the course itself (Grey *et al.*, 1996). A critical stance is also reflected in the choice of analytical frameworks introduced to students, whether deconstructionist (Townley, 1994) or applying feminist inquiry and cultural critique (Hughes, 2000).

Whichever critical perspective is applied, its characteristics are likely to include:

- questioning assumptions and taken-for-granteds, asking questions which are not meant to be asked;
- foregrounding processes of power and noting how inequalities of power intersect with social factors such as race, gender or age;
- identifying competing discourses and the sectional interests reflected in them; and ultimately
- developing a workplace and social milieu characterized more by justice than by inequality or exploitation.

With regards to process critical methods, recent influences from radical education (Giroux, 1992), feminist pedagogy (Weiler, 1991) and critical theory (French and Grey, 1996) have given fresh impetus to the development of more participative, less hierarchical approaches to teaching and learning. Approaches such as the learning community (Reynolds, 1999), or more critical interpretations of action learning (Willmott, 1997; Rigg and Trehan, 2003), apply a critical perspective in both content and method, reflecting longer-standing influences of educators who have 'called into question the political and normative underpinnings of traditional classroom pedagogical styles' (Giroux, 1992: 65). So, for example, the learning community (Reynolds, 1999) is participative in that it offers an opportunity for choice in the direction and content of learning through shared decision-making within the course. Students involved in this approach, as they would be in 'critical action learning', have an opportunity to base their learning on their professional experience and to select the ideas with which to make sense of it. The 'learning community' and 'critical action learning' therefore, illustrate possibilities for both a methodology and a curriculum, which reflect a critical perspective in HRD. Not only is conceptual content and its application based on critical perspectives, but methods, procedures and relationships are developed in ways which are consistent with them.

Opening the complexity of tutor and student relations to critique has rich potential for learning experientially about power, as it is exercised, for example, by tutors over resources, structuring the agenda or controlling assessment. Through process radical pedagogy, a critical approach to HRD also exposes managers to the ways in which discursive practices are deployed to express dominant values, beliefs and ideas, in order to convey meaning (van Dijk, 1997). As such, critical pedagogy offers managers different resources on which to draw to make sense of and to enact their practice. The significance is to address discursive closure: how, as Francis and D'Annunzio-Green (2004) describe it 'orders of discourses set boundaries upon managers' construction of meaning'.

■ Up to this point

So far in this introduction we have explored what is meant by 'traditional HRD', by looking at four conventions: its purpose, the core assumptions of human behaviour and relations, underpinning representationalist organization thinking, and customary pedagogical approaches to the teaching of HRD. We have also described what is commonly encompassed by 'a critical turn' or being critical. In the next section we will argue why it is time to critique the critical turn in HRD, in the sense of holding the experiences of working with critical perspectives as HRD practitioners and educators up to the critical spotlight.

The rationale for a critical pedagogy is that HRD practitioners ought not only to be conscious but also to be concerned that their interventions within organizations, whether as educationalists, as internal HRD professionals or as external HRD consultants, impact on the ways organization members make choices and take actions which ultimately have political consequences on the environment, on exploitation of people or on extremes of wealth and poverty. In this sense, the rationale has been that it is no longer acceptable that HRD practitioners allow themselves, or those they work with, to maintain the illusion that their choices and actions are without political consequences.

■ Beyond orthodoxy – time to critique the critical turn

Above we have outlined four arguments for a critical turn in HRD:

1 The purpose of HRD has been overwhelmingly dominated by performative values, preoccupied with improving performance of individuals and/or organizations.
2 HRD has been over-reliant on humanistic assumptions about individual identity and self.
3 HRD has typically been informed by representationalist organization perspectives that limit thinking about research and practice.
4 The HRD curriculum has traditionally been disseminated through traditional pedagogical methods, with minimal attention to issues of power and emotion in either the learning process or the wider implications of HRD practice.

Despite the increased interest in a critical perspective on HRD, there is a dearth of empirical experience on expediting critical HRD. Nevertheless, in the background, a number of practitioners and academics have been quietly working with critical approaches to learning and development and have built up a degree of experience of the possibilities, dangers and constraints of critical HRD.

A core rationale for this book is to draw on the experience of some of those who have been trying to expedite critical HRD and in reflecting on that experience to deploy a critical gaze on the principles and claims of critical HRD itself, lest they themselves become unquestioned orthodoxies. Already in the public domain there are some significant critiques which we wish to highlight here, namely, problematizing critical reflection, a fervour for reflection and self-development that borders on moral evangelism, and a failure to integrate emotions and power in the teaching and learning process.

A primary critique is that critical reflection is not so easy to expedite in practice as to articulate in theory. Firstly, there is the potential for students to resist engagement in critical reflection, because to do so would be to question their professional identity, challenge their source of status (Reynolds, 1998) or run counter to the pressures to conform to organizational ideologies (Jackall, 1988). A second main critique is that practitioners and students find critical theory 'irrelevant, unreal and impractical' (Reed and Anthony, 1992: 607) or simply impenetrable (Reynolds, 1998). A further danger relates to the potential adverse psychological and social consequences for individuals of engaging in critical reflection, as Reynolds cautions: 'It can prove unsettling, mentally or emotionally and a source of disruption at home or at work. It carries the risk to employment and even – if we include stress related illness – to life itself' (1998: 16). Brookfield (1994) describes the dissonance produced by critical reflection, as the 'darker side' of such an approach and Reynolds (1998) warns of the production of cultural misfits, facing 're-entry' problems on their return to work, feeling frustrated or powerless with their new awareness. Perhaps most pessimistic are Alvesson and Willmott (1992) speculating that 'enhanced ecological consciousness and greater freedom and creativity at work – likely priorities emerging from emancipatory change – may result in bankruptcy and unemployment (1992: 448).

A second interesting but concerning trend has been a new moral evangelism within HRD. Reflective practice has become almost obligatory within HRD, but the instrumental reflections of 'what did I do', 'what did I learn', 'what would I do differently' have been found to be limited. In a search for more challenging self-development tools, critical self-reflection has seen considerable recent growth. Fundamental to this has been the assumption that through critical self-reflection individuals become conscious of the oppression of, or constraints on, their lives and take action to bring about change for the better. Advocates of critical pedagogy, such as Freire, argue that criticism is the pedagogic route to conscientization, where conscientization is the 'Process in which men (sic) not as recipients, but as knowing subjects, achieve a deepening awareness both of the socio-cultural reality which shapes their lives and of

11

their capacity to transform that reality' (Freire, 1970, cited in Cavanaugh and Prasad, 1996: 89.) For Fay (1987: 90), critical education provides:

> 'The means by which people can achieve a much clearer picture of who they are, and of what the real meaning of their social practices is, as a first step of becoming different sorts of people with different sorts of social arrangements.'

However, the use of critical self-reflection has several implications and raises questions of 'why', 'how' and 'with' 'what assumptions?' within HRD? Perriton (2005) has argued that some practitioners and theorists within the HRD field speak about development in an evangelical way and without admitting to the existence of boundaries, an end point to the process or people's rights to say 'No more'. She argues there is a view that 'development' is an inherent good and therefore can never do harm in excess.

The third critique we want to advance here is to maintain that much of HRD pedagogy, even that which is intended to support a more critical approach, does not provide a structure or educational processes adequate to the task of working with, and developing an understanding of, emotions and power within HRD. Traditional mainstream HRD practice ignores emotions and power or contributes to their suppression. Alternative HRD pedagogies, while less hierarchical and placing more emphasis on personal and professional experience, tend to unquestioningly advocate the value of consensus, which either tends to deny power dynamics or attempts to assimilate them and the differences they are derived from (Trehan and Rigg, 2002).

This is a starting point for going beyond orthodoxy in critical HRD. But as experience of working with critical HRD has grown in recent years there are more lessons to draw. The aim of this book is to present accounts from HRD practitioners who have been working with critical HRD ideas in practice, in their classroom teaching, with corporate clients and as organization members. The collection is both about critical HRD and beyond critical HRD, in the sense of going beyond a simplistic unquestioning, non-reflexive advocacy of critical orthodoxy.

■ Structure of the book

The book is divided into four parts covering themes of:

- A critical turn in human resource development
- In the workplace
- Constraints in the classroom
- Critique of critical orthodoxies.

To aid the book's use for teaching, each part starts with its own introduction to the core themes and ends with a set of activities.

Part One: A critical turn in human resource development contains three chapters that present further arguments for why it is time to go beyond performative and humanist traditions of HRD. In the first of these, Sally Sambrook makes play on the word 'critical' to ask whether it is now a critical time for HRD? Structuring her discussion through a series of questions she further explores the themes of this opening chapter, of what is HRD and what is meant by being 'critical'. But she goes further in raising additional important questions about critical HRD, specifically, why be critical; is it just academics and not practitioners who have the time and space to be critical, and is it ethical to teach practitioners to be critical if their performance-orientated work context renders this problematic? As such, her chapter both advocates reasons for critical HRD and raises challenges to it.

In Chapter 2, Tim Hatcher repudiates many of his earlier ideas and publications around ethics and HRD, arguing that ethics as it has been described and practised in HRD has done little to enhance the profession and has in fact helped to maintain it in an oppressive state. Drawing on concepts of deep ecology and social ecology he offers proposals for the profession to develop into a 'deep', sustainable profession.

Jim Stewart pursues questions of ethics in Chapter 3, starting with a challenge that the study of business ethics is in itself flawed. He presents the proposition that, contrary to a common view that training and development activities are inherently 'good', HRD is of itself an ethical and moral endeavour.

Part Two: In the workplace, contains three chapters that explore tensions and contradictions of working with critical perspectives of HRD in the workplace. Beverly Metcalfe and Christopher Rees in Chapter 4 offer a rare scholarly examination of the role that gender can play in conceptualizing the terrain of HRD inquiry and in unveiling the way in which constructions and reconstructions of gender in organizational spheres can impact the role and status of HRD practices and concerns. In Chapter 5, Helen Francis draws upon a critical discourse perspective to explore the discursive and socially constructed nature of HRD, in the context of a specific case of a firm moving towards a flatter, team-based organizational structure. The relationship between line managers and HRD practitioners and the role of line managers in co-creating HRD practice are explored. The role and power of language in creating meaning, and therefore in changing meaning, is highlighted as a potential alternative to research that has been dominated by normative and unitarist assumptions in which tensions inherent in work organizations and the management of HR are downplayed or ignored.

In Chapter 6 Jean Kellie explores how HRD providers to corporate clients have to grapple with the competing demands of academic enquiry, with its emphasis on question and critique, and the expectations of the profession with its overtly instrumental orientation underpinned by a belief in a tools-and-techniques approach to the practice of management. She suggests that as corporate clients become more confident in influencing the management education curriculum and business schools become responsible for achieving 'outreach' targets there is a need to explore the pedagogical and epistemological issues raised by the shifting domains of management education and management development. In doing so, this chapter develops themes concerning what constitutes 'relevance' in management education.

Part Three: Constraints in the Classroom, is a set of experiences of adopting critical approaches to method and content in teaching HRD in a classroom setting, as distinct from that for a corporate client. In Chapter 7 Lisa Anderson and Richard Thorpe examine three critical epistemologies, namely critical social theory, postmodernism and critical realism, and their potential usefulness as a 'tool for thinking' (McLaughlin and Thorpe, 1993) in an action learning situation. They present an account of a part-time MSc programme, in which theories of both action learning and critical management were integrated to practice to encourage HRD managers to be more critically reflective of their work and their workplace. Chapter 8, from Claire Valentin, seeks to examine how a critical management perspective can inform pedagogical practice in management education, notably in a Master's level programme in HRD. She asks whether, given the increasingly instrumental and performative trends in university education, critical management theory and research can become a tool to understand and inform/transform practice? Chapter 9, by Brendon Harvey explores the dilemmas and tensions involved in working in creative ways with students in the course of their professional studies, in the wider context of their working lives and under the external scrutiny of a professional validating body. In particular he presents examples of using different forms of writing that explore alternative ways of sense-making.

In all the previous parts authors write reflexively about their own practices, but the fourth part **Critique of Critical Orthodoxies** explicitly aims to go beyond simply advocating a critical turn to elucidate some of the limitations and hypocrisies within critical HRD practice. In Chapter 10, Valerie Owen-Pugh gives an alternative interpretation of Lave and Wenger's model of learning, drawing attention to the shadow-side of communities of practice, and arguing that the ubiquity of oppressive aspects of social engagement has remained largely undeveloped and unrecognized. In particular, she draws on the work of Norbert Elias to extend theorizing on subjectivity, power and agency within communities of practice. In Chapter 11, Leonard Holmes asks whether 'the learning turn' in education and training is a liberatory paradigm or an oppressive ideology. He argues that the rhetorical presentation of the case for the learning turn often relies upon claims about both its liberatory and its pragmatic potential, but that conceptually and theoretically the 'learnerist' paradigm will be shown to have serious flaws. The chapter examines how the notion of the learning process as individualized activity, separated from the relationship aspects of teaching, has been and is increasingly being used to alter the balance of control over what should be learnt and how.

In the concluding chapter, Chapter 12, 'Going beyond a critical turn – hypocrisies and contradictions', the editors ask where next for critical perspectives on HRD? They revisit the multiple perspectives on critical HRD, review the aspirations and threats surrounding the field, and explore what going beyond a critical turn means for theory and practice. The chapter's intention is to illuminate some of the assumptions and taken-for-granteds which are in danger of becoming an orthodoxy in critical HRD.

▉ Using the book

This book will be of interest to people in a number of different HRD areas, including organization-based practitioners, independent consultants, lecturers and researchers.

The book takes a critical stance, which is precisely what is required at postgraduate level and for CIPD professional development. It stands in contrast to the majority of books on training which are typically prescriptive, managerialist and focused solely on organizational goals, ignoring those of other stakeholders, and society more widely.

The text can be used in a number of ways. There are practical illustrations of putting critical HRD into practice in three different contexts: as professional development, within workplaces and within the classroom. Each will provide the reader with examples they could use in practice. For those who are interested in the theoretical ideas and debates the collection provides an original set of insights into the potentials and pitfalls, expectations and concerns, of advancing a critical turn on HRD in practice. It offers a bridge between theory and practice and the final part, in particular, advances thinking on future questions for critical HRD.

Notes

1 Enron, the US energy company that collapsed amid scandal in late 2001, evaded billions of dollars in tax with the help of 'some of the nation's finest' accountants, investment banks and lawyers, as reported by the Bateson report, February 2003, commissioned by the US Senate Finance Committee.
2 In 2002 a jury in the US found accountancy firm Arthur Andersen guilty of obstructing justice by shredding documents relating to the failed energy giant Enron.

3 WorldCom, the telecom firm, filed for bankruptcy in 2002 after uncovering $11bn in alleged accounting fraud. In 2003, the company itself and six former employees including the ex-chief executive and former chief financial officer, were charged with 'executing a scheme to artificially inflate bond and stock prices by intentionally filing false information with the Securities & Exchange Commission'. (Source:Accountancy Age.com, 28 August 2003)

4 In 2002 the former president and founder of biotechnology firm ImClone Systems was indicted for fraud in an alleged insider trading scandal. He was accused of providing information to family members that enabled them to sell shares before the price fell.

5 Millions of people in the UK are thought to have been mis-sold mortgage endowment policies during the 1980s and 1990s. Policies were inappropriate for their situations and needs and advisers who sold the products did not fully explain how the endowments worked, the market risks or their suitability for an individual's circumstances.

Part One

A CRITICAL TURN IN HUMAN RESOURCE DEVELOPMENT

Introduction to Part One

Readers will find a set of activities at the end of this and each subsequent part. These activities are not intended to be mandatory or prescriptive, or indeed to be used exclusively as part of academic programmes, though we have as editors selected the content of the book to be relevant to advanced students of the subject. The activities are intended to help readers use the book to make better sense of, and develop a more informed personal understanding of, what 'critical HRD' might mean to them in the varying contexts in which they study and practise HRD. In that respect, the activities are designed first to assist in simple comprehension of what might be new language and concepts for some and second to develop their analysis of critical HRD through application of those concepts.

Each part also has an introduction similar to this one. These serve the purpose of setting the scene for the chapters that follow in each part. Some attempt is made in the part introductions to identify emerging themes and arguments. However, readers will soon realize that the content of individual chapters are capable of multiple interpretations and therefore provide a rich source of debate. We have no wish as editors to close off that debate or to present ourselves as arbiters of what are the 'correct' or most 'useful' interpretations to be taken from chapters and sections. Therefore the introduction to each part is again intended simply as an aid to understanding and further analysis, and perhaps to inform subsequent debate. Such analysis and debate will be the key to learning from the book rather than didactic expositions from the editors.

We have named this first part 'A critical turn in human resource development'. This reflects our view that while the use of the concept of 'critical' is now fairly well established in relation to the study of management and organization, and to a lesser extent management learning, it is only in very recent years that the concept has been applied to HRD. The use of the word 'turn' is then perhaps meant to imply a process rather than an established entity in that 'critical HRD' has yet to achieve the same acceptance in academic study and professional practice that the concept of HRD itself has over the past 15 years or so. It might also suggest a continuum rather than a dichotomy. This latter point is important since in critical management studies there is often an impression of 'either/or' where 'critical' is presented as an alternative to other approaches such as 'functional' with negative connotations being attached to the alternative to critical. The whole expression 'a critical turn' also has other associations. It mirrors that of 'linguistic turn' which expresses both the source and implications of modern, in an historical sense, and postmodern, in a philosophical sense, sociological and psychological analyses of human and social experience. For example, what is referred to as 'constructionist' in the former and 'constructivist' in the latter analyze human and social action in ways which draw to some extent on postmodern philosophy which emphasizes the role and significance of language. But this is only one way of distinguishing 'critical' from non-critical approaches. Earlier approaches and theories such as those which are commonly placed under the broad umbrella of 'critical theory', and which do not rely on the 'linguistic turn' in formulating their concepts and analytical tools, are also applied in producing critical analyses in management and organization studies, and are similarly applied in critical HRD. Thus, the word 'critical' can have multiple and various connotations and has no settled meaning. We have not imposed or even suggested a singular meaning of 'critical' to our contributors. The purpose of this first part is therefore to highlight the varying understandings of 'critical' that can be and are generally applied, and then to feature those that are particularly applied to the study of HRD as a conceptual category.

The first chapter by Sally Sambrook provides the most significant contribution to achieving the first purpose. Through exploring a series of questions she demonstrates how the question 'What is HRD?' continues to generate debate and difficulty which she links to the different discursive (or theoretical) traditions writers and practitioners in different countries draw from, in particular their contrasting ideas about individuality and organizations. The chapter examines a range of meanings that can be attached to 'critical' and explores the implications of a number of these for research and practice in HRD. Drawing on key critical models, Sally Sambrook holds both her own research and HRD generally up to scrutiny to question how it is done, how it is researched and who is involved. The chapter argues that the notion of 'discourse' and associated analytical tools are particularly relevant to HRD since HRD is enacted through 'talk'. This argument draws on the 'linguistic turn' in making the case for the use of discourse analysis and so might be said to be in that tradition in making the case for critical HRD.

The following chapter by Tim Hatcher takes more from critical theory in providing its critical analysis of HRD theory and practice. This is a much more political and sociological critique of the claims and purposes of HRD at societal as well as organizational levels. The chapter itself represents a personal polemic and as such is in the broader tradition of critical writing. The same is true of the final chapter in this part by Jim Stewart. Here there is more definite focus on concepts from ethical theory rather than the broader application of sociological, political and economic arguments present in Hatcher's chapter. That said, both adopt a normative rather than exclusively analytical approach.

Stewart though might be considered more radical in the sense of attempting to incorporate research and writing from the natural sciences more explicitly in making the case for an ethics of HRD. Part of the unstated premise for this attempt is the view that such research and writing is too often ignored in the social sciences and thus in their application within HRD and the wider study of management and organization.

The three chapters here in some ways set the scene for the rest of the book. While in no sense comprehensive, they do present the main themes, approaches and concepts which are then applied in the rest of the book. Some of these themes include the following:

- the nature and meaning of 'critical HRD';
- the consequences of HRD practice for society, organizations and individuals;
- the moral base of HRD;
- the legitimization of HRD practice;
- ethical dilemmas raised by HRD practice.

It will be useful for readers to bear these themes in mind as they read the chapters in this part and those in subsequent parts. While none may be directly addressed in a particular chapter, more than one theme may be an unspoken presence and may be helpful in making sense of the arguments presented in individual chapters. The themes may be considered the 'big' questions which have been present all along in HRD but which are only recently being posed. Alternatively, they may be considered as outside the remit of HRD research, theorizing and practice. And there may be other positions on them. Addressing these themes as the book is read and the activities are undertaken will support a personal view being taken and a position being adopted.

Chapter 1

Exploring the notion of 'time' and 'critical' HRD

Sally Sambrook

▇ Introduction

In this chapter, I explore the concepts of 'time' and 'critical' HRD highlighted in the title in several ways. One way is to examine the term 'critical' from various perspectives relevant to the study and accomplishment of HRD in the manner of 'critical thinking' and identify that the 'time has come' for such an approach. This suggests that HRD has evolved and is now developing into a new phase, one associated with a critical perspective where underlying assumptions about the purposes and practices of HRD are challenged. This provides a conventional examination of the chronology (time map) of HRD and compares this with other related academic subjects, particularly management and organization studies. Although it has existed in the American vocabulary for more than 30 years, HRD is still an emerging concept with a history of around only 10 to 15 years in the UK. However, despite its more mature existence in the US, the concept has only recently been considered from a critical stance (see, for example, Elliott and Turnbull, 2002). So, perhaps it is time to begin a critical analysis of HRD.

But why? It is 'timely' to do so, in the sense of 'it is about time we did this' for several reasons. As it matures, the practice of HRD is an increasingly important aspect of organizations, economies and communities, and as such merits a careful consideration of both its espoused and enacted aims and activities. Also, over time, we can now look back and perhaps critique early research for treating the concept of HRD as unproblematic, for tending to neglect defining what we mean by HRD, for omitting to consider how it exists or stating its purposes, thus raising ontological and philosophical questions.

However, another way to address the question in the title is to examine whether HRD is facing a 'crisis,' hence this might be a 'critical time'. Because the very term 'HRD' is becoming a contested label, this suggests 'now is a crucial time' to think more critically about this concept.

A further way is to explore whether HRD professionals 'have the time' to consider critical HRD. In organizations with a focus on targets, efficiency, return on investment, etc., is it feasible – or even ethical – to suggest HRD practitioners should question the rational logic of a performance orientation? It might be time for academics to ponder critical HRD theoretically, but is there time for practitioners to enact this in their workplace?

■ Aims

This chapter focuses on four aspects of 'critical' and has four related aims. First, to provide a brief historical and theoretical perspective, I ask the question: *What is HRD?* Here, there is a brief review of the emergence of HRD and its development to reach a 'critical turn'.

Second, to explain how we might adopt a critical perspective in HRD, I ask: What do we mean by *being critical* and *critical thinking*? I begin by exploring what 'being critical' might involve. Then, I examine the term 'critical' from the related academic fields of study in management and organization, and identify some of the strands of critical thinking. This section provides ways of conducting *critical analyses* of HRD practice, drawing upon critical thinking from other disciplines or fields and carefully considering how this might apply to learning and development activities. We might add here the notion of *finding* time to critique HRD practices and ask whether practitioners have the time and space to engage in critical thinking.

Third, to address the orthodox methodological treatment of HRD as an unproblematic concept, I ask: *How can we research HRD from a critical perspective?* This section introduces a *critical methodology* to the study of HRD, offering an examination of HRD research from a 'discourse' perspective. Here, I critically examine my own approach to researching HRD. I challenge the utility and validity of my conceptualization of HRD as a social and discursive construction to help practitioners think critically about their HRD activities (Sambrook, 2000, 2001). I explore the complex and often contradictory discursive constructions of HRD and also identify other emerging discourses of HRD.

Fourth, to bring our critical thinking right into focus, I ask: *What is critical to HRD at this time?* I argue it is perhaps time to consider some aspects that are *critical* to the very concept and continued existence of HRD. There is a potential crisis looming regarding the actual label appropriate to capture the diverse and dynamic features of work-related learning and development. Another crisis could emerge out of the distinction between those 'being critical' and those Others[1] that are 'not.' Instead of a separate section, I discuss these two issues throughout the chapter, weaving them into the various arguments. Finally, I offer some conclusions – both conventional and critical.

But first, it is important to be clear about the two key terms used here. We can think of *HRD* in many ways – as an academic subject, a discipline or field of practice – but, to avoid a lengthy debate, I shall refer to it here as a concept, as a way of thinking about activities and articulations associated with developing people in organizations. Similarly, we can think of the word *critical* in many ways, and in this chapter I seek to explore some of these and consider their relevance to and relationship with HRD, offering some contrasting definitions of 'critical'. Again, the notion of 'time' is woven into the discussions of both.

■ What is HRD?

It is possible to suggest that 'HRD' is a term created (by academics) to differentiate strategic and business-oriented learning and development activities from old-style training and development (T&D). That is an old debate, but one that has not completely been resolved, and which could prove critical if not. Why? If the label HRD continues to be used to refer to both T&D and contemporary learning and development activities, how can we convince stakeholders (government, business partners, learners, etc.) that the 'real' HRD is indeed more strategic and business-oriented? However, more recent concerns focus on whether the term 'HRD' itself is the most appropriate label to capture contemporary learning and development activities. So, what is HRD?

Usual practice is to begin with a definition of HRD, but this is problematic as Lee (1998) and McLean (1998, 1999), amongst others, suggest. Indeed, Blake (1995: 22) argues that 'the field of human resource development defies definition and boundaries'. Although we still cannot agree (McLean, 1999), and we are unclear about what it 'is', we continue our attempts to investigate HRD, so that we may better understand, teach and practise it. One way of investigating HRD is to consider its purpose(s).

From a UK perspective, the purpose(s) of HRD can be defined as 'supporting and facilitating the learning of individuals, groups and organizations...' (McGoldrick *et al.*, 2002: 396). Bates *et al.* (2001), American researchers, note that: 'The purpose of HRD is to enhance learning, human potential, and high performance in work-related systems.' This definition hints at the performance orientation. Thus, already it is possible to detect different discursive resources being employed to define this complex, dynamic and emerging range of activities, and the dichotomy between learning and performance. Given its longer American history, much HRD literature tends to be dominated by this performance orientation and situated within a unitary organization perspective, avoiding any hint of the tensions inherent in work organizations (see, for example, Swanson, 1995; Torraco, 1999). From this perspective, HRD is portrayed as an unproblematic and unifying model (Swanson, 2002) and can be studied in much the same way as traditional management practice, adopting a normative and idealistic rather than critical orientation. The focus is generally on identifying means of improving production efficiency, with little regard to organizational issues viewed from a pluralistic perspective, such as the political dimension manifest through the contradictory needs of employers and employees, and implicit power imbalances, for example. As the study of the concept of HRD matures, researchers now detect other discourses, including the public relations (PR) role of HRD in promoting corporate social responsibility (CSR) and its more humanistic and emancipatory role (Rigg, 2005; Turnbull and Elliott, 2005) in both helping individuals with their own aspirations and transforming the socio-political structures in which they exist.

In the early stages of the evolution of a new area of academic study and specialist practice, it was perhaps appropriate and attractive to attempt to research HRD as an unproblematic concept. Early research, for example, focused on identifying HRD roles (McLagan, 1989) and means of improving HRD activities. However, this approach neglects to define what we mean by HRD, by omitting to consider how 'it' exists or stating its complex and contradictory purposes. This raises (at least) two key issues – one ontological, the other philosophical. Later, I attempt to address these issues by critically evaluating my research that conceptualized HRD as a social and discursive construction, to connect ways of thinking, talking about and practising HRD (Sambrook, 2000, 2001). By conceptualizing HRD in this way, the focus is on developing methods of researching and understanding how HRD can be talked about and accomplished through selecting particular discursive resources to construct personal realities of this occupational activity. This approach might be considered 'critical' in that it acknowledges the politics, complexities and ambiguities in studying this emerging subject.

As an emerging field, it could be argued that HRD research is characterized by both ontological uncertainty and methodological hegemony. First, we cannot agree on what HRD *is*, or *should be* (Lee, 1998; McLean, 1998; Swanson, 1999; Walton, 2002). Thus we must accept the partial and situated nature (Elliott, 1998) of how we conceive and construct our knowledge of HRD. Secondly, much 'credible' research aims to treat this complex occupational practice as any other 'natural' phenomenon by conducting positivist research to measure, count, explain, propose causal relations and predict future outcomes. This approach can be useful in answering some of our questions, but not all. Instead, there are now calls for other ways of 'seeing' and researching HRD, drawing upon more interpretive philosophies and innovative methods (Valentin, 2005). We are entering a time where 'being critical' could be considered a contribution to developing such new approaches. Such an approach acknowledges – or takes into account – the various academic disciplines that underpin the field of HRD, such as psychology, economics and systems theory (with their associated proponents, discourses and theoretical contradictions), and the various stakeholders involved in the practice of HRD (with their associated roles, discourses and agendas). Thus, the political nature of 'doing HRD' is exposed, whether through how HRD has been talked into (and possibly out of) being – in universities, consultancies or other work organizations – or the various ways in which HRD is talked about (and thus thought about) in organizations, courses, textbooks and journals. Epistemologically, we can critically examine new methodological ways of helping us know and understand HRD. These themes – the political and epistemological nature of doing and research HRD – will be familiar to 'critics'.[2] However, there are other dimensions to being critical and critical thinking and these are reviewed next.

■ What do we mean by 'being critical'?

It is useful to start with a straightforward dictionary definition. The *Concise Oxford Dictionary* (www.askoxford.com/concize_oed/critical?view=uk) provides six definitions of the word 'critical':

> **critical** adjective **1** expressing adverse or disapproving comments or judgements. **2** expressing or involving an analysis of the merits and faults of a literary or artistic work. **3** having a decisive importance in the success or failure of something; crucial. **4** extremely ill and at risk of death. **5** Mathematics & Physics relating to a point of transition from one state to another. **6** (of a nuclear reactor or fuel) maintaining a self-sustaining chain reaction.

The first, in a negative sense, suggests providing comments that criticize or find fault. The second broadens this notion to include analysis from which to provide both positive and negative comments. The third moves away from the notion of *judging* things to the idea of something crucially important, something that could influence a decision that has to be made, perhaps when facing a *crisis*. The fourth refers to the state of something that might be about to expire. The fifth focuses on a particular, and significant, phase in the development from one state to another. The sixth suggests being able to sustain something!

■ How might these relate to HRD?

The first two appear to relate to our role as developers, where being critical suggests being skilled in, and providing, criticism (such as judging merit or pointing out faults). This is a pertinent label for those involved in developing people, whether academics or practitioners, who seek to facilitate and provide feedback on learning. As academics, it is our job to be critical of and 'judge' the work of students and peers, and ourselves. This is related to the notion of '*critique* ■ noun a detailed analysis and assessment. ■ verb (critiques, critiqued, critiquing) evaluate in a detailed and analytical way,' (www.askoxford.com/concize_oed).

The third definition refers to the nature of a crisis and some might argue that HRD is in a crisis given the debate about whether the label adequately reflects the broad and diverse range of activities associated with developing adults in the work context (Walton, 2002, 2003; Ruona, 2000, 2002). So, 'HRD' appears to be a subject moving towards, if not already in, a state of crisis, particularly concerning the utility of the term itself. Here, being critical can be defined as being decisive for good or ill. So, despite these robust arguments for and against a change in name, perhaps we do need to make a decision about the label HRD. Some advocate decisive action regarding the retention or rejection of the term. However, if we cannot agree on this, we might risk moving into the fourth definition of being in a critical state and the possible demize of HRD as we currently know it. Perhaps, to avoid this, the fifth definition suggests the term critical can refer to marking a transition from one state to another and such debate might mark the transition from a taken-for-granted acceptance of HRD as orthodoxy towards a new, critical approach as evidenced by a 'critical mass'[3] of researchers and practitioners. This 'turn' might indeed mark the maturing of HRD into a fully-fledged academic area of study and a recognized profession (see, for example, the Chartered Institute of Personnel and Development, www.cipd.org.uk). Another way to trace this transition, as HRD further develops, is to analyze research publications, both in terms of the quality of their content and critical thinking and their location, for example, whether in HRD or mainstream (management/organization studies) journals (Poell and Wasti, 2005). Another way might be to examine the links being made between critical HRD and 'big topics' such as leadership (Trehan, 2005). The final definition might refer to our ability to sustain ourselves as an academic subject, discipline and field of study, and address any looming crises (whether to do with our label or being colonized by other, more established academic subjects, such as management/organization studies).

So, these initial definitions help us think about two dimensions of HRD: an area of our practice – evaluation; and the overall state and status of our occupational activity – whether it is facing crisis or making the transition to a critical phase and sustaining its evolution. However, the term is also used in a different way to define a particular approach to studying phenomena, including teaching and researching an academic subject such as HRD. This is explained next.

■ What do we mean by 'critical thinking'?

In his editorial for the journal *Discourse and Society*, Billig (2000: 291) notes:

> 'The term "critical" is itself an interesting one. As language analysts, we should not shy away from examining (critically examining) the terms that we use to describe our own work and, indeed, our own identity.'

As HRD professionals, perhaps it is now time to examine both the terms 'HRD' and 'critical' that we use to describe our own work and identity. I have already suggested that, in terms of our identity as HRD workers, there is a potential crisis looming regarding the actual label appropriate to capture the diverse and dynamic features of work-related learning and development. Perhaps, 'critical HRD' might be a better label. In his critique of the critical, Billig (Ibid.) argues that,

> 'Basically, when academics apply "critical" to their own paradigm, discipline or theory, the label tends to signal two related messages: (a) the new paradigm/discipline/theory includes social analyses, particularly the analysis of social inequality; (b) the "critical" paradigm/discipline/theory is opposing existing paradigms/disciplines/theories, which among other failings, fail to address social inequalities. As such, the critical paradigm signals its "other" – the mainstream, apparently uncritical paradigm.'

We can apply his argument to HRD and its emerging criticality. With the increasing interest in critical HRD, are we becoming critical to address inequalities, for example, in access to learning and development opportunities? Do we wish to distinguish ourselves from those 'Others' who do not?

Theoretically, the concept of critique can be traced back to the 18th century to the work of Kant and Hegel. Kant is associated with the epistemological dimension, challenging 'reason' and 'rationality' and questioning how we might know anything and what subjective forces influence our claims to knowledge (Burrell, 2001: 13). This suggests we need to think about 'what' is knowledge and 'how' it is constructed. Hegel is associated with the social revolutionary dimension, seeking an end to illusion and the alienation of human beings from themselves (Ibid.). This suggests we need to think about 'who' uses knowledge and 'how', perhaps to emancipate people. We can interpret 'critical' in several ways – from the basic level, which implies furthering 'knowledge', to the level of social commentary, with the potential of effecting emancipatory outcomes. Here, we need to think about our own practices – as HRD academics and/or practitioners – and the (potentially oppressive or emancipatory) effect they have. Critical theory 'seeks to highlight, nurture and promote the potential of human consciousness to reflect critically upon such oppressive practices, and thereby facilitate the extension of domains of autonomy and responsibility,' (Alvesson and Willmott, 1996: 13).

A distinct interest in 'critical' theories emerged in the 1960s, a shift described by Ulrich as the 'critical turn.' This use of the term is similar to the 'linguistic turn' referring to the transition from perceiving language as the means of *reflecting* reality to the means of *constructing* reality. This turn, or transition, refers to our 'new' understanding of the use of language in the social construction of reality. The critical turn refers to our 'new' understanding of the use of critical thinking in studying academic subjects, disciplines and fields of study. Ironically, and a play on words, critical thinking involves *reflecting*, but on one's practices and relationships, and those of colleagues, communities and societies, and their impact on each other.

In the academic world, many disciplines or fields of study assert a critical paradigm, such as critical management or critical psychology. The use of the adjective 'critical' appears to convey the characteristics of both maturity and difference in the given discipline. For example, management has evolved from early idealistic and normative prescriptions (such as the work of Taylor and Fayol) to a more realistic/descriptive orientation (through the work of Mintzberg and Stewart) and more recently to a critical stance (see Burrell, 2001). We might consider where HRD currently fits in this evolution. We could argue that HRD has moved beyond idealistic and normative prescriptions (such as the training cycle) to a more realistic and descriptive stage. However, to what extent have we reached the critical stance? This and other texts (Elliot and Turnbull, 2005) and journal articles (Sambrook, 2004) provide examples of a move in that direction.

In organization and management studies, there is an established history of thinking 'critically' (Thompson and McHugh, 1995; Alvesson and Deetz, 1999; Alvesson and Willmott, 1996). Burrell (2001) reviews this work and notes that critical theory is associated with challenging 'rational' organization practices and replacing them with more democratic and emancipatory practices. It is also concerned with: identifying weaknesses and limitations of orthodoxy; the need for self-reflexivity; the empowerment of a wider range of participants to effect change and explanations of social phenomena that are multi-dimensional; and recognizing the tensions in and contradictions of managing and organizing. This might sound rather negative, in terms of *rejecting* managerialism, *exposing* the shortcomings of management and adopting an *oppositional* stance. Indeed, when I was trying to explain to a student what it might mean to be critical, his response was – 'Oh you mean cynical, finding fault in everything.' Burrell might prefer to call this pessimistic. However, the key words associated with a critical perspective seem to be: challenging contemporary practices; exposing assumptions; revealing illusions; and questioning tradition. Being critical means recognizing the messiness, complexities and irrationality – rather than the sanitized reason and rationality – of organizational practices. More recently, there has been critical thinking about human resource management (Keenoy, 1999; Legge, 1995). However, as Elliott and Turnbull note (2005:1),

> 'despite the influence of the critical turn in management studies on HRD in the UK, HRD has nevertheless neither been subject to the same degree of critical scrutiny as management and organization studies, nor has it gathered together a significant mass of followers that might constitute it as a "movement" in its own right.'

Yet, we can observe the critical perspective now beginning to emerge in HRD (McGoldrick *et al.*, 2002; Elliott and Turnbull, 2002a, 2005). For example, at the AHRD 2002 Conference, the first 'critical' session was organized. The organizers explained the rationale behind their innovative session:

> 'We are concerned that the methodological traditions that guide the majority of HRD research do not allow researchers to engage in studies that challenge the predominantly performative and learning-outcome focus of the HRD field...We seek to unpick the assumptions behind the performative orientation that dominates much HRD research ... We therefore perceived the need to open up HRD theory to a broader range of methodological and theoretical perspectives.'
>
> (Elliott and Turnbull, 2002a: 971)

From a research perspective, being critical can be interpreted as an attempt to overcome the dualistic nature of methodologies in the natural and social historical sciences (a post-paradigm agenda). This methodological perspective is explored later in the chapter.

Having briefly considered the evolution of critical thinking in management studies and its apparent emergence in HRD, we can now turn to consider 'what' we are critiquing. Mingers (cited in Burrell, 2001) identifies four critiques: those of rhetoric, authority, tradition and objectivity. Applying these to HRD, we might consider the rhetorics and realities of HR practice (Legge, 1995; Watson, 1994; Sambrook, 1998), and whether these are one and the same thing rather than one or the other. We might also challenge traditional HRD practices, such as the training cycle or the 'sheep dip' (everyone gets trained whether they need to or not) approach, which are based more on ritual than evidence. We might consider the use and abuse of power and authority when designing learning interventions, identifying training needs and 'sending' people on courses. Finally, we might consider how we know and understand HRD through our approaches to research and whether this should be more democratic, involving our partners in co-constructing new knowledge.

Burrell (2001) identifies six strands to a critical approach, and it might be helpful to consider their relevance and utility when applied to HRD. Each of these strands can be thought of as particular discourses or ways of framing what we consider to be critical. Burrell (2001: 16) notes that these strands are interrelated and still only provide a partial understanding of critical theory.

The six strands are: political, iconoclastic, epistemological, investigative, revelatory and emancipatory (2001: 14–17). Burrell and colleagues accept the first four, but are 'much less happy' about the last two. However, these seem to be the two key themes of early critical theories – the struggle for emancipation and the search for 'the' truth. So, how might these six strands relate to HRD?

From a political perspective, we could consider who are the stakeholders involved in HRD, who influences HRD, in what ways and for what gains? Also, we could ask whether HRD is part of HRM or a separate functional and strategic area reporting directly to senior management? If HRD is considered a subset of HRM, then HRD specialists serve the interests of organizations first and individuals second. In the academic arena, perhaps HRD specialists are struggling for their own academic space and freedom, distinguishing themselves from HRM or vocational education, or whatever. I have argued (Sambrook, 2001) that HRD might have been talked into being to serve the needs of academic career development, by creating valuable resources with which to trade in the organizational political arena such as new job titles and new products, for example post-graduate programmes and textbooks. In the practitioner arena, Vince (2005: 27) argues that we need to ask, 'what function HRD has within the political systems of organizing, how and why HRD provides mechanism for the control and manipulation of organizational members and what role fear (or other such powerful emotion) plays in defining how HRD is and is not done.'

From the iconoclastic perspective, critical thinking might focus on identifying what lies behind the 'dominant imagery and icons' of HRD. For example, symbols such as *Personal* Development Plans or *Individual* Learning Accounts might suggest a *humanistic* orientation, but what is their underlying purpose? Many would argue this would be *performance*. Trying to identify what lies beneath the dominant imagery can be achieved by attempting to unpick and break down the signifiers and symbols used in organizational life, including the 'right phrases' associated with a particular HRD discourse. This critique could involve discourse analysis, examining what discursive resources are being used, by whom and to construct which dominant image. So, despite the rhetoric of a humanistic orientation, HRD could be exposed for its exclusively performative objective and disregard for personal development. Critique here employs iconoclasm to debunk conventional myths (Burrell, 2001: 15), in this case, of HRD.

The epistemological perspective considers what constitutes knowledge and what methodologies are accepted in constructing how we 'know' HRD. Critique here is about asking how does HRD exist and how can we learn about it? This, in turn, raises questions about research methodologies. Turnbull (2002) identifies the difficulties associated with developing 'newer' perspectives as alternatives to the dominant positivist philosophies and accompanying quantitative methodological approaches. As researchers and 'thinking performers', we need to develop a critical lens through which to explore and develop interpretative approaches. These might include problematizing the concept of HRD, using qualitative methods, examining the role of 'the researcher' and their relationships with 'subjects', and exploring values, morality and ethics in HRD and HRD research, discussed elsewhere in this text (see Chapters 2 and 3). Perhaps now is the time to challenge the dominant approaches, actively promote those currently emerging, and ask – to what extent is this work 'critical' and how does it contribute to a deeper understanding of HRD? As well as adopting a critical reflection on the work and methodologies of others, it is also perhaps time to take the opportunity for self-reflection and consider to what extent our work is reflexive. Some argue that good research and researchers *are* critical, even if the 'label' is not used. However, a further question might challenge the extent to which more 'critical' knowledge actually pervades organizational practices. Trehan (2004: 23), for example, notes that 'while examples of critical pedagogies are accumulating, they seldom exhibit corresponding changes in HRD practice.'

The investigative perspective focuses on uncovering what others take for granted, and dealing with issues of human concern that are often neglected because they are suppressed and excluded from the agenda (Burrell, 2001: 15). Here, we can investigate what we actually 'mean' by HRD rather than taking this for granted, perhaps by questioning those who (powerfully) decide what HRD should mean, and then explore what this in turn might mean for those exposed to HRD. For example, questioning the label HRD suggests an investigative critical dimension. At the 2002 AHRD conference, the Town Forum was the arena for a debate on whether the label HRD was appropriate for the activities it attempted to encompass. Walton (2002) clearly believes that one term – HRD – cannot be used to mean many things to many people, whether it be 'theories' or organizational activities. Walton argues that 'the label we use to designate our domain is a major factor contributing to the creation of such a barrier,' (Ibid.: 1). Yet, Ruona (2002: 2) argues for retaining the label whilst we attempt to gain increased clarity of HRD. She argues that 'a major barrier for HRD professionals is that our work and what we stand for are not yet well understood by others. Some would argue that we do not yet well understand ourselves either. As a profession, we have not done a very good job working to identify who we are, what we stand for, and what we can do for those we serve.' Re-labelling at this stage would only cause, both within the field and perhaps signal to those outside, further confusion – and what would it be replaced with? But, does this matter and to whom?

Being critical could also be about searching for 'the' truth about HRD, given the disagreements about what 'is' HRD and the reluctance to first define (Lee, 1998) and then accept/retain this term. We could also attempt to identify how HRD is talked about (some might describe this as the ideology or rhetoric) and how it is accomplished through talk – but is this any more 'real'? Is it possible, or even desirable, to attempt to reveal a single truth about HRD? There are multiple and often-contradictory constructions and discourses of HRD, offering partial, ambiguous and dynamic meanings and understandings of those activities and actions currently talked of as HRD.

Finally, being critical could be associated with struggling with the issue of whether HRD is – or *should be* – emancipatory. There is an inherent tension between reconciling the needs of individuals and those of employing organizations, so how could HRD emancipate? This relates to the political dimension (Vince, 2005). Should HRD interventions serve the purpose of freeing humans – perhaps from capitalist exploitation and employment degradation? What is HRD about, and whose needs do academics and practitioners serve? Some might even ask whether HRD might be emancipated from HRM.

To summarize this section, critical thinkers adopt an *oppositional* stance (Burrell, 2001: 14) by rejecting traditional approaches to, for example, HRD practices, and exposing their shortcomings. These shortcomings can include a neglect of the political dimension, an acceptance of what is taken for granted, an inability to investigate the views of the suppressed or excluded, a naïve adherence to conventional means of knowledge creation and associated research methodologies, and the search for the single truth. I explored some of these issues implicitly in my doctoral research (Sambrook, 1998). Here, I considered the problematic ontological nature of HRD (what is the nature of HRD and how can we sense it?) and conceptualized HRD as social and discursive construction and as discursive action (Sambrook, 2000, 2001) to enable academics and practitioners to analyze how HRD is thought about, talked about and accomplished through talk. What constitutes knowledge here is not quantifiable and statistically significant measurements, but constructed accounts of what it is like to be an HRD worker, what HRD work involves and how this is achieved. I critically evaluate this next, drawing upon the themes from this brief review of 'critical' literature. I explore how 'critical' this approach was in terms of the political, iconoclastic, epistemological and investigative issues identified earlier (Burrell, 2001: 14–17).

■ How can we research HRD from a critical perspective?

HRD can be investigated from many perspectives (see, for example, Swanson 1999 and McLean, 1998, 1999), focusing on its contested roots in the disciplines of economics, psychology and systems theory, for instance. These approaches tend to describe and model HRD practices, without stepping back to consider the problematic ontology of HRD, which might be thought of as one of the first stages in adopting a critical stance. I took such an approach in my early research (Sambrook, 1998).

The idea that HRD could usefully be thought of as social and discursive construction emerged during my doctoral research. Here I was faced with the ontological difficulties of establishing what HRD *is*, and the consequent methodological problems of how to sense and measure this *thing* (critiquing the objective). So, it seemed more feasible to focus on what HRD practitioners do and, more interestingly, how they talk about what they do – in that there could be differences between what they *say* they do and what they actually *do* (an investigative perspective). Linking these two ideas, it seems that much of what HRD practitioners *do* is *talk*, hence the notion of discursive action emerged. When talking of HRD, it is possible to examine:

- how HRD has been *talked into being* – that is how it has been invented or socially constructed;
- how 'it' is *talked about* – that is how we draw upon particular discursive resources, or ways of framing how we think about and articulate our sense-making of HRD;
- how 'it' is *achieved through talk* – that is through HRD practices such as delivering training, persuading, advising, consulting and formulating strategies, etc.

The notion of HRD as discursive action is an attempt to bring together the two concepts of HRD as 'action' and HRD as just 'all talk', when the two are intertwined in the accomplishment of HRD (critique of rhetoric versus reality). We can study HRD as *discourse* by analyzing how 'it' is written and talked about – by senior managers, HRM specialists, HRD practitioners, managers and other employees, for example. We can then investigate if there are communal discursive resources being used amongst these diverse stakeholders or whether there are mixed accounts of HRD. This would help us understand how different agents think and speak of HRD. Thinking critically, this approach helps give voice to the potentially excluded or suppressed (employees, trainees), thereby offering more democratic involvement in the research process, co-construction of knowledge and possible emancipation. We can also study HRD as *action* by analyzing how 'it' is practised through talking, whether through the very tangible stand-up delivery of a training session in a classroom or the more obscure behind-the-scenes discussions about how learning and development activities can add value or contribute to achieving business objectives. However, rather than focus on these two ideas in isolation, it is important to acknowledge that the one can influence the other. How senior managers think about HRD can influence how it is practised within a particular organization (highlighting the political dimension). Conversely, how it is practised can influence how organizational members perceive HRD. This leads to the notion of HRD as *discursive action* – a complex socially constructed concept with real consequences – something that is both enacted and negotiated. This is a new way of knowing HRD (a critique of epistemology through more interpretive research methods that acknowledge the subjective).

■ The original study

The original study, and focus of this current critical exploration, formed a programme of doctoral research conducted between 1995–98. Given the rise of the concept of HRM in the NHS during the early 1990s, the intention was to explore the emergence of the associated concept of HRD. The purpose was to explore how HRD was talked about and accomplished through talk in the context of the UK National Health Service (NHS). Ethnographic research was conducted in two Trust hospitals. This involved:

■ semi-structured interviews with more than 20 practitioners (managers and specialists) to elicit their accounts of HRD;
■ participant and non-participant observations during meetings, training interventions and other daily work activities; and
■ a review of internal documents such as mission statements, strategies, policies and job descriptions.

Referring back to the notion of discursive action, what emerged from the original study was the need to explore how discourse influenced action and vice versa. For example, organization members' accounts can be influenced by formal documents such as strategies and mission statements, which may articulate the dominant voice(s) within the organization. It is by gathering and studying accounts of how HRD is talked about – in conversations and documents – and by listening and observing the talk associated with doing HRD that we can access how HRD has been talked into being and is accomplished through talk. It is useful to analyze the 'espoused' ways of thinking about HRD – such as its strategic role and integration with business strategy, articulated in formal documents – and compare these with the daily, 'theories in-use' or ways of thinking about and accomplishing HRD, for example, through limited budgets or being perceived as distanced from business operations.

The overall object was to explore the emergence of HRD in the NHS. This was achieved by constructing four specific research questions to investigate meanings attached to the term HRD by the various stakeholders involved, including nurses, managers and HR practitioners.

1 *Why* has the concept emerged and what are the intended purpose(s) of HRD?
2 *Where* is HRD located in an organization and *what* are its structural components?
3 *Who* is involved in HRD?
4 *How* is HRD practised in NHS Trust hospitals?

These questions focused on HRD and strategy, HRD and structure, HRD stakeholders and HRD practices, products and services. Thematic analysis of the various interview transcripts, observations and documents, integrated with a parallel critical review of academic literature regarding these themes, eventually led to the construction of a typology of discursive resources – *Tell*, *Sell* and *Gel* (see Sambrook, 2000, 2001 for a full account).

However, how 'critical' was this approach in terms of the political, iconoclastic, epistemological and investigative issues identified earlier (Burrell, 2001: 14–17)? From a political perspective, how much (or little) power did I have as a doctoral researcher and how might this have influenced participants' responses? I was fortunate to be able to interview a wide range of stakeholders involved in HRD and there were tensions between those who influenced HRD strategies (senior management, the HR directorates and HRD practitioners) and those who 'received' and implemented HRD policies and procedures, usually line managers. There were tensions in terms of the 'location' of the HRD function. Usually, HRD was a part of HRM but one senior OD practitioner thought OD (Organization Development) should be a separate functional and strategic area reporting directly to senior management. Within the complex NHS organization, there are many different professions with their own developers. Medical education was a separate entity. Often, nurse education and professional development was the responsibility of the nursing function. Where nurse development was part of the wider HRD unit, some nurse developers disliked their association with HR and felt this diminished their credibility on the ward (Sambrook, 1998).

From the iconoclastic perspective, this research could be considered critical in that it tried to identify what lay behind the (potential) HRD myth. This was achieved by exposing both flawed rhetorics and realities, that is by carefully analyzing what was discursively articulated (the espoused vision, strategies and values) and what was discursively accomplished (how practitioners talked about HRD and what I observed of their enacted practices). This was an attempt to go beyond the 'rhetoric' and sanitized accounts to reveal the 'real' roles and activities of HRD.

From an investigative perspective, the research focused on exploring what HRD and non-HRD practitioners 'meant' by HRD and exposing some of the issues that could be neglected because they are suppressed and excluded from the HR agenda, such as how nurse developers felt about being located in the HRD unit. I was able to investigate what practitioners 'mean' by HRD by questioning those who (powerfully) decide what HRD should mean (HR directors, HRD managers) and then asking line managers and other non-HRD developers what HRD meant to them and what it was like to be exposed to the 'official' HRD. For example, there were tensions about the 'directive' role of HRD specialists when line managers were keen for greater autonomy, and tensions about the purpose(s) of HRD – whether to meet organizational/service, professional and/or individual needs.

The epistemological perspective considers what constitutes knowledge, and what methodologies are accepted in constructing how we 'know' HRD. My own ethnographic research could be considered novel in that I emphasized the co-construction of emergent knowledge and the polyvocal dimension of the research story. I experienced some of the difficulties associated with developing a new perspective as an alternative to the dominant positivist philosophy and accompanying quantitative methodological approaches, through the comments from (positivist) journal reviewers, for example. Linking this with the political perspective, I examined my role as 'researcher' and my relationship with 'subjects' and 'declared' some of the difficulties of becoming close and then having to leave the field, as is consistent with a reflexive approach.

From a revelatory perspective, I accepted that there was no single truth of HRD, even within this one distinct context. Multiple stakeholders articulated multiple constructions of their realities of HRD. From this, I was able to construct the typology, illustrating three different ways of thinking and talking about HRD within these two hospitals.

From an emancipatory perspective, reflecting back, I could be indulgent and claim that this research emancipated me – from an orthodox and positivist stance. I stumbled and struggled to find 'another way' to conduct research, one that fitted with my own values, interests and philosophical orientation. Also, I think I can say that many participants might have felt emancipated from their engagement in the lengthy research interviews. At the end, many expressed relief at being able to talk about issues that were otherwise 'off' the agenda. Many spoke about the therapeutic value of being able to 'let off steam' and many thanked me for the stimulation and opportunity to think more critically about their own practices and the effects these might have on others (often for the first time). This suggests there is little time for a reflective, let alone critical, approach to HRD within the daily work routine. Yet, I also encountered nurses 'trapped' in HRD roles and departments, suggesting oppressive practices to gain 'structural' efficiencies and improved performance.

■ A critique

So, I have managed to neatly apply Burrell's (2001) strands of critical thinking to my research. However, being critical – in the sense of judging the quality of my work as I might one of my students – there were limitations in this study. Firstly, I would raise the issue of multiple discourses. In the original study, I identified (or, more honestly, *constructed*) three distinct discourses. Perhaps there were more, but I failed to consider these once I had devized a neat tritypology. Secondly, the typology could be considered limited as it has been constructed out of discursive resources used in a particular context – specifically

Trust hospitals, within the UK National Health Service. Is the typology situation specific? Perhaps not, when we consider that the detailed literature review conducted by Garavan and colleagues (1999) also identified three distinct perspectives. However, that is not to say that there might be other discourses employed in other distinct contexts. For example, Kessels (2002) notes that HRD practices vary between large and small enterprizes and between private and public sector organizations, and highlights the sharp controversy (and possibly language used) between employers and employees. He also notes the merger between vocational education and HRD resulting in a 'fuzzy idea, a blurred structure... (which) doesn't fit in the formal HRD discourse'. However, this raises the question of what *is* the formal HRD discourse? In addition, it might be useful to consider other aspects of HRD that I did not pay enough attention to, such as the purpose(s) of HRD – whether instrumental, emancipatory, performance-oriented or humanistic, for example.

In this chapter, I have attempted to apply some of the characteristics of a critical approach to the study of HRD and in particular provide a brief critique of early research that attempted to adopt a critical perspective. As it draws to a close, I offer some conclusions, both conventional and critical.

■ Some conventional conclusions

HRD appears to have taken a critical turn, with researchers engaging in an emerging 'critical' approach to the study of activities and discourses associated with learning and development. This chapter has examined the term 'critical' from various perspectives relevant to the study and accomplishment of the concept of HRD. Being critical can be understood in many ways, each relevant to the emergence and current 'state and status' of HRD (Stewart, 2005).

My own research attempted to contribute to this more critical investigation by suggesting that there are diverse and distinct ways of thinking and talking about HRD and accomplishing HRD through talk. Of course, theoretically, we have debated whether HRD is a stool or a centipede (McLean, 1998) and whether HRD theory is real or imagined (Swanson, 1999), acknowledging the various academic disciplines from which our understanding of HRD emerges. However, why continue to draw upon these strange (dominant?) images and the dominant orthodox disciplines and their conventional ways of knowing? This chapter has introduced and developed critical strands from management and organization studies to help develop our understanding of what HRD might both achieve and 'mean' to practitioners and other stakeholders. By examining discourses associated with 'being critical' as well as the emerging and eclectic discourses of 'HRD,' I hope to have contributed to a deeper understanding of HRD by evaluating why it is a 'critical time' for HRD.

Some critical conclusions

From a personal perspective, and trying to critique my own work, is my approach critical? From a critique of my early research, perhaps I *am* becoming critical – from the investigative, epistemological and revelatory perspectives, in particular, although there are elements of the political and iconoclastic strands, as well as hints of the emancipatory. But critical research also needs to transfer into practice. Such research raises important questions for critical practitioners. However, thinking again about the title of this chapter, we could inquire whether practitioners 'have the time' – as well as the will and power – to ask such questions and engage in critical thinking. Academics might have the 'luxury' of time to conduct research and think about critical HRD. But, 'doing' critical HRD is not an easy option. This raises a further question: is it ethical to 'teach' critical HRD in the classroom when it might be problematic, if not polemic, for practitioners to attempt to practise this in performance-oriented organizations?

Also, if I am becoming critical, then why? Perhaps because there is an opening for critical thinkers in the academic HRD market! Interestingly, Billig (2000: 292) suggests that for 'young academics the critical paradigm is the major paradigm in their academic world... The young academics will acknowledge the work of eminent "critical" figures... Thus, the critical paradigm takes on the style of the established paradigms, as it establishes itself in the academic market place.' Being relatively young in terms of my 'time' as an academic, perhaps 'becoming critical' is a question of positioning myself in the academic market. As a marketing orientation permeated the UK National Health Service, HRD practitioners in the case study hospitals had to sell both their products and themselves. Similarly, academic discourse is subject to market forces, and 'Our use of "critical" can function as a "brand label" or "unique selling point"' (Billig, 2000: 292). But we must be careful that as we sell ourselves as those critiquing Others, we must ensure we also adopt a critical eye upon our own work.

If 'we' are being critical, then conventional HRD is the Other – perhaps the 'performance junkies'. This potential split (or exclusivity?) was evident and questioned during the 'innovative' session at the 2002 AHRD conference, where some argued that *being critical* is synonymous with *good* research, and not a separate or higher level 'thing'. However, Billig (2000: 291) suggests that, in their dispute with the Other, 'the critics present themselves battling against an entrenched orthodoxy.' Initially, the critics are the iconoclasts, the unconventional, the minority view. Yet, in their battle, the effective critical thinkers can develop a successful paradigm, which 'not only has its own journals ... but its own conferences, textbooks, graduate students, research grants and even undergraduate courses. Its leading advocates will hold senior, well-paid, tenured positions' (Ibid.). It could be argued that the successful and conventional HRD paradigm has all of these, whilst the 'critical' paradigm is only just beginning to emerge, with 'innovative' sessions appearing in conference programmes (Elliott and Turnbull, 2002a), new streams appearing in critical conferences (Trehan, Rigg and Stewart, 2002) and books being published (Elliott and Turnbull, 2005; Rigg *et al.*, 2007).

Finally, I suggest it *is* time to explore what is critical for HRD. First, we can ask 'is it a *critical* (crucial?) time for HRD?' Perhaps it is – there are vociferous (academic) debates about how we label 'learning and development' activities and how this shapes our identity. There are tensions between the potentially conflicting purposes of what we currently understand as HRD, and the possible division of the community into 'critics' and 'Others'. Secondly, we could ask '*is there* time for critical HRD?' The first question has been discussed drawing on theoretical developments in critical thinking and empirical research. However, the second question has not been fully answered, suggesting we need to find time to investigate to what extent practitioners have time to engage in critical HRD and what impact this has.

Acknowledgements

I would like to thank the University Forum for HRD for funding this project. An earlier version of this chapter is published in the *Journal of European Industrial Training* (Sambrook, 2004) and was awarded Outstanding Paper of the year.

Notes

1 Those that consider themselves to be 'critical' are distinguished from 'Others' who represent more 'conventional' and perhaps 'uncritical' approaches to HRD.
2 'Critics' or 'critters' are terms used in the UK to define academics engaged in critical thinking.
3 'The minimum amount of resources required to start or maintain a venture' http://www.askoxford.com/concize_oed

Chapter 2

The fallacy of ethics and HRD: how ethics limits the creation of a 'deep' profession

Tim Hatcher

Being ethical, moral and caring about people and the environment is daunting in a world filled with conflict and hatred on a global scale, where species and cultures teeter on the brink of destruction, where new surveillance technologies infringe on our privacy, where corporations dump people like garbage and are more powerful than governments, and where commerce is hell-bent on unchecked expansion. Although not all people or organizations behave irresponsibly or unethically, it seems we have come to the point where we must act in order to save the profession of HRD from being swept up in this morass of hatred, destruction and injustice.

In an attempt to offset this deterioration, within just the past decade and for a handful of HRD scholars and practitioners including myself (Hatcher, 2002), ethics has begun to play a budding role in helping to develop the profession, creating normative standards for professional conduct and providing moral guidance for research and scholarship. While these are worthy goals, it is my contention as a recently converted polemicist to repudiate many of my earlier ideas and publications around ethics and HRD and to suggest now that ethics as it has been described and practised in HRD has done little to enhance the profession and has in fact helped to maintain it in an oppressive state. Thus, there is a fallacy that ethics enhances the profession of HRD in responsible or sustainable ways. This chapter will address this fallacy by first describing the business-entrenched ethics that HRD is currently practising and researching. Secondly, a discussion is offered about the inadequacy of concepts that ethics scholars have identified as supportive of ethics, such as sustainability and environmentalism, and finally, borrowing from related concepts of deep ecology and social ecology the chapter offers proposals in order for the profession to separate itself from its oppressive state and develop into a 'deep', sustainable profession.

■ The practice of ethics in HRD

Philosophical ethics is the study of right and wrong conduct within a defined environment. Also called moral philosophy, it involves systematizing, defending, and recommending concepts of right and wrong motivation and behaviour. Applied ethics attempts to solve moral dilemmas within a particular context or conflict. The diversity of approaches to applied ethics can provide choices when professionals are faced with decisions about values. The choice of ethics can also limit the practical as well as moral worth of the activity or outcome. The context in which ethics is applied serves to set boundaries and establish limitations. As examples, feminist ethics helps us understand right and wrong within a feminine point of view while business ethics is restricted by neo-classical economics that governs organizations in the global marketplace.

Throughout this chapter I discuss ethics from both academic and applied contexts. Business Ethics (note capitalization) as an academic subject is differentiated from the ethics of business as practised in work-related settings primarily through a separation between the norms and cultures that industries and organizations develop and defend, and the knowledge and understandings that individuals obtain through academic study and then hopefully transfer to behaviours and working values. These personal ethics may then become part of the norms and values that people bring to particular industries and organizational cultures. Although differentiated, there is a potential relationship between Business Ethics and the ethics of business.

Additionally, my interpretation of the terms capitalism and neo-classical economics require clarification. I take a narrow view of these terms as values that focus on the short term, development, economic-over-ecosystem, reductionist, exploitative, and exclusive versus sustainable, conservation, life-over-economics, holistic, diverse and inclusive. See Table 2.1, Comparison of business and ecocentric paradigms, later in this chapter, for further concepts that illustrate my idea of capitalism and neo-classical economics as business paradigm.

Business Ethics and the ethics of business

Continuous moral dilemmas sensationalized in the media highlight the need for ethics, especially within commerce and organizational contexts. 'Business ethics continues to have a marginal status in both the theory and the practice of commercial organizations' (Sorrel, 1998: 15). Underlying reasons for the need for business ethics include:

- the public's expectations that businesses act ethically;
- the possibility of harm to people and the environment;
- to comply with the law (e.g. the Sarbanes-Oxley Act in the US);
- the protection of employees' safety and health;
- to promote personal morality (Post, *et al.*, 2002).

While certainly not an exhaustive list, these explanations point to responsibilities that business has to its stakeholders.

Ethics as practised in business is by and large inept in tackling complex moral dilemmas in today's global work environments. A rationale for this lack of effectiveness includes:

- the philosophical nature of Business Ethics,
- common concepts that limit Business Ethics and the ethics of business, and
- contextual limits to the ethics of business.

Each of the three reasons is briefly discussed.

Philosophical nature of Business Ethics

'Some at least of its practitioners have taken the position that [ethical] theory is of little or no use in the solving of those real-life ethical problems' (Kaler, 1999: 207). This may be, in part, due to its theoretical nature and, unlike ethics in medicine and law, its failure to solve many real-world ethical problems. Dean added, 'There is a gap between the theory and practice of business ethics' (1997: 1638).

The theoretical nature of ethics as applied in business may also be attributed to the teaching and training of Business Ethics. De Rond (1996) suggested that ethics teachers are grounded in either moral philosophy or theology, not business or commerce, and thus are too far removed from real-world concerns of business to provide realistic and balanced guidance to practitioners. The philosophical nature of Business Ethics is also responsible at least in part for the lack of development and application of universal moral standards or codes that might bring some direction and stability to the practice of ethics.

Common concepts limit the usefulness of Business Ethics

Closely related to the philosophical nature of Business Ethics are the theoretical foundations that have been criticized as limiting Business Ethics' usefulness. It is not possible in this brief chapter to discuss all of the many and varied theoretical concepts that are considered foundations for Business Ethics. Included here is a discussion of stakeholder theory, a concept that is referenced consistently and with some frequency in the Business Ethics literature.

Stakeholder theory suggests that a firm has many constituents such as stockholders, employees, the public, communities and the environment which it should serve and that are affected by organizational decisions, processes and outcomes. Limitations of stakeholder theory include the legitimacy and conflicting needs of each stakeholder. The extent that each stakeholder has legitimate relationships with a firm and how a firm responds to such relations is a potential source of conflict. Not all stakeholders have equal status. Managers may find themselves caught between the needs of various stakeholders. For example, allocation of resources becomes problematic when the requirements of an environmental regulation conflict with the needs of employees.

Contextual limits to Business Ethics and the ethics of business

Add to this theoretical and conceptual ineffectiveness increasingly global, technological, developmental and consumer-driven contexts and it becomes apparent that business ethics has major constraints in providing a basis even for minimal ethical conduct.

Globalization and technology have caused new and unanticipated problems and opportunities that outpace contemporary ethics of business; witness its inability to address the recent breakdown in moral leadership and ethical practices within Enron, WorldCom, Shell, British American Tobacco, Tyco and others. Economic globalization is challenging ethics. Cultural and religious diversity make application of moral standards across continents and on a global basis difficult. Technologies that are testing the ethics of business and Business Ethics include those related to security, surveillance and employee privacy and confidentiality. Development as unimpeded economic growth and the conversion of people into rabid consumers, especially in the West, are strongly opposing the values that enhance humanity through sustained growth.

'Our very notions about the way the world works are based on what we have come to regard as the primordial urge to exchange goods with one another and become propertied members of society. We are an "experience" economy – a world in which each person's own life becomes, in effect, a commercial market.'

(Rifkin, 2000: 4, 7)

HRD and Business Ethics

Several scholars suggested that HRD has moral responsibilities and is an ethical endeavour (McLean, 2001; Chalofsky, 2003; Stewart, 2003a and b; Woodall, 1996; Hatcher, 2002); that the processes and outcomes of HRD contain values, morals and ethical implications. In support of these contentions a recent review of HRD-related scholarly publications revealed a lack of discussion on ethical theory in HRD. This review included scholarly publications from 1998–2003 for the following: Academy of Human Resource Development (AHRD) annual conference proceedings, *Human Resource Development Quarterly*, *Human Resource Development International*, *Advances in Developing Human Resources*, *Human Resource Development Review* and *Performance Improvement Quarterly*. A content analysis focusing on ethical theory and ethics and HRD theory revealed that of the hundreds of publications reviewed there were none with a specific focus on ethical theory in HRD and only four publications were located that specifically discussed ethics and HRD theory (see Swanson, 1999; Swanson and Holton, 2001; Hatcher, 2003; Stewart, 2003a and b). There were however several publications on ethics and HRD (see Russ-Eft, 2003; Stewart, 2003a; Aragon and Hatcher, 2001). A conclusion that can be drawn from this limited review is that ethical theory is not an overt concern to many HRD scholars and that ethics has played a superficial role in HRD to date. This lack of focus on ethics has many causes. However, a credible basis that has been raised here is the unquestioned reliance of HRD on business ethics which has not served to expand HRD as a moral or sustainable profession. HRD is compliant and a 'handmaiden' to neo-classical economics. This limits its influence beyond the organization, reducing provisions for a humane workplace or depreciating workplace democracy (Dirkx, 1996; Hatcher, 2004c). HRD has provided modest leadership in business ethics. It has been accused of being complicit in corporate wrongdoings and HRD has assisted in fostering less than ethical behaviours. 'It does appear that an institutional ethical vacuum or "moral hole" has been created' (Cornelius and Gagnon, 1999: 227).

It is increasingly obvious that the ethics that we either choose or inherit as part of the business contexts in which we find ourselves as our governing points of view and normative guidelines influences how we approach or carry out HRD-related practice and research. Adhering to a Business Ethic or the ethics of business based on neo-classical economics limits how organizations react to the environment, to the bottom line on a balance sheet. The result is HRD practice ill conceived to fully address the critical nature of values, morals and ethics that sustainable professions require.

Common concepts of HRD define it as organizationally bound. What is right and wrong within organizations is characterized as the ethics of business. Thus, HRD research and practice occurs within and is moderated by and dependent upon Business Ethics and the ethics of business. As stated previously, Business Ethics has contributed little to alleviating unethical practice. As a result, my question: 'To what extent has Business Ethics or the ethics of business added value to HRD?' is a valid and important one.

Due to its inherent 'good', HRD is likely to come under ethical scrutiny (Woodall and Douglas, 2000). Stewart added 'the basic confusion at the heart of business ethics [the ethics of business] is the false belief that business decisions and activities can be separated into ethical and non-ethical issues. The two are interrelated' (2003a: 92). He also said, 'HRD is, in and of itself, an ethical endeavour' (Stewart, 2003b: 83). The business approach to ethics has tended to be observational and based on external reflection, with few recommendations for change (Cornelius and Gagnon, 1999). Business Ethics has not provided a catalyst for morally sound work-related behaviours nor for the evolution of ethical norms for the HRD profession. And even though several sets of codes of ethics and standards of ethical behaviour exist (Russ-Eft and Hatcher, 2003), the promise of normalizing ethical behaviours remains unfulfilled. Without an HRD-specific ethic we have been compelled to engage in an existing ethic that has emerged from the capitalist market-economy and business environments in which most HRD professionals ply their craft (Hatcher, 2002).

This section outlined criticisms of general business ethics and ethics in HRD that are important to understand why business ethics cannot be considered crucial in HRD achieving its goals. To the extent that business ethics is not applicable, concepts that have been identified as important to HRD in achieving its goals are also important to discuss and analyze. The next section discusses sustainability and environmentalism as ethically-related ideas that, like business ethics, have been discussed but in reality have done little to enhance ethical consciousness or behaviours.

■ Sustainability and environmentalism: limits to ethics

Despite the growing public concerns over ethical *faux pas* of leaders and corporate-controlled environmental disasters, the field of business ethics offers little evidence of its positive influence on socially responsible organizations. To reiterate, in HRD ethics has been largely ignored when compared with other research topics. Although not a *carte blanche* indictment of HRD, it does symbolize the focus of HRD on economic performance and learning. As suggested earlier, one reason for this lack of focus is the narrow business-orientation of contemporary ethics in HRD. To the extent this is true, it is instructive to identify other concepts that may reinforce or substitute for business ethics.

Sustainability and environmentalism are concepts closely related to ethics that have legitimacy in the business literature and are important to firms in achieving their overall goal of doing the right thing. The problem is that they fall into the same category as business ethics when we attempt to apply them to the development of a profession such as HRD that seeks to create sustainable and humane work environments.

A major criticism of business ethics is its lack of sustainability:

'Neither profit nor market share nor mere reputation seems capable of providing the kind of substance that can fuel a morality over the long term. Profit and market share may not be unimportant, but perhaps should be subordinate to a deep-rooted loyalty to creating value.'

(de Rond, 1996: 55)

While this rhetoric appears *prima facie* to address the issues addressed by moral conflicts with a focus on profit and values, decidedly human issues, it fails to place *Homo sapiens* within the larger rubric of nature. Moral theorists have made the case that the utilitarian metric of pain and pleasure and moral reasoning are strictly human traits and that only humans should have moral status. An ethic inclusive of environmental issues facing organizations and long-term organizational sustainability as an outcome has been seen as crucial in other disciplines such as environmental economics. Attempts have been made to institutionalize ethics within business through compliance with environmental standards and seeking outcomes of ethics programmes such as sustainability. In other words, organizations have chosen to address environmental compliance and sustainability in an effort to highlight their intent to 'do the right thing' and flaunt their ethical 'character'. But, again, the manner in which environmentalism and sustainability have been conceptualized and manipulated within global commerce has thus far proven that neither is capable of reaching its full potential.

This conceptualization is based primarily on the logical-scientific and minimalists' idea that by viewing the environment equal to other stakeholders, such as employees and stockholders, will bring long-term benefits to the organization. However, this commonly-accepted approach to environmentalism is based on the notion that nature is a commodity to be used and that passing on long-term costs to the public – as in the case of the tremendous costs of managing the millions of tons of appliances, Styrofoam, automobiles and other consumer products that will be with us for millennia in our landfills – is acceptable. Another example is the externalization of workers' injuries that occur as a result of slow exposure to toxic chemicals even with workers' compensation and other government support. These costs are still primarily borne by the individual, families and the community, and not the responsible organization(s).

Organizations pursue environmentalism and sustainability only if it is in their self-interest and only if they can avoid litigation, retain shareholder value or profit in some economic manner. They accomplish this distortion by a blind faith that technology will continue to provide an infinite source of raw materials and natural resources. This egocentric, 'compassionate capitalism' suggests that 'humans are above nature and that the environment is an object – an assemblage of things – which obeys immutable laws, and that those laws can be discovered and subsequently used for human advantage' (Purser *et al.*, 1995: 1066). Sustainability of this type is a 'classic case of doublespeak', focusing more on a narrow economic view of organizations tied to the status quo. One of the problems with sustainability is the wide-ranging manner in which it is perceived and defined.

There are many definitions of sustainability. Holmberg and Sanderbrook (1992) identified some 70 definitions and Dobson (1998) found at least 300. The Brundtland Report 1987 definition by the World Commission on Economic Development is arguably the most commonly cited. It states that it is development that meets the needs of the present without compromising the ability of future generations to meet their own needs. Yet, this definition uses the human being as the unit of measurement with an emphasis on equality of economic opportunities for the future (Purser *et al.*, 1995).

Peter Singer (1975) and others have made a case against this 'speciesism' by insisting that unequal treatment of all living things is equivalent to disparate treatment of people of different races and genders. Holding no moral significance for non-humans is analogous to the way slaves are treated. Slaves have no moral significance because they are seen as 'less than' their owners. 'This way of treating people is called racism, but we could just as well substitute the word speceisism in regard to the manner in which nonhumans are treated' (Buchholz, 1993: 64). For some this is illogical because non-human beings cannot make moral choices. However, all living things have an intrinsic good of their own and thus qualify as moral subjects. Regan (1983) and Des Jardins (2001) explained this as ethical extensionism that proposes a hierarchical ordering of individuals within species (rather than ecosystems) with humans at the top and determining the value of nature only through human attributes.

Ecosystems do not exclude human culture. Rather, they include culture and thus human values. So, healthy ecosystems include human values that support ecological integrity. Only an *unhealthy* ecosystem requires human intervention through environmental management, upkeep and repair.

The notion of sustainability in business has focused on sustainable competitive advantage at the level of the firm (Srikantia and Bilimoria, 1997). Business scholars have defined sustainability in various ways. For example, Pfeffer (1994) defined sustainability in terms of investing in people as sustainable advantage while Collins and Porras (1994) suggested that sustainability promotes organizational survival. Senge (1990) implied sustainability as related to an organization's ability to learn or to die due to a 'learning disability'.

To date, sustainability in business has been generally viewed within a tactical to strategic time line (as compared to non-business definitions) as a competitive advantage, and 'conforming to the values and interests of established business institutions in reinforcing individualistic, market-driven, competitive economic growth' (Srikantia and Bilimoria, 1997: 390) by focusing on long-term performance gains. This commerce-oriented definition is in stark contrast to characterizations of sustainability in non-business disciplines such as ecology and environmental economics.

Non-business approaches to sustainability reflect a 'holistic concept of human welfare that recognizes the primacy of nature' (Jacob, 1994), and is concerned about the well-being of the planet as a whole and a conscious attempt to live in harmony with nature, thus providing a higher quality of life, especially for people living below the poverty level (Hickling, 1994; Hatcher, 2002). Non-business approaches also tend to maximize non-material dimensions of humanity including spiritual, social, psychological, political and ecological aspects that span an extensive intergenerational time horizon.

Srikantia and Bilimoria (1997: 394) point out that:

'These differences in the conceptualizations of sustainability illustrate the isomorphism engendered in the business literature by a dominant corporate paradigm, a distinct interpretative frame that homogenizes every phenomenon that is brought within its spotlight of inquiry.'

See Table 2.1 for a summary of differences in the business paradigm and the more ecocentric paradigm discussed here.

Table 2.1 Comparison of business and ecocentric paradigms

Business paradigm	Ecocentric paradigm
Dominance over nature; nature is an instrumental resource	Humans are part of and seek harmony with nature and not overseers. All life has intrinsic value independent of human usefulness
Ample natural resources are available and should be used by humans and organizations	Natural resources are limited and should be conserved and use limited
Strategic time horizon (typically less than ten years)	Intergenerational, extended time horizon. May be epochal
Economic hegemony	Human and non-human well-being is goal
Disenfranchisement	Organic wholeness
Individual metric	Community and ecosystem metric
Competition	Cooperation
Centralized control/authority	Democracy
Success measured in terms of financials	Success measured in terms of human welfare and sustainability
Any available technology as progress and solutions	Appropriate and sustainable technologies only
Monopoly of life and ideology	Diversity of life and ideas

HRD has had little focus on sustainability or environmentalism and, with a few exceptions, little has been written about the role of the environment or ecosystem within HRD. But, even if HRD embraced environmentalism and sustainability, the way that they have been defined and used within economically-oriented organizations would not significantly advance the profession.

A more sustainable approach to HRD is to view human beings as equal to, not above or superior to, or apart from other sentient beings and living entities; that nature is not a product to be used or is there for the sole use of humankind, but that we are stewards of nature. This shift in our paradigm from 'human'-centered to 'eco'-centered is a radical and complex concept.

What this revolutionary idea might mean to the profession and what we can do to achieve this transformation as a strategic goal is discussed next.

■ Building a 'deep' HRD

If the profession of HRD chooses to remain subservient to Business Ethics and the ethics of business, it will remain a 'handmaiden' to capitalism and thus superficial in terms of its ability to achieve sustainable outcomes. The tenets of deep ecology and social ecology are used here as analogies to suggest that approaches to the environment can be either 'shallow' or 'deep'. Generally speaking, deep means great in degree, intense or profound. When coupled with ecology it differentiates a deep versus shallow view of the environment as intrinsic versus instrumental. Deep ecology also requires the judgement of all stakeholders including nature and non-human species as morally considerable.

Deep ecology is attributed primarily to the work of Arne Naess (1973) Aldo Leopold (1966) and George Sessions (1985), and their attempts to describe a 'deeper, more spiritual approach to nature', and of most import to HRD, 'a more sensitive openness to ourselves and nonhuman lives around us... asking more searching questions about human life, society, and nature' (Devall and Sessions, 1985: 65). To date, HRD has done too little in terms of incorporating these kinds of holistic sensibilities into its research and practice. Even though I have previously made the case for a focus on environment, spirituality and eco-centric HRD (Hatcher, 2002, 2003, 2004a) the time for the profession to seriously investigate where it falls on a continuum between 'shallow' and 'deep' is well past due. In order for HRD to become 'deep' will require the profession (research, scholarship and practice) to assume a different attitude towards how its processes and interventions impact upon people and equally upon the ecosystem, and what effects its outcomes have on people as part of the environment. Through piecemeal, single-issue reform or change measures such as sustainability and environmentalism, as Bookchin, a well-known social ecologist suggested, problems that lead to human antagonism with nature emerge from 'within social development itself, not between society and nature' (1990: 32). Thus, environmental problems, while including technological and political issues, are primarily social problems. Global warming, among others, exists not because people have anthropocentric points of view, but because they dominate each other and colonize the social and natural worlds as mere resources for power and profit (Best, 1998) – what Habermas (1987) called colonization of the life world.

Social ecology is the most dominant concept in eco-anarchism. It suggests that the domination between people is the root cause of environmental destruction. 'The notion that man must dominate nature emerges directly from the domination of man by man' (Bookchin, 1991: 65) that reduces the planet to a resource for exploitation. Only under capitalism does this domination of people transfer to domination of nature. 'Owing to its inherently competitive nature, bourgeois society not only pits humans against each other, it also pits the mass of humanity against the natural world. Just as men are converted into commodities, so every aspect of nature is converted into a commodity, a resource to be manufactured and merchandised wantonly' (Bookchin, 1971: 63).

To become a 'deep' profession will require not only a radical shift in how we define the profession and its principal points of view but also a militant approach to actions and interventions. In terms of definition and points of view, borrowing an idea from my friend and colleague, Neal Chalofsky, what would it mean if HRD were removed from its organizational context; if we chose to view HRD as a set of interventions or actions that might act upon an individual, a group, an organization, a work system, an ecosystem, a region, or a culture for the specific outcome of enhancing sustainable development, potential and healthy growth? To date we have defined HRD as learning and performance within an organizational context, with little or no thought of its long-term consequences or to what end (with the possible exception of improving instrumental performance or learning tied to strategy). Are we so egocentric and anthropocentric that we limit our purview only to 'organizations' and to those entities that have feelings, a purpose and conscience, in other words, sentient beings? And what of the validity of the definition of organization and 'sentient' in today's world of virtual organizations, temporary employment and smart machines, biotechnology, and the probability that human cloning is a reality? Is this semantics or simple wordplay that fails to benefit us?

These abstractions and reifications take shape only in what Bateson called the epistemological fallacy of the separate 'I', an independent, 'self' that carves out identify and boundaries that are based only on linguistic convention (Bateson, 1972). The same can be said for organizations and professions which take shape within social cognitive spheres. We maintain these identities through social consensus, collective conscience and mental spaces that are malleable; they tend to transform over time. Professions encourage this discourse through socialization that tends to support the economic *status quo* and seldom provides an opportunity for meaningful questioning of the dominant socio-economic system.

A re-definition of the contexts that HRD is embedded within could potentially provide several results. Firstly, it would mean that we are not bound solely by economic or social practice or theory nor would we be isolated to a capitalistic worldview. Secondly, we would see HRD as having potential to develop learning, performance and meaning within individuals and 'others' as part of any abstract collective not necessarily that of a identity-bound or rational organization or system. Thirdly, this would expose the profession to

Bateson's (1972) idea of 'other' and Buber's (2000) notion of 'I and thou' to include the environment and non-human species and allow us to finally understand that what we do to ourselves we do to nature that sustains us. (For those unfamiliar with Buber, he proposed that we have two types of relationships: the 'I–It' relationship where we treat 'others' as objects and the 'I–Thou' relationship where we recognize 'others' as living beings rather than objects.)

If we remain tied to organizations and corporations in particular we remain defined by socio-economic contexts. As a fallback, less radical position, what if we choose 'work-related systems' instead of no context whatsoever in which to situate HRD? Work could be outside the organizational context, associated with family or an individual for example. But does this mean that we cannot help develop skills that enhance our leisure time or however we define the opposite of work? This is still HRD. So, if we choose organization as our context then we denigrate the individual; but, we cannot actually isolate an individual from his or her associations and interconnections with 'others' including 'other' sentient beings. It is hard to conceptualize a profession that is not situated within or to some extent beholden to some level of organization. What we must fully grasp is the degree to which contexts influences our ethics and our ability to achieve sustainability or a healthy relationship with nature and to consider seriously HRD without an organizational context.

To further the questioning of the organizational context, we should begin to identify to what extent HRD has a responsibility to ensure sustainability based on the outcomes, products or services that our organizations provide to society and the ecosystem. When organizations are faced with a decision between ethical 'ought' and economic 'musts', it seems clear which path they will take (Buchholz, 1993). Thus, HRD as subservient to economically-focused organizations is forced to either ignore or acknowledge outcomes, whether good or bad. But, the nature of the work being done cannot be ignored when we assume a more ecocentric and sustainable approach to HRD. Ethics training in an organization that is economically successful through the production of bombs or products that foul our air is a win–lose situation paramount to scrubbing the deck of the Titanic.

I suggest that an individual's choice of employment may not always be within his or her sphere of influence. But, to achieve a 'deep' profession requires more than a simple ethical sense or awareness of the products and services that we help to develop. It requires a commitment to eradicating organizations that produce or provide products or services that cause environmental damage or negatively affect the health and safety of people and/or non-humans. Again, this does not imply that individual HRD professionals are required to seek employment only in 'good' organizations. This is a personal ethical choice. What I am suggesting is that the profession takes on a commitment to meeting a stated goal of reducing and ultimately eliminating the use, manufacture or sale of products or services that cause environmental damage or health and safety hazards, and to provide support for professionals that choose not to aid 'bad' organizations. One way to accomplish this goal is to adhere to universal guidelines such as the CERES Principles (Coalition for Environmentally Responsible Economies: www.ceres.org) and to support through *pro bono* work or consulting those organizations that are responsible and honestly working towards sustainable outcomes.

Our definition of sustainable ought to reflect an ecocentrism that moves us beyond competitive advantage and towards embracing holistic indicators of human welfare (Srikantia and Bilimoria, 1997). These indicators include environmental, social, psychological, material, economic and spiritual well-being. It also requires us to take more responsibility in our associations with technologies; to cooperatively develop and support only those technologies that sustain quality of life and to help transfer these technologies and ensure equity across organizational, cultural and gender boundaries.

If we choose sustainability as our mantra this makes us a *part of* and not conquerors of nature. This is a 'base of moral awakening, analogous to the form of social change that corrected the evils of child labour and human slavery' (Purser *et al.*, 1995: 1073). Based less upon a question of 'What can I do?' and more upon an 'attitude of reverence for life, a respect for nature, which is concerned more with the question of "What kind of person do I want to be?"' (Des Jardins, 2001). But again, this will require radical changes in the way we conceptualize and practise HRD. As Kuhn (1962) and Barker (1992) suggested, theory development and shifts in our paradigms do not occur all at once nor do they occur quickly or without conflict. Instead, there is a long struggle that involves deconstruction of existing theory, a pointing out and acceptance of the incommensurability of competing paradigms of nature and business, and finally development, retrofitting and testing of alternative ways of thinking.

The current paradigms of HRD are learning, performance and meaning. Business ethics is focused on right and wrong conduct within a performance paradigm and as long as some return or value-add is obvious learning too remains an instrumental value. Yet, for people as employees, meaning like values is of paramount importance. Business ethics has well-established characteristics, for example, codes of ethics and cases. What it fails to accomplish is to provide a truly non-instrumental or non-fiscally-based way to address issues of morality and meaning. The failure of business ethics to sufficiently take into account the importance of meaning is what gives rise to 'other'-ethics that might result in an HRD-specific ethic. Adding values beyond the economic, towards meaning might be a beacon call for an HRD-ethic as a valid ethical theory (Hatcher, 2003). I believe that this is an example of and justification for the deconstruction of existing theory.

HRD-ethics would also provide the profession with a better way to address humanistic issues such as human rights and global contexts. An argument against HRD-ethics is that it has no conceptual foundation; that just because a profession chooses an ethics does not necessarily mean that it has a solid conceptual base. However, a case can be made that HRD-ethics already exists. The definition of ethics being right and wrong conduct implies that descriptive (cases) and normative (codes) characterizations of such conduct is explicit and at least to some extent accepted within a defined context. The more distinct HRD is as a profession separate from and not dependent upon business the more defined the context.

Finally, a new HRD ethic is more relevant today. Business ethics was a better fit when HRD was more confined to simply training and a primarily remote and esoteric field of study as a minor part of human resource management (HRM). However, in the current work environment this approach jeopardizes the enhancement of values and moral behaviours. In addition, HRD-ethics can sensitize us to specific HRD-related ethical problems such as human and non-human rights. Similar to ethical relativism, HRD-ethics viewed from a relativistic stance provides a lowest-common denominator approach to ethics; that is, that the context of HRD dictates an ethic. The more changes in context HRD is asked to operate within, the more applicable a specific ethic becomes.

An assumption made in this brief discussion of ethical theory is the organization as economic entity; that firms are rationally operated for wealth maximization. Their purpose is to produce goods and services that maximize financial performance. As a result, the predominant ethic within business is one that supports this economic goal. Concepts of sustainability and environmentalism that are related to and support business ethics were also discussed. However, these concepts have not been fully embraced. Even if acknowledged by the HRD profession, I suggest that because of their partisan focus on economics they would not enhance the profession to the extent that we might assume. The myopic views of ethics and supporting concepts offers HRD a narrow approach to morality. This is likely to be complicit in corporate wrongdoings and has assisted in providing environments that support unethical behaviours. Trying to adhere to a business ethic based on neo-classical economics results in HRD practice and scholarship ill-conceived to address fully the critical nature of values, morals and ethics in today's actual and virtual realities. A metatheory of ethics as a foundation for HRD may lead professionals to view their practice as a moral imperative versus an instrumental outcome, no matter how economically important the result.

This chapter addressed Business Ethics, the ethics of business and supporting concepts such as sustainability and environmentalism within current economic organizations and how they fail to enhance HRD. Radical shifts in how we view our profession in terms of contexts and justifications for a new HRD-ethic were discussed. These actions are necessary in order for HRD to separate itself from the morass of ethics as applied to business and to enhance the profession in efforts to achieve sustainability.

Chapter 3

The ethics of HRD

Jim Stewart

◼ Introduction

Taking an ethical stance is one way of being 'critical' (Fenwick, 2005). To do so questions and challenges the value assumptions that inform the practice and profession of management. However, as others have argued (see Hatcher in Chapter 2 of this book; Short and Callahan, 2005) such questioning and challenging is often within a frame of reference which itself accepts as given truth the beliefs which are fundamental to the economic system within which management is conducted and managers operate. If we accept that HRD practice and HRD professionals are, to some extent at least, operating in the sphere of 'management' then the same will be true of them. And therefore critical HRD from an ethical perspective will be similarly limited by accepting those beliefs as given truths. So, there is a need to go beyond the orthodoxy of accepting those beliefs in order to be truly 'critical'. This argument provides one element of the context of this chapter.

A second element of the context is the assertion that HRD research and theorizing has neglected the moral and ethical dimension of HRD practice (Perriton, 2005). I made such an assertion myself in the first issue of the journal *Human Resource Development International* (Stewart, 1998) and called for more attention to be paid to the ethics of HRD in the pages of that journal and elsewhere. I am glad to say that has happened although linking those two statements is not meant to imply either a causal relationship or personal credit. It is rather to recognize that the situation is now different and many more HRD researchers and writers are giving attention to ethics now than was the case in the late 1990s (e.g. Bates *et al.*, 2002; Hatcher, 2002; Douglas, 2004; Fisher, 2005; Lee, 2005). However, some of that work still reflects the first element of the context in that the fundamental beliefs of the economic system are the accepted frame of reference. What we have then is a situation where attention to the ethics of HRD is greater than it used to be, though still not extensive, but which is still mainly, but not exclusively, informed by what might be termed conventional frames of reference. I believe that the situation arises from a lack of acceptance of what I consider to be a basic truth of HRD practice and I want here to make the case for that truth.

The purpose of this chapter is then to demonstrate the truth and validity of the following proposition:

HRD is, in and of itself, an ethical endeavour.

A few words of explanation on the proposition will be helpful. The word endeavour is chosen to mean 'effort towards a goal'. I am confident that most readers will grant the premise that that is characteristic of HRD. What can be at issue though is the nature of the 'goal' and of the 'effort' and that begins to bring into sharp(er) relief the arguments in support of the proposition. My understanding of the word 'ethical' is that it describes phenomena in which moral values are implicated and in which, therefore, moral choices have to be made. So, I do not use the word 'ethical' to mean moral or good (see also Fisher, 2005). I use it to describe my view that the practice of HRD requires moral choices to be made.

The proposition represents the main opinion that I wish to express in this chapter. Additional opinions will be hinted at if not fully argued. A logical approach to the argument will be to say something about HRD, then something about ethics and then to bring those together to demonstrate the truth and validity of the argument. Broadly speaking, that will be my approach. I will though be saying some things about ethics when the main focus is HRD, and vice versa. However, I want to begin with an additional argument. It is one which is of some relevance to both elements of the context but in particular the first. It is simply that the study of business ethics, which to some extent sets the agenda for the study of ethics in HRD, is seriously flawed, and that is because it accepts the frame of reference within which business and management is conducted.

■ Business ethics – a flawed concept

I want to begin this section with a controversial opinion. It is simply that the study of business ethics is certainly wrong, at best confused and at worst just plain daft. My reasons for this opinion can be illustrated by two examples. The following is a quote from one of the early and still leading writers on the subject of business ethics:

'Business is driven by values. Some business values are commercial and technical...
Often, the values are clearly moral values as when companies declare their policy to
be "responsible".'

Donaldson (1992: v)

The implication of this argument is that it is possible to distinguish between moral and non-moral values in business and management. And, that commercial or technical issues and decisions have no moral dimension. If we then add that a basic assumption of free-market economics is that pursuit of profit is the most fundamental of commercial, or technical, values in business then according to Donaldson's argument and position, this is not a moral value and so morality need not enter the variables influencing decisions. It follows from this that those commercial or technical decisions on sourcing manufacturing, for example, in third-world countries using child labour for less than subsistence wages, have no moral implications. Taken to a logical conclusion, such a position would also endorse working conditions which provide high risk to health, or even life, as similarly not needing to trouble the moral conscience of decision-makers. Therefore the basic 'business of businesses' does not have a moral or ethical dimension.

Donaldson's position is illustrative of the kind of thinking which leads the literature on business ethics to focus only on some aspects of business and management to the exclusion of others. My second example from a more recent piece of work (Davies, 1997) is fairly typical of the kinds of issues addressed by the business ethics literature. These are:

■ sustainability
■ corporate governance
■ social responsibility
■ whistle blowing.

In my view then, the basic confusion at the heart of current understandings of business ethics – a confusion which makes that understanding wrong and, on occasions, just plain daft – is to view the activities of business, and the decisions and actions of those who manage them, as separable into ethical and non-ethical issues. I personally find it impossible to conceive of any aspect of business and management which does not have a moral dimension. The confusion I see as arising from the opposite view may in part explain why Tom Sorrell (1998: 15) can make the following observation:

'Business ethics continues to have a marginal status in both the theory and the practice of commercial organisations at the end of the 1990s.'

According to the moral philosopher, Mary Midgley (who I will return to later), the same might be said of ethics itself as a field of study. It is not just business ethics that is marginalized. Midgley (1996: 14) has this to say:

'For many highly educated people, in fact, ethics is enclosed today in a ghetto that shuts it off altogether from the rest of the intellectual scene.'

The views expressed by Midgley and Sorrell on ethics in general and business ethics in particular, suggest reasons why the ethics of HRD has been in the past a neglected field of study. One of the first and most influential pieces of work on ethics and HRD was done by Professor Jean Woodall and her colleague Danielle Douglas. They have this to say on the ethics of HRD:

'Training and development activities are perhaps the area of HRM policy and practice that is least likely to come under ethical scrutiny, invariably being presented as intrinsically "good activities".'

(Woodall and Douglas, 2000: 116)

This suggests that the ethics of HRD was indeed a neglected topic. As indicated in the introduction though, that is less the case than in the recent past. The quote implies a particular reason for that previous neglect. A conversation I had recently with a senior HRD practitioner suggests a different reason. He offered the following opinion:

'The ethics of HRD isn't it? There aren't any are there?'

When pressed, this practitioner elaborated by arguing that HRD served managerial purposes and therefore adopted whatever approaches or methods worked in particular circumstances without needing to consider ethical implications. Logically therefore HRD can indirectly support the exploitation of child labour and still remain inherently either 'ethically good' or 'ethically neutral'. These two quotes on the specific case of the ethics of HRD – one from an academic text and one from a practitioner – illustrate the confusion inherent in current understanding of the topic. And it is this confusion that, in my view, explains the first element of the context of this chapter. It is because the basic rationale of free-market economics remains unquestioned and unchallenged that 'ethics' is separated out of mainstream business and management research, thinking and writing. The notion that some activities of management, and of managers, have an ethical dimension and others do not arises from an acceptance of the frame of reference that believes maximizing profit, or surplus in other contexts, is a prerequisite for continued success. Thus the ethical dimensions of that belief are not examined. This separation is also evident in work on the ethics of HRD. Writers such as Douglas (2004) and Perriton (2005) focus on particular and specific aspects of HRD practice for an ethical analysis, rather than HRD itself as an ethical endeavour. This may also be partly explained by the basic assumption articulated by Woodall and Douglas that HRD is inherently 'good'. The paradox of course is that the particular and specific examples illustrate the false logic at play in separating activities into those that have ethical implications and those that do not. I hope that I have made clear the confusion at the heart of business ethics which in turn has implications for and impacts on the ethics of HRD. It is in any case now time to return to the proposition.

A theory of HRD

To demonstrate the truth and validity of the proposition, I have to first establish what it is I mean by the term HRD. My starting point here is that there is no theory of HRD. There has of course been much theorizing on the concept and so my position on the subject, in common with that articulated in the previous section, will not be without controversy. It can though be easily established by reference to two recent reviews of the literature of HRD. The first concentrated primarily on the US-based literature and reached the following conclusion:

> 'Without a focus on the theoretical foundations of research and practice, HRD is destined to remain atheoretical in nature.'
>
> Hatcher (2000) quoted in McGoldrick et al. (2002)

Working with Professor Jim McGoldrick and Sandra Watson, I recently completed a review of the literature which encompassed both US and European sources. The following quotes come from that work:

> '[this] suggests that HRD has not established a distinctive conceptual or theoretical identity.'

> 'This variety of perspectives demonstrates vividly that there is no dominant paradigm of HRD research.'
>
> (McGoldrick et al., 2002)

My main point is that there is no theory of HRD. I want to go further. In my view, there is no possibility of a theory of HRD, at least not in the sense that I understand the concept of theory. More importantly, I also believe that we do not need a theory of HRD and for a very simple reason. As I intend to show later, HRD is concerned with influencing, some might say shaping, human behaviour. HRD therefore rests on theory which is concerned with understanding and explaining human behaviour. And we have quite enough of those without adding to that confusion!

To justify the previous assertion, I could at this point include an examination of theories of human behaviour by addressing the perennial 'nature versus nurture' debates and, in particular, attempts to produce a unifying theory in what is known as socio-biology. My reasons for adopting that focus are that I have read and been influenced by the science of ethology since the early 1970s and I am a persuaded evolutionist as well as a social scientist. However, I do not have the space in a single chapter to do justice to those theories and debates. I do though want to briefly mention that I fail to be impressed by the latest attempt to unite biological and social explanations of human behaviour through what is termed evolutionary psychology, and I am sceptical about either its power to unite the biological and social sciences or its validity in explaining human behaviour, for two reasons. Firstly, it fails to unite biological and social theories since it gives dominance to the former over the latter. In fact, it does nothing to unite the disciplines since it simply provides biological explanations for social behaviour. This leads to my scepticism on its validity which rests on some of those explanations. According to evolutionary psychology, there are valid biological and evolutionary reasons why men do not do housework. It is not our fault or even our conscious choice apparently – it is genetically determined! Two other examples of male behaviour illustrate what is in my view the absurdity of these arguments. Firstly, the existence of the 'glass ceiling', which describes men denying women promotion opportunities, is actually the result of Darwinian evolution; secondly men raping women has its cause and explanation in the same process. I have both moral and intellectual reasons for rejecting such arguments, but I will leave readers to ponder what they might be as the chapter and argument develops.

As a long-standing amateur student of ethology, and convinced evolutionist as well as social scientist, I do support the principle and the possibility of a unifying theory of human behaviour. And there is one which I find persuasive, not least because it synthesizes much of my own thinking and many of my opinions. The theory has been argued very cogently by Patrick Bateson and Paul Martin (2000), and their argument is represented in Figure 3.1. A number of points need to be made about this diagram:

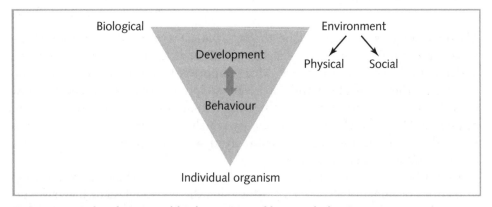

Figure 3.1 A developmental biology view of human behaviour

Source: An interpretation of Patrick Bateson and Paul Martin (2000) 'Design for a life: How behaviour develops'

1 It does not appear in the book by Bateson and Martin; it is my interpretation of their arguments.
2 The diagram is meant to demonstrate a strong and interactive relationship of mutual influence between development and behaviour; a point of obvious significance to HRD.
3 Both development and behaviour are influenced by biological factors which create both potentialities and limitations.
4 These potentialities and limitations of behaviour and development are influenced by experience of and in both physical and social environments.
5 Factors unique to the individual organism also influence behaviour and development.
6 In the case of human beings at least, these individual factors include agency; that is the exercise of choice and free will so that neither behaviour nor development is fully determined by either biological or environmental factors, or exclusively by their interaction. Individuals are active agents in their own development and behaviour.

I can illustrate these arguments with the simple example of my height. The reason I am 5'5" is because of the complex interaction of the factors in Figure 3.1. Biologically, I was destined to be never less than say 4'11" and never more than say 5'9" when fully grown. The physical environment influenced my growth through the living conditions, including the availability of food of varying types, I experienced during the development of my height. Of those available, the choice of food I actually consumed was influenced by people in my social environment – parents, siblings and peers, for example. So too were the forms of physical exercise I chose to engage in, or not. In the end, I exercised some choice on food consumed and exercise undertaken and so exercised agency. All of which lead to my arriving at 5'5". My height is an example of physical development. It illustrates though that even that aspect of development is influenced by behaviour and agency. Bateson and Martin (2000: 238) make the point thus:

'In reality, developing organisms are dynamic systems that play an active role in their own development.'

This point has obvious implications for ethics. Without agency, the notion of ethics has no meaning or value. Bateson and Martin make an additional important point for my overall argument. It is that, for human beings at least, learning is a critical factor in influencing development and behaviour. And that learning is both a biological and social phenomenon. They have this to say about learning:

'It seems likely that the initial rules for learning are themselves unlearned, universal and are the product of Darwinian evolution.'

(Bateson and Martin, 2000: 76)

'Behaviour, in particular, becomes adapted to local conditions during the course of an individual's development, whether through learning by trial and error or through copying others.'

(Ibid.: 8)

These two quotes suggest a biological propensity to learn through a process which depends on experiences in a physical and social environment, and which has social outcomes in the form of both individual behaviour and social relations. This has obvious significance and implications for HRD.

■ A model of HRD

I have argued so far that HRD is concerned with human behaviour and that developmental biology provides the best understanding of human behaviour that we have to inform the practice of HRD. It is now time to be more precise about what I mean when I use the term HRD. I developed a model of HRD in the early 1990s. Since then, I have discussed the model with many colleagues and students, receiving many comments and suggestions. So far though, I have not had reason to change the model. It follows from and is based on the following definition:

'Human resource development encompasses activities and processes which are **intended** to have impact on organisational and individual learning. The term assumes that organisations can be constructively conceived of as learning entities, and that the learning process of both organisations and individuals are capable of influence and direction through deliberate and planned interventions. Thus, HRD is constituted by **planned interventions** in organisational and individual **learning processes**.

(Stewart, 1999: 17)

Three points arise from the definition:

1 The last sentence contains the essence of the definition.
2 The highlighted words are critical. Interventions abound in everyday experience, but only those which are intended, deliberate and planned constitute HRD practice or processes.
3 There are two key components of HRD practice: interventions and learning processes.

The resulting model is shown in Figure 3.2.

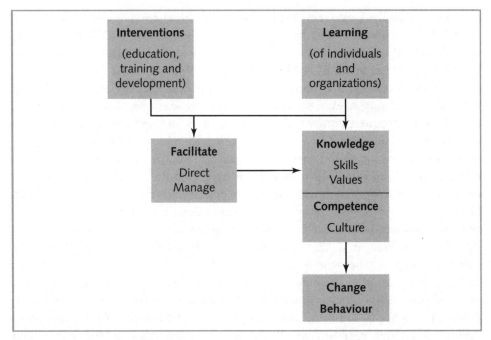

Figure 3.2 A model of HRD

Some explanation of the model is necessary. There is no direct connection between interventions and learning because there is no necessary and certainly no causal relationship, which a direct connection might suggest. For human beings, learning is a biological imperative and we learn naturally in the same sense as we breathe naturally; we are born to do so. Moving down the right side of the model, both biological and social understandings would support the view that learning is an influencing factor on behaviour. I do not believe and nor do I wish to claim that behaviour is linked in a direct causal relationship with learning. But, I do believe and claim that learning is a significant influencing factor.

Turning to the left side of the model, it suggests that interventions constitute HRD practice. Various labels are used to categorize different types of intervention. Here, despite my view that debates on defining different categories are often sterile and of no value (see Stewart, 1999), three commonly recognized categories of education, training and development are used. I use these simply because the categories *are* commonly used and understood, a point which can be illustrated by two examples of applying the first two categories. Firstly, if I require an operation then I would much prefer a trained surgeon to an educated surgeon. Secondly, I am very happy for my child to receive sex education in school, but there is no way I am going to approve sex training! These amusing (hopefully!) illustrations conceal the problematic of distinguishing the categories, a point reinforced by the lack of such an illustration for development.

While the focus of interventions is learning processes, they serve three separate but related purposes. The first is to facilitate learning. This simply means to make the particular content of learning more likely and easier than it would be otherwise. The second is to direct learning to achieve particular and specified outcomes rather than others. The third, to manage the resources allocated to facilitating and directing to achieve efficient and effective utilization. It is recognized that these purposes suggest a performative orientation for HRD. However, in my view, this does not necessarily equate with performance objectives in organizations. Such a suggestion arises only if we apply the beliefs informing the view that 'the business of businesses is business'. If alternative beliefs are applied then the focus and nature of performance can be different and can, for example, encompass notions such as 'world citizenship' (see Short and Callahan, 2005). This point also illustrates that my use of 'organization' is deliberately loose. It is not meant to imply for-profit business organizations or even perhaps 'organization' at all. Rather, the intention is to focus on social collectives as distinct from individuals.

What links interventions and learning are the mediating factors specified in the centre of the right side of the model. Within HRD practice, these factors are seen to be the outcomes of learning which, in turn and in part, influence behaviour. At the individual level, these factors are referred to as knowledge, skills and values, or, sometimes, attitudes. At the organizational level, the notion of competence encompasses knowledge and skills while the concept of culture stands for attitudes or values. Thus, they might just as well apply to a charity, a school or a social enterprise. These distinctions, between knowledge, skills and values, or between competence and culture, are, as we will see later, of the same form as the categories of interventions. That is, they are analytical devices with some useful applications rather than representations of any true or experienced reality. One of the useful applications is to allow me to express another of my opinions.

The traditional focus of learning in higher education (HE) has been and remains subject knowledge. That has and does provide the content of learning. Over the past ten years or so, there has been a growing emphasis in the UK on skills of various forms, especially those related to what is termed 'employability'. Currently, we who work in HE are required to specify our intended learning outcomes in terms of both subject knowledge and a range of skills sets. It has always struck me as strange that little attention is either demanded or paid to values. Certainly at the levels of modules, courses and programmes almost no debate occurs on the values that the learning experiences actually do, or might wish to, develop in students. Unlike knowledge and skills, we are not required to identify or specify attitudinal or value outcomes in our descriptors. I find this situation more than a little worrying. The chapters later in this book examining HRD work in the classroom are of relevance to this point and, I think, a step in the right direction.

To return to the model, the box at the very end provides the ultimate rationale for HRD practice. This is simply to change behaviour. The purpose of HRD practice is to take an individual or collection of individuals with an existing set of behaviours through a planned learning experience, so that those behaviours are changed. This is as true of higher education as it is of practice in employing organizations. Changed behaviour is the success criteria of HRD. Or, perhaps more accurately, an increased range of behavioural options and choices.

The previous sentence has, for me, ethical echoes which I hope are apparent to readers. They are similar to those sounded by the phrase 'effort towards a goal' earlier in the chapter. The echoes also signal that it is now time to turn our attention to the subject of ethics.

■ The nature of ethics

The fundamental focus and purpose of ethics is succinctly expressed by Bowie and Duska (1990: 3):

> 'Ethics... is a study that attempts to shed light on the question "What should one do?".'

While these authors provide a useful summary of the focus and purpose of ethics, they go on to mistakenly create a distinction between serious and non-serious questions and issues which have, according to them, serious or non-serious consequences. The notions of 'serious' and 'non-serious consequences' are of course problematic. This can be illustrated by the example given by Bowie and Duska (Ibid.):

> 'not putting oil in one's car ... will not have serious consequences.'

An example which, in my view, also illustrates their mistake. The consequences of not putting oil in a car will include the car itself becoming scrap and therefore a waste of the earth's resources and the adding to of physical waste which has to be dealt with in ways which add to environmental problems. As with issues in business ethics, I find it difficult to conceive of questions or issues which do not have 'serious consequences' and so I would argue that the question, 'What should one do?' does not require any qualification. The distinction is in any case in the same category as those drawn in business ethics and so is an illustration of the same logical flaw.

Apart from the problem of identifying issues that matter and those that do not, the most vexed question in ethics is perhaps whether or not there are universal answers, in the form of 'natural law', to the question 'What should one do?' My position is that there are indeed universal answers which are, literally, based on natural law. The form of that natural law is very well expressed by Andrew Brown (1999: 79):

> 'Humans are naturally idealistic and altruistic among many other, sometimes contradictory, things.'

Brown's use of the word and concept of 'natural' is the same as I used them previously in relation to learning; behaving in an idealistic and altruistic manner is, for human beings among some other animals, a biological imperative. He reaches his conclusion based on a review of debates in evolutionary biology. This position is also argued very persuasively by the moral philosopher Phillippa Foot (2001) in her book *Natural Goodness* and so it has both scientific and philosophical credibility. The implication is that the natural law determining what is ethical, in the sense of being 'right' or 'good', is behaving in an idealistic and altruistic manner. Brown's quote implies though that we, as human beings, are also naturally the opposite of idealistic and altruistic; we are also materialistic and selfish. But, without that contradiction and the existence of agency, there would be no possibility of choice and therefore the question posed by Bowie and Duska as the central focus of ethics would not arise. Nor indeed would the need for any natural law to guide answers to the question.

The position suggested by Brown and argued by Foot finds support in the work of Gorringe. He relates ethics to the meaning and value of life which, according to Brown and to Foot, must in part have a biological answer. Gorringe (1999: 9) then goes on to argue the following:

> 'We, as humans, are fundamentally concerned with what is life conserving... what it is that promotes human well being,... that makes for joy, creativity, security, the flourishing of love and happiness... Whatever promotes all these things is good; whatever destroys them is bad. Therein lies our ethics, our morality, and the foundations of what we call social justice.'

It is clear from this quote that Gorringe is arguing universal answers and a natural law. If we accept that by 'fundamentally' Gorringe means 'natural' in the same sense as Brown and as Foot, then Gorringe too is making the same case in relation to a biological imperative towards idealistic and altruistic behaviour as the basis of the natural law. Gorringe (Ibid.: 19) calls on support from what may seem a strange authority in this context when he cites Hayek:

'Hayek recognises that the altruistic virtues are deeply ingrained, perhaps innate.'

As with Brown and, in particular, Foot, Gorringe (Ibid.: 31) relies on the view that human beings are social animals as the basis for arguing the centrality of altruism to ethical questions:

'Sociological and psychological studies, however, seem to confirm Aristotle's view that we are indeed community animals. We are not "individuals" but persons in relation to each other. The only absolutely "individual" thing about us is a corpse.'

Interestingly, what we have in this quote is a philosopher using the social sciences to support a position argued by the natural sciences. We can add the words of another scholar and writer to provide further support to the argument. Umberto Eco (Eco and Martini, 2001) argues the existence of what he refers to as 'universal semantics'. These might be referred to as 'natural understanding' if not 'natural laws'. In addition, Eco goes on to argue that these universal semantics provide the basis for a 'natural' ethical system. And, he further argues that the social nature of human beings is at the centre of that ethical system. This is apparent in the following quote:

'and the ethical dimension comes into play when the other arrives on the scene… Just as we couldn't live without eating or sleeping, we cannot understand who we are without the gaze and reaction of the other.'

(Eco, 2000: 93–4)

According to the moral philosopher Mary Midgley, Darwin himself argued a position very similar to that of Gorringe. Midgley's summary of Darwin's argument is presented in Figure 3.3.

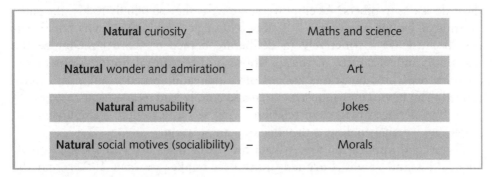

Figure 3.3 Darwin's contribution
Source: Based on Mary Midgley (1996)

The use of the word 'natural' here is again as I have used it consistently in this chapter. Darwin argued that the list of characteristics on the left is part of our biological make-up and heritage. These biological characteristics find corresponding cultural expression through the activities and aspects of social life listed on the right. But, as Midgley points out, and as Brown implied, Darwin suggested additional biological characteristics, especially in relation to social motives. We are altruistic but we are also selfish. We do cooperate but we also compete. This creates conflicts and the need for choices to be made. As the following quote illustrates, Midgley (1996: 98) argues that without those conflicts there is no choice and therefore no need for ethics.

> 'It is the conflicts which give rise to the need for rules and priorities, and therefore for morality.'

Midgley's analysis and argument supports that of Bateson and Martin; biological imperatives do not deny the existence and role of human agency. For Midgley, agency is the basis of freedom. And it is the freedom to choose that creates both the need for and the focus of ethics. So, what choices are faced in HRD practice and what can guide them?

■ Implications of ethics for HRD

In this final part of this chapter I want to examine the connections between ethics and HRD. I think there are three important implications for HRD that arise out of what I have said about ethics. The first is I think pretty obvious. If the rationale, purpose and success criteria of HRD are changed behaviour, two sets of questions need answering. First: What is the desired or required behaviour? How will current behaviour be changed? Second: As students, are we content to leave those decisions to others? As employees, are we willing to blindly follow the paths determined by our employers? I think and hope not. And, if not, why not? I suggest because we instinctively (a deliberate choice of word!) recognize the essentially moral nature of the questions and the moral implications of the answers. Sadly, the questions are not often or readily posed in the form I have framed them here. This can just as often and readily lead to unethical answers. As Timothy Gorringe observes in relation to my second example – employers and employees – managerialism is the ethic of manipulation.

The second implication arises from the distinctions drawn between knowledge, skills and values. I argued in my first book, (Stewart, 1991), that the distinction is a useful analytical device rather than an accurate representation of reality. The concepts themselves can be related to psychological theory which distinguishes three domains of experience, as illustrated in Figure 3.4.

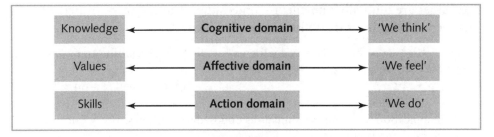

Figure 3.4 Psychological domains of experience
Source: Based on Stewart (1996)

The domains of experience – and the distinctions between knowledge, skills and values – imply that 'we think, feel and do' separately. In my view, this is inaccurate and misleading. We actually experience all three at the same time and do not ourselves, in our lived experience, draw those distinctions. And, not only do we 'think, feel and do' all at the same time, what logically follows is that our thoughts, feelings and actions are mutually immanent. This argument is represented in the model in Figure 3.5.

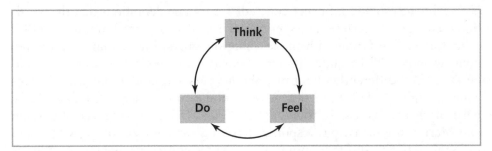

Figure 3.5 Think, feel, do

What follows from Figure 3.5 is that any and all HRD interventions will have an impact on values. It is irrelevant that the intended purpose is to merely pass on knowledge, and a lecture, for example, is a common means for achieving that kind of intended purpose. Since the supposed distinction and separation of knowledge, skills and values do not reflect or represent the reality of lived experience, it is not possible to design or conduct an intervention that is value free or neutral. Therefore, HRD always has impact on values and, consequently, always has an ethical content and dimension. This view is not of course universally held and some recent work on the ethics of HRD reinforces the assumed distinction between 'reason' and 'emotion' (Perriton, 2005). However, the premise which supports my argument – that knowledge, skills and values are mutually immanent – finds support in the work of two authors I have cited already, as the following quotes illustrate:

'The behaviour of brain-damaged patients reveals how crucial the emotions are in real-life decision-making.'

(Bateson and Martin 2000: 243)

'Communication … is, among animals as opposed to machines, always an emotional as well as an intellectual business.'

(Midgley 1996: 138)

We now turn to the third and final implication. It concerns the nature of interventions. Intervention is an interesting word and concept. It is used, I believe, to hide the real implications of what it means to 'intervene'. The *Oxford English Dictionary* uses the word 'intervene' to define 'interfere', and vice versa.

'Intervention'	'Interfere'
Interference, especially by a state in another's affairs	Meddle, obstruct a process. Take part or intervene, especially without invitation or necessity

We might with some confidence conclude from these definitions that the words 'intervene' and 'interfere' are synonyms. But, if I say that I am, as an HRD practitioner, interfering with the learning of others, rather than intervening, your response will be quite different. Something seems not quite as it should be. You 'feel' differently about me, about yourselves and about what is happening within my HRD practice. A very good example of where this might be particularly the case can be found in Lee (2005). Using the language of Bateson and Martin, non-conscious responses have a greater impact on conscious and rational analysis, and they more quickly enter conscious awareness. Why is that? I would argue it is again an 'instinctive' stirring because of the ethical nature of HRD practice. The simple question, 'By what right does one person interfere with the learning of others?' highlights the ethical dilemma inherent in HRD practice. Generating the question by using the word 'interfere' also, I would argue, supports the view that morality is a central component of the human condition. Your, indeed our, response to the word is, in that sense, entirely 'natural'.

A final observation on the word 'intervention'. It is commonly used in the medical profession. That profession pays significant attention to its ethics. Perhaps they recognize the connection with 'interfere'. HRD practice though is still faced with the question, 'What should one do?'

■ A categorical imperative

I have so far attempted to show how things are in relation to HRD and ethics, and the connections between them. Assuming some success in that task, does describing how things are allow me to argue how things should be? According to enlightenment thinkers such as David Hume, the answer to that question is a straightforward 'no'. We cannot make statements on how things should be based on how things are. This rests on the distinction drawn between empirical and normative statements. What I have argued so far should suggest that I have problems accepting that distinction and, therefore, the logical conclusion that follows from it. In other words, Hume was and is wrong. Mary Midgley agrees with that statement. So too does Timothy Gorringe, who has this to say on the subject:

> 'This distinction [between positive and normative studies] was specious from the start because the distinction between positive and normative science itself represents a value judgement.'
>
> (Gorringe, 1999: 44)

> 'fact and value belong together, and not only can we derive an "ought" from an "is", but we can also derive a categorical imperative from the way things are.'
>
> (Ibid. 59)

My earlier argument on the immanent nature of knowledge, skills and values supports the position so forcefully argued by Gorringe. Taking support and permission from Gorringe's position, I now want to offer a categorical imperative for HRD practice and practitioners. And, it is important to note that I continue to include academics working in higher education, in any and all subjects and disciplines, in my definition of HRD practitioners.

The categorical imperative follows, I believe, from the arguments I have presented in this chapter. It is though also based on an insight from Mary Midgley that I hope many readers will agree with. Midgley writes the following in her book:

> 'Our unity as individuals is not something given. It is a continuing, lifelong project, an effort constantly undertaken in the face of endless disintegrating forces.'
>
> (Midgley, 1996: 23)

Midgley is referring to the sense of self, to personal identity. Supporting the constant struggle to maintain that sense and identity is, I think, promoted by the values of cooperation and altruism. This is the basis of the categorical imperative I want to promote for HRD. It is put very well by Bateson and Martin (2000: 254):

> 'The best gift that can be given to a child is the happiness that comes from being able to cope successfully in a complex world.'

If we substitute the word 'child' with the word 'person' we have, nearly, a categorical imperative for HRD. The practice of HRD ought to serve the purpose suggested in Bateson and Martin's words. It can best achieve that purpose by promoting the qualities listed by Gorringe – joy, creativity, security, etc. – which, in turn, are more likely if the idealism and altruism identified by Brown are also promoted by and through HRD practice.

There is though a limitation to the imperative as it stands. Coping successfully in a complex world is a valuable and worthwhile aspiration. But, as we have seen, HRD is about change. And, as we have also seen, humans have the gifts of freedom and agency. As Karl Marx advised, it is not enough to understand the world; the point is to change it. So, any final categorical imperative for HRD will not only reflect the sentiments in the quote from Bateson and Martin, it will also embrace changing as well as coping with the world.

A syllogism and a closing

I want to close the chapter with a final argument in support of my original proposition. The argument is in the form of a syllogism. To be valid, a syllogism has to have a logical construction. I am confident it has, but readers can be the judge. To be true, a syllogism has to have premises which are true. I rely on the authority of Watson for the truth of the first premise and on the work of two major UK writers on HRD for the truth of the second premise. The work and status of all three mean that we can accept the premises as being true. The syllogism is as follows:

> 'Organising and managing is, through and through, an ethical and moral endeavour.'
> (Tony Watson, 1994, 1998)

> 'Human resource development is an organising and managing function.'
> (Rosemary Harrison, 1998; John Walton, 1999)

> 'HRD is an ethical and moral endeavour'

> QED

This chapter has had the intention of arguing a particular position on the ethics of HRD, expressed in the form of a proposition. If I have demonstrated the truth and validity of the proposition, it does not follow that I believe or claim to have provided the last word on the subject. There remains much work to be done but, in common with Lee (2005), I do not mean in the form of producing ethical codes of practice, even if they have some place and value. Much of the work will be by individual professionals working out their own position. Unlike Lee though, I do not believe that we are the single 'authors of our own world' or believe in the relativism that implies. But, just as a code of practice cannot be imposed or policed in any meaningful sense, even if it can be remembered and recalled at the point it is needed, so too can a categorical imperative be ignored. Understanding the current ethical positions of HRD professionals will be another area of important work and that being done by Bates and Hsin-Chih (2004), and by Fisher (2005), albeit from different perspectives, will provide significant advances on that understanding. Such understanding will be useful in helping professionals work out their own positions. In the end though I believe we have to move on from the unquestioning acceptance of the 'orthodoxy' of free-market economics before real progress in achieving the inherent potential of HRD practice can be achieved. A potential which I believe arises from the inherent ethical nature of that practice.

Activities for Part One

1 (a) Construct a rationale for your personal understanding of the notion of 'critical' as it applies to the study and practice of HRD.

(b) Examine your rationale in the light of the arguments presented in the chapters in this section. Explain how those arguments either support or challenge your rationale.

(c) Discuss your results with colleagues. Review your personal understanding and rationale in the light of your discussions.

2 (a) Select and describe one *major* or *significant* HRD intervention with which you are currently involved.

(b) Evaluate the extent to which the intervention can be said to be congruent with the principles of critical HRD.

(c) Discuss the results with colleagues and determine any changes you wish to make to future interventions.

3 (a) Select one chapter from this section.

(b) Produce a thorough analysis of the strengths and weaknesses of the arguments presented in the chapter.

(c) Present your analysis to colleagues to facilitate debate on the pros and cons of the arguments.

(d) Identify the implications of the results of this activity for the professional practice of HRD.

Part Two

IN THE WORKPLACE

Introduction to Part Two

This part has the title 'In the workplace'. This is a somewhat arbitrary way of distinguishing it from the next part. Here the focus is on professional practice in an employment context. What we mean by this is that the decision-makers on HRD practice are employed in non-educational work organizations and that the recipients of that practice are in the same employment position. So, those two features are the defining characteristics of what we mean by 'in the workplace'. That being the case, an educational setting for the HRD intervention is not excluded and this is illustrated by the inclusion in this part of the chapter by Jean Kellie. But the chapters in this part have a primary focus on HRD as practised in non-educational work organizations. This context might be argued to be the assumed, or 'default', position of what is meant by HRD. Such a view is though highly questionable. Work by all of the editors has included examination of university programmes and not just those designed and delivered for corporate clients. The model of HRD proposed by one of the editors back in 1992 included all educational practice as within the meaning of HRD and this shared understanding is applied in the next part of the book. In addition, national policy in relation to education, training and development is now widely accepted also to be encompassed by the concept of HRD, even though separate terms such as 'vocational education' and 'training' are also applied. It is therefore useful, if not necessarily always easy or precisely accurate, to apply the term 'workplace' to denote a particular category of HRD practice and one which is distinguishable from others such as education or national policy.

Despite the arguments above, it is probably the case that workplace HRD is the most significant in having an impact on the lived experience of the largest number of people. And, as part of that impact on individuals, on the social relations that form a central part of that lived experience. It is certainly the case for modern Western nations that work organizations are a significant component of the social structures within which people live their lives, irrespective of their role in the creation, co-creation or re-creation of those structures. It is also probably the case that one outcome of what is usually referred to as globalization is that this is true of more and more nations and greater numbers of people. So, workplace HRD is 'critical', in the sense of important and significant, for a 'critical approach', in the many other senses applied in this book, to its study and practice. Workplace HRD though may also be the most difficult, contested and challenging context for application of critical HRD. This is because, among other reasons, unstated and therefore unquestioned assumptions provide the basis for ongoing operation of work organizations. These assumptions are in turn derived from related and equally unstated and unquestioned assumptions that inform the political economy within which work organizations widely operate. The simplest and clearest examples of the latter are those of classical economics and political philosophy which are used to underpin a capitalist economy and liberal democracy. These generate a rationale for HRD which focuses on performance – of individuals, organizations and national economies – and a legitimization of this derived from managerial as well as political authority (cf. Stewart, this book). Thus a 'performative' approach becomes the dominant paradigm underpinning HRD professional practice and the same paradigm informs the majority of research and theorizing undertaken by academics.

The chapters in this section question and challenge this dominant paradigm. Beverly Metcalfe and Christopher Rees draw on recent feminist critiques of traditional understandings of gender as well as research in the field of 'diversity' and difference to examine established power structures in work organizations, and the role of HRD practice and practitioners in either perpetuating or challenging those structures. They argue the case that the growing use of HRD in attempts to transform organization cultures makes this issue particularly important, especially since within change programmes related to managing diversity the stated aims are often to do with equity which, in turn, has clear connections with power relationships. The focus on organization change is continued in the chapter by Helen Francis. Here though Francis utilizes the 'linguistic turn' and the tools of discourse analysis to explore the nature of the 'reality' of organization change in the context of a specific case. The relationship between line managers and HRD practitioners, and the role of line managers in co-creating HRD practice, are explored. The role and power of language in creating meaning, and therefore in changing meaning, is highlighted as a potential way in to questioning taken-for-granted assumptions and so challenging and shifting established structures. The related potential of HRD in such processes is also explored. The final chapter in this part by Jean Kellie shifts the focus to HRD which occurs outside of the workplace but which certainly remains a central part of workplace HRD strategy and practice. This focus is on university-designed or validated programmes which lead to recognized qualifications but which also meet the demands and 'needs' of workplace learning and development. Kellie specifically applies the notion of 'relevance' to examine the often conflicting desires of those commissioning such programmes and those charged with their delivery and/or validation. The third partner in these programmes, i.e. the participants, is not forgotten and the often conflicting or competing organizational contexts of employer and

provider of higher education is argued to be a key factor influencing participants' development. Drawing on a number of case studies, Kellie's chapter
highlights the possibility of alternative paradigms to that of performance but also
the difficulties for those attempting to provide a voice for those alternatives.

Some of the main themes of the chapters in this part are the following:

- the centrality of power and power relationships in practising HRD in the
  workplace;
- the role of language and meaning in constituting HRD and so in influencing
  power relations;
- the varied and varying roles of stakeholders in the HRD process;
- the potential for application of alternatives to the performance paradigm.

These themes are not to be seen as exclusive or even the most important.
Others are certainly possible and readers are encouraged to identify their own
after reading the chapters. That said, those listed above are offered as a starting point and to be borne in mind when seeking to identify the implications of
this part for professional practice.

Chapter 4

Feminism, gender and HRD

Beverly Dawn Metcalfe and Christopher J. Rees

■ Introduction

Within the field of HRD there is little scholarly examination of the role that gender can play in conceptualizing the terrain of HRD inquiry or in unveiling the way in which constructions and reconstructions of gender in organizational spheres can impact on the role and status of HRD practices and concerns. Equally, the field of HRD has seen little in the way of critically inspired scholarship (with the exception of McGoldrick *et al.*, 2002; Elliot and Turnbull, 2003). Given the growing number of organizations that are attempting to assimilate diversity values as central to their corporate identity, there is thus a timely need to reassess the intersections of gender and HRD research within a more critical management framework. The aim of this chapter will be to highlight how and why the gender lens can assist both practitioners and academicians in explaining HRD processes, as well as consider the dominant gender discourses that are embedded within HRD literature. The discussion will draw on critical management learning research within organizations (e.g. Acker, 1998; Calás and Smircich, 1999) and women's studies and feminist theory (e.g. Weedon, 1999; Jackson, 1999; Grosz, 1994; Bartky, 1997; Butler, 1990, 1993, 1995) which emphasize the fluidity of gender as a social and analytical category.

The chapter will discuss the importance of the critical study of gender and its relationship to the theory and practice of HRD. Three key themes underpin the analysis:

1 It has been well documented that HRD practitioners are predominantly women (Bierema, 2001; Smith, 2000), yet it is also documented that HRD practitioners often wield limited organizational power and decision-making influence (Hanscombe and Cervero, 2003; Praechter, 2003; Abrahmason, 2001).

2 There is also some evidence that a growing number of HRD specialists are key players in organizational transformation programmes and ultimately have a strategic influence on the development of working cultures that support difference and diversity.

3 Feminist writings have moved beyond essentialist notions of male and female and have highlighted that gender is a continually negotiated and relational category (Butler, 1995; Gherardi, 1995; Weedon, 1999).

Drawing on the writings of feminist and women's studies scholars in philosophy and education, social constructionist approaches in particular, I highlight the importance of the body in management and organization learning, the formation of particular power relations for educators and learners, and the significance of reflexivity in informing management knowledge and practice. These observations raise questions concerning the epistemological foundations of HRD knowledge and pose a task for scholars to utilize critical methods of inquiry in order to ensure that gender and equity issues are unveiled within dominant HRD writings. Thus, what does it mean to say that HRD writings may be gendered? How can we understand the gendered and political dynamics of doing HRD? What are the differences for doing HRD in a male and female body? It is these questions that this chapter is mainly interested in.

The organization of this chapter proceeds as follows:

- The first sections provide a review of the gender and HRD literature and a summary of the importance of critical management studies and feminist poststructuralist principles.

- The remaining sections of the chapter highlight how a feminist poststructuralist lens can be adopted in HRD research, namely the body in HRD, power and discourse in HRD and finally reflexivity in management learning and education.

- The chapter concludes with some suggestions for future research and policy development in gender, equality and HRD.

Gender and HRD

Before examining the interrelations between HRD and gender it is first important to attempt to define HRD within the context of this chapter. HRD and its knowledge and practice boundaries have been the subject of much debate

recently (McGoldrick *et al.*, 2002; Metcalfe and Rees, 2005). HRD has historically been concerned with training and development in an organization, and
incorporates individual development, organization development and career
development (Lee, 2004). As management and organizational commentators
have noted, however, the field of HRD has expanded beyond training and
development to include a strong connection to corporate strategy, individual
responsibility for learning, an extension into team learning, internal consultancy, organizational learning, knowledge management, as well as the
nurturing of the intellectual capital of an enterprise (Easterby-Smith and
Cunliffe, 2004; McGoldrick *et al.*, 2002). Recent scholarship has also started
to move beyond organization *bounded* learning and development by unravelling the socio-cultural context within which learning occurs as well as
examining the dynamics of learning societies and national HRD strategies
(Metcalfe and Rees, 2005). The interest in feminist critiques of HRD is associated with these broader debates to open up HRD intellectual inquiry. In this
chapter, HRD is not conceived as a fixed or static category, or as a functional
HR activity, but as a social and political process which is concerned with
exploring all learning scenarios that attempt to develop organizational and
individual capabilities (McGoldrick *et al.*, 2002). While acknowledging that
HRD activities are many and varied the discussion in this chapter focuses primarily on management education and development processes.

Gender and feminist inspired critiques are an established area of inquiry
within education literature; one that has only recently begun to be assessed in
HRD (Hughes, 2000). Recent HRD investigations have provided useful
insights into how HRD research has tended to ignore feminist research agendas as a tool for analysis (Bierema and Cseh, 2003; Bierema, 2001; Simpson
and Lenoir, 2003), and also how gendered power relations in organizations
can impact on the role of male and female HRD managers (Hanscombe and
Cervero, 2003). Bierema and Cseh's (2003) study, published in the journal
Human Resource Development Quarterly, provided a detailed review of the
Academy of Human Resource Development scholarship and attempted to
assess to what extent a feminist or gender lens was part of their study. They
found that of the 655 articles analyzed only 10 per cent incorporated gender as
part of the analysis. Significantly, however, they noted that their intention was
to provide a summary of research rather than explore the *gendered construction* of HRD theories and practices, and suggested that this avenue of research
needed to be further developed (2003: 19). Similarly, Hanscombe and
Cervero's (2003) research examined the ways in which practising male and
female HRD managers exercised power in their role and found that power and
decision-making was interpreted in gendered ways. They found that power
and influence was also related to the seniority of HRD practitioners as well as
the significance that HRD played in corporate culture. They called for

researchers to draw on wider literature bases (including feminism and psychology) to ascertain insights into the gender differences and experiences of 'doing HRD'. Acknowledging there is a 'critical turn' in HRD research (McGoldrick *et al.*, 2002; Lee, 2004; Elliot and Turnbull, 2003), there is thus agreement within the Academy to incorporate gender as an analytical category in order to advance HRD intellectual inquiry. Following Bierema and Cseh's suggestion therefore the following discussion evaluates developments in feminist theory and gender and organization analysis in order to see how they can aid critical assessment of HRD.

▓ Gender and organization analysis

Joan Acker's theory of gendered organizations (1990; 1998) systematized more than a decade of insights by researchers in the area of organization, labour markets and gender. Acker (1990) unravelled the gender assumptions that underlie the process of gendered organization by showing how organizing principles assume a disembodied and universal worker. However, this worker was usually a man so that: 'men's bodies, sexuality, relationships, from procreation to paid work are subsumed in the image of the male worker' (Acker, 1990: 139). Joan Acker (1990: 146) suggests that to say an organization is gendered is to say that:

> 'advantage and disadvantage, exploitation and control, action and emotion, meaning and identity are patterned through, and in terms of a distinction between male and female, masculine and feminine.'

The gendered organizational paradigm, at least thus far, has continued to be a lively arena for ongoing theoretical debate within critical management studies (e.g. Calás and Smircich, 1999; Gherardi, 1995; Gherardi and Poggio, 2001; Britton, 2000). Indeed, Fondas argues that contemporary management writings culturally produce the 'institutionalisation of a feminine ethos' (1997: 275) revealing that 'gender is not peripheral to researchers' understandings of management: gender is part of the very conceptualisation of management' (1997: 275). These insights have been especially lucid in poststructuralist analysis.

▓ Feminism, gender and critical organization research

Poststructuralist theorizing has greatly influenced many disciplines in the social sciences (Gherardi and Poggio, 2002; Alvesson and Skoldberg, 2000). Poststructuralist writings have destabilized grand master narratives and questioned the masculinist knowledge bases of organization research (Alvesson and Willmott, 2000; Metcalfe, 2003a). Feminist poststructuralist modes of inquiry (across the social science disciplines) in particular have opened up the possibilities for evaluating gender construction processes in more diverse and fluid ways (Metcalfe, 2003a). Feminist theorizing has always tended to facilitate new ways of thinking and seeing, and spearheaded social and economic change (Hughes, 2000). However, the injection of post-modern theories into, and within, feminist sociological and feminist philosophical discourse has been met by both enthusiasm and resistance. Indeed, the relationship between feminism and poststructuralist modes of thought has been an 'uneasy' relationship (Calás and Smircich, 1999: 660; Mumby, 1996: 262) There is, as Judith Butler (1990: vii) remarks, 'a certain sense of trouble, as if the indeterminacy of gender might eventually culminate in the failure of feminism.'

How then can we conceptualize the characteristics of poststructuralist feminism? Mumby (1996: 261) neatly summarizes six key themes underpinning feminist poststructuralist modes of inquiry:

1 a critique of dominant Western forms of rationality;
2 a rejection of representational views of language in favour of a view of language and discourse as constitutive of reality and experience;
3 a questioning of any universal truths;
4 a decentring of the Western subject in favour of a subject who is fractured and discontinuous;
5 a focus on power and domination;
6 a focus on difference and the 'other' embraced in a concern for marginalized groups.

Acknowledging the debt owed by the gendered organization framework which Acker provided, feminist poststructuralist organization theorizing reveals the tensions and contradictions at the ideological, structural and identity levels so that gendering dynamics be read as 'gender in process'. (This of course mirrors the theoretical framework proposed by Acker (1990).) What this brings to the fore is the different levels of analysis involved in gendering so one is aware of the cultural construction of an occupation as well as how individual workers themselves construct the importance of the meaning of their work (Weedon, 1999). As Britton nicely puts it, gender and organization studies should consider the ways in which:

'gender segregation and gender inequality are reproduced by a dialectic between gendered organization structures and the situated performance of the gender of individual workers.'

(Britton, 2000: 431)

HRD getting critical?

The forgoing analysis has implications for researching management learning and education. Sylvia Gherardi argues that gender is an inescapable part of the deep structure of human life and interaction, and need not necessarily imply inequality and hierarchy. For her the challenge in organizations is to unveil ways in which gendered behaviours may be enacted and exhibited without reproducing inequality, which would allow workers to do one gender and avoid second serving the other (1995: 128). Postructuralist insights of HRD would mean unravelling the ways in which structures of HRD themes produced gendered effects. The way in which HR and personal development is occupied by predominantly women may communicate strong signifiers of a feminized profession and associated lesser-than status. Equally, cultural preference for specific types of training intervention (problem-solving and decision-making in management processes) and the components of management curriculums (Sinclair, 2005; Simpson and Lenoir, 2003; Smith, 2000) may reinforce gendered values and competencies. For example, Sinclair's (2005) work on the 'masculinization' of the MBA found that both women themselves and feminism(s) tended to be marginalized. She found that this was related to ways in which the curriculum had been underpinned by masculinist forms of knowing and knowledge.

A key area that has been omitted in the literature is the ways in which the individual identity positions of management learners and HRD specialists has been constituted and reconstituted within different organization spheres. A common theme associated with postructuralist approaches is that work experiences are not associated with the whole fixed self but are formed through the discursive invocation of a person as a man or a woman, and that gender-differentiated practices rely on the circulation between subjectivities and discourses that are available. Bierema's (2005) recent study to some extent is useful in showing the fragility of the self for HRD professionals.

Bierema examined how the setting up of a women's network in the headquarters of a Fortune 500 corporation in the US did not necessarily assist women's professional development and advancement; in fact, she found that potentially they can have negative consequences for women's organization status and promotion prospects. It is generally assumed that women's networks promote learning via, inter alia, enabling women to navigate different power structures in an organization. The network in Birema's study was primarily intended to tackle what was perceived to be unequal representation for women especially in senior management levels and create opportunities for sharing ideas about career development. Although Bierema's work was not positioned within a postructuralist framework, a postructuralist lens based on Ackers' framework (1990; 1998) can help identify gendered formations of inequalities.

At the structural level of analysis the network was divisive as not all senior managers became involved and there was reluctance to publicly declare one's commitment to the network. At the cultural level the lack of openness and commitment to the network was in part based on what Bierema calls the patriarchal culture which emphasized dominant forms of hegemonic masculinity (Britton, 2000). Helping to shape and constitute these forms of gender relations are overarching 'discourses' that create reality and meaning systems for organizational actors. The dominant 'network discourse' that Bierema discusses is one related to 'company performance' not strategies associated with women's development. Thus, the language used to describe the women's network and the central meaning of the network is understood in terms of assisting corporate strategy, not as a policy or practice that can assist women's development.

This performance discourse has been central to much theorizing about diversity management initiatives – social rights and obligations are now transformed into corporate opportunities for competitive advantage (Vince, 1996). These gendered structures and gendered cultural practices meant that managing an HRD identity was problematic for women. At the individual identity level women revealed tensions and contradictions in trying to carve an appropriate professional work identity. On the one hand, women's subject position was constituted via involvement in the network and supporting women's issues, through sharing knowledge and information and working together. On the other hand, women did not want to be positioned as 'recipe swapping male bashers' or appearing to 'need help' (Bierema, 2005: 216) and tended to articulate their professional association as important for promoting company strategic issues. This 'silencing' of gender strategies reaffirms the ambivalent process of managing identity work and highlights the ways in which gendered power relations are intertwined with everyday social and organization practices. Overall, Bierema (2005) found that the organization was what she termed 'gender conscious unconsciousness' – that is, women participants showed some awareness of gender inequalities, but were unwilling to articulate gender disparities openly, nor were they committed to change or action.

There is evidence therefore that HRD researchers are starting to get more critical but few studies have tended to 'position' themselves as adopting a critical stance or adopting particular insights from specific social theory research. In order to expand on how we can read HRD through a poststructuralist lens, and specifically a feminist poststructuralist lens, in the following section we outline developments in feminist poststructuralist theory and show how they have implications for HRD thinking and practice. It should be noted that references are primarily drawn from feminist sociologists since advances in the understanding of gender relations are more detailed within women's studies writings since, paradoxically, organization and management scholars have tended to be highly selective in their use and application of gender theorists (Metcalfe, 2003a, 2003b).

■ Gender, HRD, and a postructuralist lens

As one would expect, feminist postructuralist research is characterized by fluidity and variability. While acknowledging that there are no unified voices within the academy (i.e management, humanities and arts academies), feminist scholars have expressed a concern with the tendency of postructuralist thought to focus on questions of epistemology and philosophy, with a corresponding neglect with the ways in which such questions are tied to wider social and political issues (Braidotti, 1989, 1996; Weedon, 1999; Jackson, 1999; McNay, 2000). Three key areas are relevant to the study of HRD and gender:

1 the body of the HRD and learning practitioners,
2 the dominant discourses and power relations in HRD, and
3 the nature of reflexivity in doing HRD.

Gender, the body and HRD

The body has been central to feminist analysis, particularly in challenging the mind–body dualism that has pervaded thinking about men, women, masculine and feminine (Grosz, 1994; Butler, 1993; Jackson and Scott, 2001). The appropriation of women's bodies does not necessarily mean that bodies cannot help explain gender inequalities (Mumby, 1996). As McNay (1992: 22) states:

> 'It is not necessary to posit a single cause of feminine subordination. Once the female sex has come to connote specific feminine characteristics, this "imaginary" signification produces concrete effects through diverse social practices. These concrete effects are not the expression of an immutable feminine essence. However, they react, in turn, by constituting the maintenance and reproduction of this symbolism and, thus, perpetuate the myth of immutable feminine qualities.'

Poststructuralists have theorized the ways in which women's bodies are disciplined, controlled, and subjugated in culturally and historically specific ways (Howson and Inglis, 2001; Irigaray, 1985, 1995; Butler, 1993; Grosz, 1994). The body can be viewed therefore as a site, and outcome, of social regulation and complex relations of power, and is significant in constructing female work identities (McDowell, 1997). How, though, can we usefully attempt to map out and differentiate the myriad of regulatory and social controls that constitute bodily/work identities? Disciplinary regimes can be conceptualized at two levels, the social and the organization.

The body and culture

At the wider cultural level, Bartky's (1997) work inspired by Foucauldian feminism suggests that female disciplinary regimes are part of the patriarchal process through which the ideal feminized body is created. She identifies three disciplinary mechanisms:

1 practices that aim to produce a body of certain size and figuration, for example regimes of dieting;
2 practices that shape the way a woman enacts bodily comportment and displays, for example, the disciplines that require women to gesture modesty rather than eroticism; and
3 practices a woman must master if she is to attain 'the proper styles of feminine motility' such as the application of make-up.

Bartky argues that these discursive practices position women in very particular ways and are self-disciplining and socially and culturally embedded. Women learn to live in their bodies as a form of 'obedience to patriarchy' (Bartky, 1997; Wolf, 1990). Bartky (1997: 149) further maintains self-discipline is a reflection of the

> 'ways in which *she* is under surveillance that *he* is not, that whatever else she may become, she is importantly a body designed to please and excite... Since the standards of female bodily acceptance are impossible fully to realise, requiring as they do virtual transcendence of nature, a woman may live much of her life with a pervasive feeling of bodily deficiency.'

Significantly, feminist theorists highlight how these regimes operate differently for men and women. Unlike women whose nakedness is passive, vulnerable and subject to penetration, the unclothed male body intimates transcendence and connects to his understanding of masculinity, of being a man, of being physical and of being powerful (see Grosz, 1994; Whitehead, 2002). Paradoxically, the physicality and materiality of men and male bodies has not averted from their association with rationality. As Grosz exclaims 'women's corporeality is inscribed as a *mode of seepage*' (Grosz, 1994: 203). The male body in organization environments is therefore more likely to be imprinted with notions of strength, power and knowledge.

The body in organizations

The way in which women's bodies represent a surface, as a *text of femininity* on which the rules and hierarchies of cultural control are inscribed, has unveiled the *gendered* nature of the role and management of the *body at work* (see McDowell, 1997; Howson and Inglis, 2001). Populist texts in the 1990s (e.g. Wolf, 1990) argued that organizations were structured and managed in such a way so as to discipline and shape the aesthetics of woman's identities, so that the preservation and maintenance of a female professional career was not only equated with competence and knowledge acquisition against masculinist norms and parameters, but also that women were required to manage corporate *professional beauty requirements* (Wolf, 1990).

Empirical studies of women's work have identified several examples of occupations in which certain properties, qualities and attributes associated with women's bodies come to be commodified in professions such as service work (Adkins, 2002, 2004; McDowell, 1997). Brewis' (2000) account of English female university professionals revealed the fluidity in body construction and reconstruction as individuals 'learn and relearn' about their bodies according to the social texts to which they have been exposed. Moreover, her study revealed how women distinguish their bodily lives from men, highlighting the 'dual status' as a source of 'human commonality *and* a source of difference' (Brewis, 2000: 21). Trethaway's (1999) study focused on a women's business networking group in the US and found that doing gender in the workplace was linked to the management of a *fit* body and *a body in control* so that the female body represented the 'potential for professional liability' (Trethaway, 1999: 445). The central theme underpinning these studies is that women have to engage in body management practices in order to be constituted as professional and that professionalism is inscribed on women's and men's bodies in quite different ways. Women who wish to be perceived as competent, for example, must look less feminine and more 'male-ish' (Trethaway 1999).

The implication of the foregoing analysis is that the body is significant in how HRD processionals understand the social self and the political and interpersonal dynamics of learning and organization development encounters (Vince, 1996). The body can also be interpreted as a cultural sign of good, average or bad performance. As Sinclair suggests, we need to analyze the interaction of power and gender with bodily constructs (2005: 97).

The body and management learning

The body is central to how educators and HRD professionals engage with/do their craft, yet surprisingly has not been extensively examined. A small number of management learning scholars have highlighted how the body of the woman teacher is 'a source of trouble for her, and others' (Swan, 2005; see also Hughes, 2000; Sinclair, 2005). Within management learning and teaching environments the particular structures and hierarchies represent important socio-cultural spaces for the ways in which bodies are marked and signed in gendered ways. As Fiske argues (in McDowell, 1997: 76; Fiske's italics):

> 'the body is the primary site of social experience. It is where social life is turned into experience. To understand the body we have to know who controls it as it moves through the spaces of our daily routines, who shapes its sensuous experiences, its sexualities, its pleasures in eating and exercise, *who controls its performance at work*, its behaviour at home and school and also who influences how it is dressed and made to appear in its function of presenting to others. The body is the core of our social experience.'

In the management education context therefore bodies are a powerful indicator of teaching competence, presence, and may symbolically represent a sense of intellectual inadequacy which many women feel, since 'woman as body' is historically and socially ascribed as the most defining feature of women's presence, in society and organizations (Braidotti, 1989; Jackson and Scott, 2001). Similar to other managerial and professional roles the bodies of women doing HRD are likely to be appraised with a high level of surveillance (Sinclair, 2005). Of course, similar assessments of management performance are made about men who do not live up to constructions of idealized notions of masculinity (Whitehead, 2002). Evaluations of teacher performance in US universities have suggested that assessments are often based on the 'performances and displays' of academics and that women tend to fare less well (Carson, 2001). Deem (2003) suggests that the new managerialism in UK universities is concerned to measure student outcomes rather than the processes of learning via rigorous systems of audit surveillance and this ultimately has gendered impacts. Similarly to US research, Deem found that female university educators are reviewed less favourably than their male counterparts. These gendered processes serve symbolically to create gendered hierarchies and position the feminine as other, lesser-than in social contexts (Irigaray, 1985).

Women's teaching has also been linked to the eroticization of the learning environment (Swan, 2005; Carson, 2001; Clegg, 1999). McWilliam and Jones state that good teaching is *erotic, passionate* and evokes *body pleasures* (in Clegg, 1999) As Sinclair suggests, management education should not be 'shamelessly reproducing a false mind–body dichotomy, or ignoring bodies in the mistaken belief that their effects will be inert' (2005: 98). In other words, 'doing HRD' and the relationships between educators and learners is as much about the gender (and race, age, ethnicity) of the HRD professional, as about the training content or client task itself.

Bringing the material body into HRD

A great deal of feminist literature on the female body emphasizes the vulnerability and fragility of women's bodies as it is marked and labelled against masculinist characteristics. In seemingly acknowledging the passivity with which women's bodies and identities have been shaped and moulded, there is a sense that women's bodies are rendered powerless. There is also a sense of *disembodiment* (see Howson and Inglis, 2001). As already noted, feminist critical management studies are largely based on Foucauldian theoretical approaches following the dominant majority of critical management researchers' interests (Fournier, 2002 is an exception). As Metcalfe (2003a) has argued 'Foucault fetishism' and 'phallic fascination' with male philosophers as an inspiration has silenced the contribution of female feminist philosophers (e.g. Luce

Irigaray, Nancy Fraser) to management thought – they certainly do not see women's bodies in such powerless, disembodied and inactive ways.

Acknowledging the usefulness of Foucauldian accounts which conceive of the body as an inscribed surface of events, women's studies scholars stress inscription on a male and female body 'does not usually mean the same thing or result in the same text' (Grosz, 1994: 156). Luce Irigaray argues that the materialities of bodily inscription be surfaced through exposing the socially different modes of social inscription (1985; 1995). In other words, women are active agents in their body/learning/work positioning – they can play with, and resist, gender identity positions (see McNay, 2000). As Grosz (1994: 19) suggests:

> 'If women are to develop modes of autonomous self-understanding and positions from which to challenge male knowledge's and paradigms, the specific nature and integration (or perhaps lack of it) of the female body and female subjectivity and its similarities to, and differences from men's bodies and identities need to be articulated.'

Following this line of inquiry, bodily insights of HRD writings should thus be aiming to capture the nature of *embodied subjectivities* as part of the process of doing and reflecting on HRD interventions. This is wonderfully argued by Elaine Swan's (2005) critique of her own experiences doing management education and development. Swan stresses that she gains pleasure from teaching management students, men in particular, and that she draws on a range of repertoires in constructing her identity such as playing with multiple notions of femininity and masculinity. She argues that 'femininity with attitude' and femininity with 'style' and 'glamour' can be conceived as a strength, and be active and liberating:

> 'Not only does glamour give me pleasure in the feeling of some sense of potency and charisma, but it also *interrupts* the highly visible and uniform embodiment of corporate masculinity in the classroom. I see this as a performance as an affirmation of femininity for women in the classroom and to the men, rather than reproducing its negation.'

> (2005: 326, Metcalfe/Rees's italics).

This disruption or interruption unsettles our understandings of feminine as weaker, submissive and shows how this 'glamour' and feminine potency can be an empowering occupational resource. The feminine body doing HRD can therefore be conceived as a form of cultural and professional capital rather than a liability (see Adkins, 2002). In her take-up of a range of performing masculinities, Swan explains how she enjoys being seen as an expert and knowledgeable. Of course as she highlights, and referred to earlier in this chapter, knowledge in the development of Western thought has been linked with men. It should again be acknowledged that corporate masculinity is not something that all men necessarily do – poststructuralist approaches show how both men and women can do multiple masculinities and femininities. The playing with different masculine and feminine work repertoires highlights the fluid and ambivalent process of doing gender and doing HRD. How you do HRD however, and the different ways bodies are culturally inscribed, highlights different forms of power relations and it is to this debate we now turn.

■ Power and HRD

Feminist poststructuralists are concerned with the role of discourse in the construction of the gendered relations of power. As such, subjectivities, power relations, forms of resistance and so forth all exist as discursive practices that are arranged in complex systems of signification (Butler, 1990; Mumby, 1996; McNay, 2000). In this context a discourse is understood to be an institutionalized use of language and language-like systems. Institutionalization can occur at the disciplinary, political and individual levels (Weedon, 1999). This means there are no overarching, totalizing explanations of gendered relations of domination – one cannot simply explain women's domination by recourse to patriarchal class systems of production. Power is exercised not from above, but rather resides in the local and individual practices of institutional life and has multiple points of origin.

A great deal of the discourse and organization literature has tended to show how discourses produce 'gendered effects' – that is, discourses discipline and shape individual gender positions (Alvesson and Skoldberg, 2000). The body discourses identified by Bartky, and detailed earlier in this chapter, are a good example. Her work has highlighted how body work discourses shape notions of professionalism and ultimately have different career implications for men and women. This is not to suggest that discourse effects are consistent. There are many discourses at play that produce gendered effects and shape dominant understandings of HRD systems and processes (Halford and Leonard, 1999).

HRD and performance discourse

There is very little scholarship that has attempted to unveil how dominant discourses are manifest in everyday HRD social practices and this research area will be a valuable arena for further inquiry. However, a prevalent theme in HRD writings is the nature of HRD interventions and their impact on corporate performance. A feminist poststructuralist reading of HRD performance discourse would allow researchers and practitioners to see how HRD can symbolically reproduce gendered hierarchies through the valuing of stereotypical characteristics/language associated with masculinity and the silencing, or not naming of, stereotypical characteristics/language associated with femininity. A good example is the recent review of the learning organization by Ellinger *et al.*

(2002). Basing their study on the learning organization framework of Marsick and Watkins they attempt to provide a critical assessment of the links between the development of a learning organization and financial performance. Their study shows that organizations that work towards establishing learning systems can yield financial benefits. However, close examination of the learning organization framework will reveal that this is conceptualized in gendered ways. Ellinger *et al.* stress that financial benefits are accrued via a 'systems' and 'control' orientation to capturing learning, with a focus on 'measuring knowledge outcomes' (2002: 7). HRD performance descriptors rely on stereotypical masculinist descriptors and practices. In this respect, 'achievement', 'control', 'measurable results' and 'performance goals' are key signifiers of HRD *outcomes*. Where is the focus on the interpersonal skills dynamics and on the nurturing capabilities – those relational and informal work behaviours that are stereotypically associated with feminine behaviours? In this account these processes are subsumed within achievement and measurement descriptors and as such are silenced and marginalized (see Calás and Smircich, 1999; Butler, 1995). This is all the more interesting as the account seemingly glosses over the *processual* and *emotional* dynamics of HRD, something which practitioners argue is central to our epistemological reasoning on HRD. Thus, discussions of 'relationship building' and 'communication', for example, are symbolically and culturally subsumed within broader masculinist constructions. This analysis complements some of the critical research of Elliot and Turnbull (2003) who highlight the performative notion of HRD theorizing, although a gender lens reinforces the ways in which this performative paradigm has been constituted along gender lines (see also Acker, 1998).

Similar arguments are presented by Russ Vince (1996) who states that the language of diversity and equality has tended to 'supplant' feminist employment and organization concerns. He argues that diversity discourses underplay differences and instead focus on change strategies and HRM performance dynamics. Through neither naming differences nor attending to the politics of the formation of identity positions, HRM strategies which focus on the business benefits and organization performance are capitalizing on diversity discourses as a means of discipline and control:

> 'Diversity in organisations is often an attempt to take the politics out of change by individualising social power relations. The inability of diversity strategies and practices to bring an analysis of *process* to bear on these issues makes diversity initiatives into mechanisms for denial and control'
>
> (Vince, 1996: 191, Metcalfe's/Rees's italics)

Diversity (and within this label gender, race, ethnicity, sexuality) is thus part of the dominant performance discourse that can discipline employee relations. Vince's commentary although not positioned within a poststructuralist framework highlights the significance of power relations in shaping management practices. Thus, the dynamics of gender and HRD is a political process shaped and reshaped by power relations. A poststructuralist lens would thus aim to unveil those voices that have been marginalized or silenced. How, though, can we give voice to the marginalized and create space for different identity positions? One way is to be aware of the importance of reflexivity in research and it is to this that we now turn.

■ HRD, reflexivity and organization change

The concept of reflexivity is key to understanding poststructuralist critiques of organization and management since it is acknowledged that the researcher contributes to knowledge-generating processes. In 'edging towards reflexivity' (Calás and Smircich, 1999) writers acknowledge that theorizing in organization is a political process, as well as permitting for a critical examination of the way 'modern (paradigmatic or foundational) knowledge has been constituted, without needing to provide for an alternative knowledge' (Calás and Smircich, 1999: 652). Cunliffe (2002) has argued that management learning and education scholars should encourage *reflexive dialogical practice*. This incorporates an acknowledgement of the self and practice as central to understanding dynamic learning processes. The principle draws on a radically reflexive stance and tries to identify the part 'we' (i.e HRD management scholars and practitioners) play in constructing the realities, knowledge structures and practices we write about, and the management education we do (Cunliffe, 2002: 47). Reflexive dialogical practice involves unravelling contradictions in learning encounters: exposing contradictions, doubts, dilemmas and possibilities so as to highlight the tacit assumptions and ideologies that are constituted in our ways of talking and social relations, and exploring how our own actions, conversational practices and ways of making sense may be created and sustained in particular ways.

The principle of dialogical critique has tended to be skirted around and flirted with in critical management studies (Metcalfe, 2003a, 2003b), yet is fundamental to literary criticism where many critical scholars have taken their inspiration. Cunliffe (2002) is presenting dialogic critique as being about an individual practitioner thinking about how they do their craft, and the knowledge they bring in doing management education and the process of reflection. This does not consider the role of the reader which is central to many poststructuralist literary critiques. The reader, as part of an interwoven moment, gives form and meaning to a text. In essence, as Derrida argues, reader, writer and text (i.e. what is written, what is) are a 'moving interplay' (Gill, 1995) coming into play at a particular time, space and social context, stressing the fragility of meaning. Like Derrida, Bakhtin (2002) highlights that knowledge is produced through the intertextuality of reader, writer and text. This in essence means that the socio-cultural and historical context of dialogue is important in interpreting meaning and signification. The result is that transcriptions systems or *heteroglossia* (Bakhtin, 2002: xix–xx) are characterized not by unity, but on multiplicity. Taking a literary criticism stance, the reader's mood and emotion experienced while engaging with a text, their gender, sexuality and ethnicity will also have a bearing on how that text comes to life and creates meaning for readers.

However, where modes of inquiry are concerned with feminist pursuits then it should be acknowledged that the practitioner's and researcher's participation in, and through, knowledge-generation processes will significantly have a bearing on writing practice and theory, especially where the dynamics involve a female researcher in a male organization or male-dominated teaching setting (Clegg, 1999; Praechter, 2003; Stanley, 2000; Ramazanoğlu and Holland, 2002). The positioning of women has been long covered in feminist methodological scholarship. Feminist standpoint theorists contend that the researcher's positionality affects all aspects of the research process – from the articulation of a research question to the analysis and presentation of the data. They argue that this influence becomes problematic when researchers occupying privileged positions in society elect to study those who are marginalized on the basis of race, sexuality, class, and gender.

Feminist reflexivity in management learning and HRD

Feminist reflexivity is based on the notion that HRD researchers' and practitioners' values should be acknowledged, revealed and labelled, and that the researcher is accountable for his/her actions (Gill, 1995). This acknowledges the nature of gendered power relations and the silencing and invisibility that women or other marginalized groups may experience. This is nicely expressed by Sally Sambrook (2002) as she reflects on writing the HRD story of her PhD which examined management processes in an NHS hospital. She argues that there is a direct connection 'between thinking and writing abut HRD' and that 'your philosophical practice shapes your flow of words' (Sambrook, 2002: 250). This engagement with the text involves 'showing myself to myself' as well as 'showing myself to the reader' (2002: 235). As feminist sociologist Liz Stanley (2000: 76) claims:

'Reading is both active and a process: it also relies heavily on intertextuality. Texts are certainly not inert and how they are structured certainly intends a preferred reading. However, readers are also active readers. We may be textually persuaded, cajoled, led and misled: but we can, and we do, also scrutinize and analyse, puzzle and ponder, resist and reject.'

However, it is important to highlight that the scope of reflective practice is limited by the contexts in which it has been adopted. In the UK, reflective practice has been implemented in professions with large female workforces: nursing, teaching and social work. The scope for autonomy in these professions is increasingly limited. Reflective practice, therefore, may be becoming a vehicle for self-surveillance and orthodoxy (Clegg, 1999), and becoming bound up with the project of 'managing a self' rather than in helping us to think critically about professional practice. These socio-political considerations provide the basis for more searching epistemological questions about the nature of professional knowledge and the characteristics of all human labour.

Implications for HRD research and practice

The preceding chapter has tried to link together feminist sociological writings and HRD writings within the management learning arena and position them within a critical management framework. Above all, the focus has been to try and challenge taken for granted and dominant knowledges in HRD and adopt a feminist lens, specifically a feminist poststructuralist lens, to aid greater understanding of HRD policy and practice. The implications for HRD researchers and practitioners are:

- that we need to think how bodies and emotions may impact the myriad of learning and organization change encounters;
- how knowledge and understanding, and ultimately research agendas, are shaped by dominant HRD discourses and power relations; and finally
- to consider the importance of reflexivity in doing HRD.

These areas of inquiry have gendered consequences in terms of how we conceive of HRD and how we carry out HRD as a practice. There are also implications for the 'voice' of HRD in broader strategic management debates. Uncovering the gendered dynamics of HRD can make space for marginalized voices and assist the discipline in forming inclusive organization learning interventions.

A central theme underpinning this chapter is how the bodies of HRD practitioners are disciplined, shaped and imprinted by specific discourses. The embodiment experienced by men and women may not necessarily always result in negative associations with body work. As we have highlighted, management and organization studies have tended in particular to problematize women's bodies. Bodies, however, are more than the effects of power: there is also the complex interaction between discourses of sexuality and power (McDowell, 1997). As highlighted, Swan's (2005) reflective account reminds us that social constructionist critiques of pedagogy are all about fluidity and variability. Doing management education and doing feminine body work can open up pleasurable experiences. Women HRD professionals, therefore, should talk more about empowering, exciting experiences of teaching managers, teaching men, teaching management studies (Swan, 2005). As Fournier (2002) has suggested in relation to critical management studies we should aim to 'flesh out gender'. As feminist sociologists have argued, Foucauldian approaches are limited since they ignore gendered processes of inscription. HRD accounts should aim to move on from assuming 'the practitioner is disembodied to one which encourages and requires embodied practice' (Howson and Inglis, 2001: 298). This will permit examination of the lived experience of organizational embodiment (of both the researcher and researched), which has been pushed to the margins of organizational analysis or excluded altogether. The concepts employed in deploying bodiliness as a medium for sociological inquiry include corporality, materiality and physicality, and emphasize the body as a site and agent in constructing subjectivities.

■ Conclusion

This chapter has attempted to provide a critique of the intersections between HRD, critical management and feminist theory in order to advance theorizing of feminist and gender themes within HRD research. Drawing principally on poststructuralist insights the discussion highlighted that:

- the body *matters* in doing HRD;
- learning about how we experience management learning work can assist practical encounters;
- the formation and reformation of gendered power relations in organizations influences the identity management strategies of individuals in HRD roles; and finally
- HRD and management educators engage in reflective practice.

Injecting feminist analysis into HRD writing is about putting women into a picture largely drawn by men. But it is also about rethinking and, in the end, about drawing a new picture in organization and management learning that includes men and women (Hughes, 2000: 51). Contributing to critical management debates within HRD research the chapter promoted the idea that HRD is a constantly evolving field (McGoldrick *et al.*, 2002) which must take account of social, moral and existential debates within broader gender and social theory literature, but also be aware of the need to inform and educate the wider practitioner community. There is an enormous challenge for HRD scholars to persevere with promoting the value for feminism and a gender lens to support HRD and organization development change interventions. As Bierema reported in her study of a women's organization network, its development was largely ineffectual. While there was some acknowledgement of gender issues being significant for management and learning, women did not raise gender and equality issues due to 'fear, denial, frustration, and exhaustion, and organizational resistance to the network' (2005: 221). This reflects the broader concerns with equality educators and specialists. That is, how do we get the gender agenda into organizational change programmes and how can we convince senior decision-makers, when feminism and equality seem almost passé, and thus insignificant. As Fondas (1997) has suggested, there appears to be a widespread commitment to not 'naming' or not 'articulating' these 'differences' concerns. The 'feminine' she stresses is often unsymbolized and unarticulated and subsumed within dominant masculinist conceptual schemes.

However, we would stress that differences and inequalities present in everyday life and education experiences provide an opportunity to learn about power and privilege in the wider society, and 'learning from difference' should assist transformation and change (Reynolds and Trehan, 2003). We would also support Swan who argues, like many women's studies scholars, that we should take pleasure in who we are. Perhaps a way forward is to strongly encourage HRD scholars of critical modes of research and investigation. Cunliffe (2002) has argued that critical approaches allow us to reframe our notions of learning as an 'active and embodied process' where all participants are 'struck' to make sense of experience in different ways. (Cunliffe, 2002: 57). While Cunliffe does not focus on, or acknowledge, gender dynamics in learning processes in her paper, the spirit of learning about, and through, difference was certainly sensed by the authors. This resonates strongly with Monica Lee's (2004) insightful observations that HRD terrain is not fixed or static but should be viewed as an 'ontology of becoming' which emphasizes the fluidity of constructionist processes. We would like to close with the words of Adrienne Rich who reminds us that we should constantly be looking at our world and our learning experiences anew, and make claim to be specifically moving towards further unveiling the feminisms and the feminine in HRD:

'A radical critique of literature, feminist in its impulse, would take the work first of all as a clue to how we live, how we have been living, how we have been led to imagine ourselves, how our language has trapped us and liberated us, how the very act of naming has until now been a male prerogative, and how we can begin to see and name – and therefore live – afresh.'

(Rich, 2001: 11)

Chapter 5

The mutation of HRD and strategic change: a critical perspective

Helen Francis

▉ Introduction

Despite a long legacy of critical thinking within organizational studies, the more specialized field of HRD has been characterized as mainly prescriptive and performance-driven in nature (Trehan and Rigg, 2005). Recently, a growing number of analysts have called for more 'critical' empirical and conceptual work concerned with understanding the discursive and socially constructed nature of HRD. This chapter draws upon a critical discourse perspective to explore these issues within a firm moving towards a flatter, team-based organizational structure, and is divided into four sections.

- Section one highlights increasing pressures being faced by personnel and development (P&D) specialists for HRD activities to be justified in terms of costs or value added, and for P&D practitioners to play a more strategic role in the form of business partnerships with line managers. It is explained that research in this area has been dominated by normative and unitarist assumptions in which tensions inherent in work organizations and the management of human resources are downplayed or ignored.
- In the second section, I examine the implications of drawing upon discourse theory for conceptualizing organization change and HRD.
- In the third section I present case study material from an in-depth investigation of changes taking place in a large manufacturing firm, SutCo, in which I trace P&D managers' experiences of introducing change over a period of four years.
- The final section draws together a number of conclusions and key learning points from this investigation, which highlight the potential of discourse analysis to provide rich insights into the dynamic and ambiguous practice of HRD.

■ Strategic partnerships and the dominance of business 'speak'

There has been much debate in recent years about the nature, meaning and justification for 'strategic' HRD (Walton, 1999; McGoldrick *et al.*, 2002).
Increasingly HRD professionals are being expected to justify their activities in
terms of costs or value added, and to play a more 'strategic role' in order that
firms may create and sustain competitive advantage (Sambrook, 2004; Stewart
and McGoldrick, 1996). This is based on growing acceptance amongst senior
managers that people are a critical source of competitive advantage, and recognition of the pivotal position of HRD professionals in developing intellectual
capital through knowledge management and development (Walton,1999,
Swart *et al.*, 2003)[1]. Modelling of HRD in this context has been diverse and
HRD has emerged as a complex and dynamic construct, which is not easy to
'unpack' through conventional research techniques. Noting these trends
Sambrook (2000, 2004) explains the potential of discourse theory to provide a
useful means for practitioners and academics to identify and analyze strategic
HRD in this context. Here, she conceptualizes HRD practice as a form of discursive action, based on the assumption that HRD is a negotiated reality of
shared meanings constructed through the medium of language. Critical of the
dominance of normative, idealistic and overly performance-oriented HRD
research, she is one of a growing number of academics concerned with the promotion and development of 'critical HRD' (Elliott and Turnbull, 2005).

Introducing the first collection of critical HRD texts within the UK, Elliott
and Turnbull (2005: 1) argue that 'the majority of HRD research does not
allow researchers to engage in studies that challenge its predominantly performative and learning-outcome focus'. In what follows, I explain that similar
concerns have been expressed within the human resource management (HRM)
field, as P&D managers have been challenged to assume the role of 'business
partner' in order to enhance their organizational contribution (Ulrich, 1997;
Ulrich and Brockbank, 2005; Moore and Patterson, 2005).

Pioneered by David Ulrich, the concept of business partnership is often used
interchangeably with the term 'strategic partner' which is one of four key roles
prescribed by him in his typology for the functioning of P&D: strategic partner, administrative expert, employee champion and change agent. While Ulrich
has recently modified these roles, the term 'strategic partner' remains, a role he
describes as one in which P&D professionals partner with line managers to
help them reach their goals through effective strategy formulation and strategy
execution (Ulrich and Brockbank, 2005: 212). This positioning of the P&D
function as a key organizational player is proving very attractive to P&D professionals (CIPD HR Survey, 2003). Noting this trend, Ulrich calls for P&D
practitioners not to lose sight of the employee champion role, which he now
describes as 'employee advocate' and 'human resource developer', and which

he views as equally important contributors to the 'human infrastructure' within the organization (Ulrich and Brockbank, 2005).

Strategic capability in this context includes being able to represent individual employee needs when strategy is debated among the management team, for example, in relation to closing a plant or expanding a product line. While he recognizes some tensions in carrying out these kind of activities, Ulrich has been criticized for seriously underplaying the issues of role ambiguity and role conflict that emerges when a person and/or P&D function performs more than one role. Guided by the belief that line and P&D managers and employees will all work collaboratively to drive business success (Ulrich, 1997; Ulrich and Beatty, 2001), his model is based on a construction of P&D policy and practice that seeks to align the psychology of the worker with business goals. It is consistent with the 'soft' developmental idealization of HRM in which employees come to identify with the organization and engage in discretionary behaviour (working beyond the requirement of the job), in exchange for job security, financial rewards, and training and development (Landen, 2002)[2].

Power inequalities and associated tensions inherent in work organizations are downplayed within this unitary organization perspective. The creation of high-performance work practices (HPW) geared to induce discretionary behaviour, is seen to be hampered by 'resistance' amongst managers and employees that is largely attributed to 'misunderstandings' rather than more fundamental differences of interest rooted in the wider social/political sphere (Watson, 2004). This construction of resistance is illustrated by the following explanation of the relatively poor uptake of HPW noted in a recent EEF/CIPD Report (2004: 5):

> 'If the benefits and nature of HPW are communicated well and better understood by managers and employees within your company then one of the key barriers to HPW can be removed, or at least substantially reduced.'

As Grant and Shields observe (2002), analysts within this genre treat employees as 'objects' to be developed/practised on, rather than 'active subjects' of P&D who seek to create their own competing 'realities' of work and organization. Their examination of P&D rhetoric in employee constructions of their psychological contracts reflects growing interest in the uptake of discourse perspectives for understanding the complexity of P&D. This uptake is linked to growing disillusionment with mainstream theories and approaches to the study of organizational change and P&D reflected in a spate of books and journal special issues in which analysts have called for more critical and reflexive research designs based on discourse analysis (Clark, 2004, Grant et al., 2005). These provide a wide range of interpretive and critical perspectives (Prichard, et al., 2004).

The research presented here draws upon one particular 'brand' of critical work identified by Harley and Hardy (2004: 393) that is concerned with the role of discourse in the construction of P&D, a constructionist approach in which critical and postmodern insights are combined and which is explained in the next section. The approach is exemplified in Trehan's (2004) examination of 'what is not being talked about in HRD' in which she describes the potential of deconstruction techniques to identify how organizational and educational discourses function to stabilize meanings and practices. She explains that the 'accepted' discourse of the HRD profession is highly unitarist and closes off opportunities for practitioners to engage in a form of critical reflection that takes account of power, politics and social dynamics.

Trehan suggests that the Chartered Institute of Personnel and Development (CIPD) plays a major role in shaping the ongoing dominance of normative P&D discourses and concurs with Reed and Anthony (1992) who call teachers to account, insisting on their responsibility to help practitioners engage with moral and social issues inherent in management practice (see also Fenwick, 2003, 2005a). The concept of 'thinking performer' launched by the CIPD as part of its new professional standards in 2002, holds out some promise for more critical reflection in educational and practitioner settings (CIPD Professional Standards, 2004). However, Francis and Keegan's (2005, forthcoming) exploratory research, involving relatively small samples of P&D practitioners and educators, suggests that the framing of the concept as it emerges into practice is currently too tightly bound with expressions like 'strategic', 'value added' and 'customer advantage', with very limited promotion of critical reflection as a *core* HR activity. Their research shows how models and vocabularies of P&D driven by the business partner concept are currently being amplified, and how dominance of business 'speak' in framing talk of P&D practice and the notion of thinking performer is squeezing out space for framing HR outcomes in terms of employee well-being and advocacy.

The unquestioning performativity noted here works hand in hand with the ongoing devolution of P&D tasks to the line coupled with the creation of more sophisticated use of on-line P&D systems and creation of centralized P&D 'service centres' that act as the hallmarks of business partnership emerging within UK organizations (Brown *et al.*, 2004). Recent research has shown that line management involvement in day-to-day people management is not without its difficulties. While Purcell *et al.*'s (2003) influential research into P&D and organizational performance points to the pivotal position of the 'discretionary role' of managers in 'bringing HR policies to life', research has also shown that line managers may not necessarily have the interest, capability and responsibility to deal with HR-related work (Fenwick, 2003; Johnson, 2005; Hope Hailey *et al.*, 2005). Francis and Keegan (2005, forthcoming) warn of the dangers involved in assuming that that line managers will have the time, the training or the interest to give priority to individual employee needs and well-being, especially when it appears to have increasingly less priority amongst P&D professionals themselves. These dangers include loss of employee trust and confidence in P&D functions to represent their interests, costs to employee well-being, disenchanted practitioners and truncated careers for P&D professionals.

■ Discourse analysis: a framework for investigating organizational change and HRD

In what follows, I explain the form of discourse analysis used to analyze the key discourses by which organizational change and associated power relations between P&D and line managers were formulated and articulated as they worked towards the creation of a team-based manufacturing system at SutCo. A cross-case analysis that depicts the broader dynamics of change in the form of multi-layered 'conversations' has been presented elsewhere (Francis, 2003; Francis and Sinclair, 2003), and captures these processes across three broad phases of change: evolution, transformation and incorporation. Here, I revisit and draw material from one of these cases in order to devote greater depth of analysis to managers' struggle around discourses of P&D, thereby capturing processes of 'recontextualization' (Thomas, 2003) – where managers draw upon and modify discourses to meet local conditions or needs.[3]

This material should be understood within the particular socio-economic context in which it emerged, during the mid-1990s. Nevertheless, it has contemporary relevance in that it presents a useful exemplar of the constitution of HRD and attendant issues of meaning, power and politics, at a time when 'critical' HRD is emerging and finding space in both academic and practitioner worlds (Sambrook, 2004). Despite the essentially political nature of knowledge construction and learning initiatives, there is a dearth of critical approaches in this area which focus on power and politics (Keegan and Boselie, forthcoming; Fenwick, 2003). Watson's (1994) study of change in a telecommunications plant and Hamilton's examination of the use of rhetoric (Hamilton, 2001) is exemplary of work in this tradition.

The 'critical' approach to discourse taken here, is rooted in the view that reality is socially constructed rather than 'given' and that discourse plays a central role in the social construction of realities (Berger and Luckman, 1966). In this sense I am interested in the action-oriented nature of discourse which goes beyond the idea of language that merely represents organizational life, to include all forms of text (verbal, written visual), together with the social practices and power relations inherent in discourse (Fairclough, 1992, 1995, 2001, 2003).

Treating discourse as a form of social practice, I recognize that it brings an object into being (e.g. a training initiative), so that it becomes a 'material reality' in the form of practices that it invokes (Grant et al., 2005: 8)[4]. This construction process includes interaction between language-in-use (text), the processes by which these are produced and interpreted (discursive practices), and the sets of material and social conditions (social practice) in which discourse is anchored (Fairclough, 1992, 1995, 2001). As social practice, discourse thus acts as a *resource* made up of a set of concepts, expressions, statements and related practices, and a set of *rules* (social structures) framing the way people apply their 'sense-making' (Watson, 1995, 2002).

Mumby (2004) explains that critical analysis of power relations is central to an understanding of social practices. She describes the organization as a 'political site' characterized by the negotiation of meanings and interest-driven discursive strategies 'that lurk beneath ostensibly consensual meaning systems' (1996: 237). Fairclough observes that the 'power of discourse is to do with powerful participants controlling and constraining the contribution of non-powerful participants in this meaning creation process' (2001: 39). He distinguishes between three types of such constraint:

1 contents – on what is said;
2 relations – the social relations people enter into in discourse (e.g. between manager and newcomer to the workplace);
3 subjects – or subject positions people can occupy, such as manager (mentor) and newcomer (mentee).

Fairclough explains that these constraints do not necessarily involve direct control in that they derive from conventions (orders) of discourse which frame how, when and why language is used. These emerge from the context under which they are negotiated which acts to provide a mixture of both choice *and* constraint to change agents (Grant *et al.*, 2005; Tietze *et al.*, 2003).

Application of the concept of 'intertextuality' is central to Fairclough's approach to the analysis of the relationship between discourse and context, and is concerned with locating text within socially and historically produced texts (Fairclough, 1992), described by Keenoy and Oswick (2004) as the 'textscape' of a discursive event. Like Fairclough, Keenoy and Oswick emphasize the need to avoid treating context as simply a backdrop to the discursive event under study, but to see it as being in a dialectical relationship with it in that 'the text actually forms part of the context and vice versa' (Grant *et al.*, 2004: 23).

Critical discourse analysis thus requires a consideration of interactions other than the discursive event being scrutinized and allows the analyst to address both micro and macro levels of analysis. While my investigation was largely conducted at a micro-discursive level that focused upon the local construction of managerial discourses, attention was given to the 'textscape' within which they were embedded, noting how this framed the emergence of dominant meanings and related discourse conventions, for instance in the boardroom, on the shopfloor, in the development of HRD practices.

My approach to intervention analysis noted here, also draws on what Deetz (1996) describes as a 'dialogical orientation'. This emphasizes the complexity and hidden points of resistance in reality construction, thereby focusing on the fragmentation and potential disunity in any discourse (see also, Alvesson and Deetz, 2000; Broadfoot *et al.*, 2004). Deconstructing texts in this way offers rich insights into the construction of organizational processes and HRD practices (Keegan and Boselie, forthcoming).

Principal textual material gathered in the SutCo case included transcripts from in-depth interviews, documentary evidence and to a lesser extent participant observation. This incorporated retrospective as well as real-time data covering the four-year period between the winters of 1991 and 1995. Following an initial interview held with a personnel manager, respondents were chosen through a process of a 'snowball sampling' technique (Mason, 1994). A total of 30 interviews were carried out with three members of the management board, three departmental heads (resourcing, management development and operations), and ten middle/junior line managers including two team leaders who were responsible for implementing the change. In addition, two group interviews were held with shopfloor employees and their 'leading hands' that provided me with some insight into participants' natural vocabulary on a topic.

Interviews lasted between one and a half and three hours and were tape-recorded. These were complemented by informal discussions with key respondents held in canteens and offices, and attendance at briefing sessions between managers and staff, allowing me to 'enter' the daily lives of managers, and helped inform the interpretation of material generated in interview, finding new connections, and shaping future interviews. In addition, full access to all committee minutes and formal reports, memos, information packs and notices about the change initiative (known as 'CFM', or 'continuous flow manufacture') provided me with a rich source of material for textual analysis.

Careful to avoid destroying the meaning of material through intensive coding, case narratives were developed that were central to the generation of insight into the complex ways in which text and discursive practices emerged as fieldwork progressed (Miles and Huberman, 1994). Consonant with Keenoy's polemic about 'HRMism' (Keenoy, 1999), I found that the integrity (completeness) of respondents' narratives and archival material would be easily lost if they were 'classified' in too mechanistic a fashion.

The following section traces the key discourses by which change unfolded within the case organization, from the initial piloting of teamworking within one product line to its diffusion throughout the factory.

◼ Case analysis

Antecedents of change

The case study focused on a 1500-strong UK subsidiary (SutCo) of a large, non-unionized, US multinational company, responsible for the manufacture of medical products. Following rationalization of operating plants in Europe, it became the recognized 'European centre' for the manufacture of certain product lines within the company and became the largest manufacturer outside the US with a sales turnover of nearly £80m in 1993.

Although SutCo had a large share of the domestic market in the UK, the top team were concerned about new competitors entering the European market and sought to maintain their competitive position through introducing team-working arrangements and new methods of manufacturing, referred to as 'continuous flow manufacture' (CFM). This study focused on changes that took place within assembly operations (which included approximately 1200 production operators).

Traditional assembly operations at SutCo were organized functionally in departments according to three stages in the production process that involved the assembly, wrapping and packing of products. A supervisor and their 'leading hand' managed each department in which operator jobs were broken down by individual operation and each production worker performed one highly repetitive task.

Respondents' accounts of these working arrangements suggested that, historically, management practices within SutCo were dominated by an approach to human resourcing that treated employees as a cost to be minimized, placed primary emphasis on the meeting of month's-end targets and was characterized by 'us and them' relations between management and workers. Described by one manager as a 'traditional engineering culture', these priorities were embedded in a hierarchical structure that allowed for close direction of operating staff and inspection of their work, and an individual output-based incentive bonus scheme applied through the use of traditional work-study techniques.

This cost-centred orientation contrasted with what one manager described as a 'welfare' approach to human resource policies, geared to induce worker consent and loyalty to the company. These were reflected in discursive practices that centred round notions of 'justice' and 'fairness', emphasis on internal promotion and high wages (top quartile of industry), and an emphasis on job security and an atmosphere of lifelong allegiance to the company.

Role of corporate discourse in the local construction of P&D

The origins of CFM appeared to stem from discursive change at corporate level that focused on the need to develop company-wide P&D strategies geared towards enhancing the loyalty, commitment and performance of employees.

These strategies were framed by the explicit need for employees to 'speak the same language all over the world (...) excellence' (Chairman's introduction to 1989 Annual Report) and mirrored the emergent enterprise discourse promoted by the then Thatcher administration (Legge, 1995).

Like the term 'enterprise' the concept of 'excellence' was ambivalent. In one sense excellence meant the development of human resource practices that allowed for employee development and growth, reflected in publicized examples of self-managing production teams in the parent company's suture manufacturing plant in France (Annual Report, 1991). In another sense the language of 'excellence' centred on the development of new manufacturing techniques, systems and procedures that could improve the efficiency and the ability of people to 'contribute to their maximum potential' (Company Annual Report).

The ambivalence of 'excellence' meant that while the discourse acted as a set of rules framing the way managers enacted corporate plans at local level, it also created space for them to alter it according to their own interpretations and interests. The following narratives illustrate how the operations director drew upon the competing managerial logics embedded in the discourse to explain his plans for introducing CFM.

The director explained that the CFM initiative was rooted in the need for 'culture change' at SutCo, which in one sense meant a break away from 'us and them' attitudes and behaviours between management and workers and a move to a 'high trust' organizational culture in which operators would be 'empowered' thereby assuming more responsibility at work rather than 'leaving their brains in the locker room'.

Alongside this imperative for developing a 'high trust' culture, the director also placed emphasis on the need for streamlining work activities to ensure 'higher levels of operator flexibility, efficiency and reduction in costs'. In this context, 'culture change' also meant compliance to new operating procedures and preparedness for operators to

'be flexible in attitude, which is also a cultural change. If there is nothing required to be done in one area, then they should immediately look around for things to do in areas where there is a bottleneck. The process is only as good as the weakest part of the process and people need to understand that and to say, "we will need to resolve that" before going to the rest room or the smoke room or whatever.'

(SutCo Director)

In this context CFM was seen to afford some 'opportunity' for employee empowerment, but this needed to be understood in light of a range of 'hard business drivers' and 'exploitation' of human capital:

'The reasons for pursuing CFM were the hard business benefits – reduced lead-time for manufacturing, significantly lower work in process – and we were looking to improve quality. These were the hard *business* benefits gained immediately on the

115

introduction of CFM, and it *wasn't* teamworking. The driver wasn't employee empowerment. Having said that, within CFM there is the opportunity to develop and exploit these to the benefit of the employee and more importantly to the benefits of the customer. The customer is not concerned whether we have teamworking, he is not concerned whether we have a high work-in-progress; he is concerned about the product being available at the right time, the right price and the right quality, compared to the competition.

(SutCo Director)

Managers' discursive struggle in P&D

I turn now to an examination of how managers at SutCo made sense of and became caught up in the ambiguities and tensions associated with opposing corporate 'logics' noted above, and the critical potential of discourse to create lines of tension around which they attempted to preserve, restructure or renew local P&D practices surrounding the initial piloting of CFM within one product line to its diffusion throughout the factory.

I found two co-existing and overlapping managerial discourses emerging from my interpretation of this research material, which I have labelled here as 'control' and 'empowerment'. These were broadly similar to the kind of 'control' (low commitment) and 'empowerment, skills and growth' (high commitment) discourses identified by Watson (1994) in his account of change within a telecommunications factory.

Control discourse

The control discourse was structured round notions of 'efficiency', 'flexibility' and 'adding value', and was signified by the development of new manufacturing designs (just-in-time) and P&D practices (incentive systems; more systematic recruitment and selection; training in inspection techniques) that could improve employee and organizational efficiency. It was characterized by notions of rationality and a mechanistic view of change concerned with altering structures and behaviours in order to improve the 'bottom line'. Talk of 'roll out charts', 'negative variances' and 'cost control' in relation to people management were illustrative of this approach and built upon 'engineering traditions' that were performance-focused, concerned with maximum utilization of labour.

Empowerment discourse

This discourse was structured round discursive concepts of 'employee development', 'involvement', 'teamworking' and 'empowerment' that signified the importance of employee growth and well-being. The discourse found expression in new recruitment, selection and reward practices in support of cell working that signalled the importance of teamworking and the creation of more varied and interesting jobs. Related discursive practices included the use of a company-wide attitude survey that measured employee morale and satisfaction and a company credo that emphasized 'respect for the individual', 'dignity', and ' fairness'. These were consistent with the 'welfare' traditions within the company geared to induce worker consent and loyalty to the company.

Establishment of a pilot cell and redrawing the boundaries between competing discourses of P&D

Groups who enjoyed a controlling influence over early decisions about CFM were those represented on a steering group given the remit for designing a strategy for change and included production, accountancy and work study disciplines, with no input from P&D staff. Chaired by the operations director, early plans produced by this group were dominated by the emergent control discourse primarily concerned with structural issues, flow diagrams and 'roll out' charts connected with the start up of a 'pilot cell'. New monitoring procedures focused on hard performance outcomes, including reduction in inventory holding costs and the costs of indirect labour. Questions about measuring more qualitative aspects of teamwork (such as personal development and cooperation) were absent at this stage.

As policy decisions emanating from the steering group were being translated into operational human resource practices, the boundaries between competing discourses of P&D were re-drawn, reflecting shifting orientations and interests of different managers. All human resource staff interviewed at that time talked of the importance of developing operator flexibility and involvement, reflected in the preference articulated by the Head of Resourcing, to promote a reward system that would encourage responsible autonomy and more varied work for cell workers, which meant

> 'moving away from the idea of a mini production department within a cell to one in which operators are given the opportunity to be accountable as a unit rather than an individual and which should be geared towards enhancing operator flexibility and involvement.'
> (Minutes of special CFM meeting between engineering and personnel functions)

This argument contrasted with those presented by work study engineers and production managers who emphasized the control of costs and development of job skills and operator flexibility 'as and when required' (Committee Minutes).

Rival interpretations amongst personnel and the line about how cells should be formed became evident in a confusing mix of discursive practices as the pilot cell was launched in the winter of 1991. In one sense, CFM was used by recruitment administrators to describe a form of teamworking that allowed for increased operator control over their own jobs and more variety at work. The job title of production operator was relabelled to that of 'cell operator' (later designated as 'team member') and the foreman position changed to team leader, signalling the importance of teamwork (the positions of leading hand and setter remained unchanged). In addition recruitment advertisements described CFM as

> 'An opportunity to increase employee involvement in the manufacturing process ... CFM is an innovative work structure that will require considerable amount of operator flexibility.'
>
> (CFM Recruitment notice)

In another sense the term CFM was used by production and planning engineers to describe a form of teamworking in which the primary focus for training was on creating a workforce with the skills needed to achieve optimum performance. Longer-term skill development training associated with notions of job enrichment or empowerment was not a priority. 'Initial training was to be in inspection techniques only and multi-skilling... to be carried out if and when necessary' (Operations Manager, Steering Group Minutes).

Respondents remarked that new recruits to the pilot cell found their initial experience of cell working was little different to traditional assembly line work. One HR manager explained that while operators had become responsible for quality inspection, there was little or no job rotation or multi-skilling within the cell, nor evidence of an empowered form of work 'sold' to recruits at the outset. She explained how cell operators expressed dissatisfaction with their experiences of cell working by 'capping their performance'. The resultant fall in output from cells led to human resource issues being placed high on the steering group's change agenda and establishment of a place for the personnel director on the committee in order to help develop a new strategy for recruitment of cell workers. In the interim, pilot cell operators continued to be paid individual incentives.

This re-positioning of the P&D function suggested a significant shift in the power dynamics of change in that it allowed for more explicit constructions of the empowerment discourse used to redefine management priorities and the creation of new strategies for developing cell workers beyond immediate skills training in inspection techniques and additional process skills. In the following section, I illustrate how change leaders (in briefing statements and speeches to shopfloor workers) drew upon creative use of metaphors to bring into play ideas that had meanings within competing discursive 'realities', in order to add more credibility to the development of more humanistic and developmental HRD practices: notably that these concerns were of 'strategic' importance based on an understanding that a concern with personal growth and employee involvement would result in greater organizational efficiency. These messages sought to create a fresh and positive view of CFM upon which 'voluntary' transfer of operators from batch to cellular manufacturing depended.

Metaphors of 'team', 'market' and 'customer' became central themes to a series of 'directors briefings' run jointly by the operations and personnel directors on the shopfloor. Written copies of these briefings indicated that the 'market' metaphor provided directors with the business case for change by drawing attention to heightened competition within the industry against which change instigators could place responsibility on employees as well as management for the success of the business:

> 'CFM is a major company policy, our survival depends on it... Our customers and our competitors are forcing SutCo to act swiftly as a world-class relay team and to adopt our new strategy of cell team working. It is important to know that becoming a member of a cell is ultimately not a matter of choice; it is a matter of necessity created by our customers' needs, and the need to compete effectively in the marketplace.'
>
> (Directors' Briefing)

> 'In time, after full training, we visualize cell members being able to make many of their own decisions within the team – how to organize themselves – to plan training events, to help colleagues, and so on. That's what employee empowerment means – just trusting employees to help manage themselves.'
>
> (Directors' Briefing)

In the above narrative, customers were characterized as a discreet identifiable entity that was *'forcing'* SutCo to 'act swiftly' in order to survive in *'the* marketplace' (emphasis added). This use of metaphor provided a critical means of conveying a congruence of interests between management and workers and placing responsibility on all organizational members on bringing in 'sufficient orders for the future employment of us all'. Moreover, unitarist statements of this kind implied that organizational goals and the means to achieve them were not open to negotiation. Supported by use of the 'team' metaphor they appeared to ignore the prevailing culture of 'us and them' noted earlier, seeking to create an image of the organization as a kind of team, united by the concern to improve 'competitive advantage'.

This 'performative rationale' (Lyotard, 1984) for teamworking was juxtaposed with competing conceptions of teamworking found in the same briefing statement that offered a future vision of teamworking, which promised more autonomy for cell operators, and more varied work, consistent with the empowerment discourse.

While the P&D director worked with the operations director to build an univocal vision and a more receptive climate for change within the organization, P&D managers became more closely involved with the line in development of recruitment and reward policies in support of the progression of the CFM initiative across the factory. These took place in the context of a 'loose' labour market that allowed the organization to be highly selective in its recruitment of staff at that time.

Construction of reward practices and reproduction of images of the 'empowered' cell

Ten months after the establishment of the pilot cell, a 'trial' pay system was established which reproduced images of 'empowered' teamworking created by personnel specialists in previous debates about an appropriate reward system for cells. All operators were paid a common basic salary[5] plus a group incentive based on quality, lead-time and output. The team bonus was a combination of everyone's performance in the cell, in output, quality and lead-time over a period of a fortnight (the cell comprised two shift groups). On this basis it promised to raise the importance of cooperative work relations and more innovative working practices, but in practice this led to considerable conflict amongst operators classed as 'high flyers', reflected in 'capping of their performance' (Internal report). These were the most highly-skilled and productive operators who were not only graded the same as those with lower skills, but also were given the same proportion of the overall team bonus to performers that were 'above' and 'below' average in the cell.

One HR manager explained that unrest amongst this group was exacerbated by the complexity of the bonus scheme and the limited opportunities offered to them by production managers (especially longer-serving ones) in respect of job flexibility and increased worker autonomy. She considered that these managers were 'too preoccupied with issues of efficiency and cost effectiveness' to allow operators to enhance their skills and be given the opportunity to 'rotate to more skilled positions within the cell'.

Change leaders downplayed these problems and instructed operators 'not to dismiss the new payment system without giving it a full trial' (internal memorandum), then proceeded to run a second series of factory briefings, which sought to promote a more positive image of CFM to organization members, and glossed over the contradictions inherent in work organizations. This was critical to senior managers at a time when the pilot phase was drawing to a close and the steering group sought to progress with CFM on an organization-wide basis. Recruitment practices in support of this next phase of CFM development are examined below.

End of pilot phase: construction of recruitment practices in support of new cells

Having formalized pay procedures, psychological testing was introduced for the recruitment of six new cells that comprised 32 per cent of operating staff.[6] Tests were in the form of a telephone-screening instrument that built upon the people-centred definition of teamworking outlined at factory briefings. Testing procedures were constructed round a conception of team and associated lists of behaviours that signified the 'ideal cell operator', such as 'being a team player'. Linked with this, job titles for cell members were re-labelled 'team member', and briefing notices to CFM applicants promised opportunities for teamworking, increased autonomy and more varied work:

- 'opportunity to enjoy togetherness feeling of being in a close-knit team;
- given special training in team-building, problem-solving, how to enjoy putting into practice some of the team's ideas;
- will be given more variety of work and be trained in other tasks for which you are suited.'

(Notice to all staff)

The discursive practices noted above provided an important means of creating a univocal and positive image of change accepted by potential recruits to cellular manufacturing, evident in the high number of applications for internal transfer into cells. One administrator involved in the recruitment process explained that applicants had high expectations of more employee development and more interesting work under CFM but these soon changed as they gained practical experience of cell working.

Operators quickly found that once transferred to cell work, team leaders made only minimal concessions to the notion of participative management and more flexible working practices. She explained that unrest over the new pay system amongst the more-skilled and more-productive workers was particularly evident, and recorded an increase in absenteeism and a fall in productivity amongst these 'high performers'. These workers continued to be paid the same as less-skilled and less-productive workers in their cell and voiced the 'unfairness' of this new system at directors' briefings (Steering Group Minutes).

Placed under increasing pressure to solve this 'productivity issue' the steering group established a 'CFM implementation team' given the task of developing P&D policies that would generate commitment and understanding across all levels of management and the shopfloor, to the principles of teamworking and employee involvement.

The CFM team included a cross-section of 17 employees from a range of functions and levels within the company and was led by a CFM project manager and training manager. Both emphasized the need to 'manage the politics of change' in an organization where production pressures remained high and where human resource matters continued to be taken 'downstream' to financial and production issues.

The CFM project manager explained that for him effective teamworking meant expanding operator responsibility beyond making routine decisions to where

'You have employees appraising each other; there is peer selection and a high level of communication amongst team members... In my view we need to spend more time encouraging people to work together, taking time out together, just talking about things in the team, in order to reduce costs and to improve quality.'

This narrative illustrates further the intertextuality of discourses framing strategies for change. While highlighting the importance of employee development and growth, it also ties the success of teamwork to business performance through a reduction in costs and its impact on product quality. Explicit 'voicing' of these performative rationales was perceived to be important by the project manager. Noting the controlling influence of finance and production disciplines he remarked that it was important for him to legitimize, in 'rational' terms, the resources being channelled into the training and development of cells. For him this meant the need to 'visibly demonstrate that empowered teams will work' and 'add value' to the business, but that this task was problematic. Consistent with earlier research (Hiltrop, 1996), it was explained that he was unable to articulate in quantitative terms, how or why his version of teamworking could affect the 'bottom line'.

In this context, the HRD manager's rhetorical establishment of the need for 'empowered work groups' became an important episode for legitimizing a heavy investment in the development of cell workers. Her 'Development Strategy' was framed by the rhetoric of 'strategic' HRD that justified the introduction of 'innovative teambuilding activities' at operator level, which would allow 'employees to make greater contributions to the business'. It gave primacy to the market metaphor which centred round notions of 'value added', 'world-class manufacturing' and 'competitive advantage', and which sought to create the perception amongst members of the steering group that the development of empowered employees was a critical and 'strategic' concern.

A cornerstone of the development strategy was the introduction of 'pilot training' for two of the longer-established cells in order that 'models of best practice' could emerge as a yardstick for further cell development. The nature of this training reflected a significant departure from traditional HR practice in two respects. Firstly, it went beyond job training in one particular process skill and aimed to develop softer people-centred skills in communication and teamworking, thus shaping attitudes and social behaviour. Secondly, training was geared to enable participants to gain a sense of ownership of the change. Importantly it facilitated more extensive upward influence amongst production employees upon the (empowerment) discourse of P&D surrounding change that had been largely absent during the design and early implementation of CFM and which is examined in the following section.

Training as a medium in the reconstitution of P&D and discursive 'subjects'

Following approval of the employee development strategy, operators and team leaders from two cells received 'pilot training' that involved two-day development workshops. Participants explored their understanding of teamwork, were asked to reach consensus about what would make for an 'effective cell' and to discuss their findings with a panel of departmental and senior managers, presenting them with an opportunity for some 'authorship' of P&D discourses surrounding change.

Course evaluation forms and accounts from the manager leading these workshops suggested that employee involvement of this nature allowed subordinates to use the language of P&D to bring managers into line with *their* expectations by challenging them about not 'letting go'. On doing so, cell operators were able partially to 'reconstitute' managerial images of CFM that had been dominated by a control-centred orientation. As one training manager explained:

> 'Sometimes their demands are very straightforward including such things as better catering facilities. Other matters include more 'teamy' things, and getting the team leaders to let go... They came up with models that emphasized people pulling together, people training each other and not just the coordination type skills. Coaching, doing all their own paperwork, deciding their own holidays, setting their own targets for example.'

These findings are consistent with Rosenthal *et al.*'s (1996: 177) study of service excellence training within a retail company, in which:

> 'The language seems to have given many a new confidence in their dealings with ShopCo, because it provides a clear and legitimate yardstick by which to assess managerial actions.'

Consistent with Rosenthal's findings, the training manager at SutCo considered that training events 'helped operators gain more confidence in talking to managers about what they felt was important', thus placing them in a better position to shape the interpretive frames of their seniors. This had important political implications at a time when, in her opinion, there was a lack of consensus and understanding amongst senior managers about 'what is meant by empowerment' and what was believed to be a 'team', consistent with comments made by a production manager who acknowledged that

> 'There was no discussion at the initial planning stage of the concept of teamworking nor the need for any radical change in reporting relationships. It was assumed that if you put people in a group they would work as a team.'

Towards the end of fieldwork there was some evidence (cited by training and production managers) of the kind of empowerment constructed at training events being realized on the shopfloor. However, younger-serving team leaders were more prepared to adopt and agree in the change effort than longer-serving colleagues who identified and were more attached to deeply-rooted values and discourse associated with that of a 'traditional' supervisor.

Differences in orientations between P&D and line managers, described earlier, were also important influences upon the dynamics of change and became more apparent as competition increased within the health sector in the mid-1990s. Corporate leaders placed increasing emphasis on the 'control' elements of excellence, putting pressure on local managers to provide data that could be used to evaluate the costs and benefits of organizational change initiatives. This influence led to an increasing concern amongst change agents at SutCo to develop more performance-focused P&D policies concerned with values of cost control rather than investment in employee development and well-being. In this context operational managers responsible for consolidating the CFM initiative talked of a lack of commitment to 'follow through' with the change effort, evidenced by switching of change leaders on the CFM team to other projects that assumed a higher profile.

▪ Discussion and key learning points

Challenging the normative and consensus-orientated assumptions underpinning much of the P&D literature to date, a growing number of academics are calling for more 'critical' empirical work concerned with understanding the discursive and socially constructed nature of HRD policy and practice. Going some way towards addressing the dearth of empirical work in this area, this chapter has sought to capture the complexity and ambiguity of HRD practice at SutCo. In this sense it might be considered 'critical' in that it invokes notions such as power and control to challenge the assumptions and 'taken-for-granteds' underpinning the contemporary theory and practice of HRD (Reynolds, 1999: 173; see also Fournier and Grey, 2000). A number of conclusions can be distilled from this case analysis.

First, Deetz's conception of a dialogic approach, combined with a Faircloughian view, provided me with a critical lens with which I was able to explore the fragmentation and disunity of HR discourses at local level and how these were embedded in the political dynamics of change internal and external to the organization. Consistent with a Foucauldian perspective on power, this analysis illustrated the inseparability of power and knowledge as texts and discursive practices emerged and fell away in importance. Discourse, in this context, is shown to be complex and dynamic, involving a rearticulation of meanings as change unfolded at SutCo. These processes of social construction were associated with changes in key 'authors' emerging within competing discourses that I have labelled 'excellence', 'control' and 'empowerment'. Exploration of this dynamic allowed me to present fresh insights into the agency role of line and P&D managers in shaping organizational change, which is poorly conceptualized in normative accounts of HRD.

Importantly the case illustrates ways in which the 'ambivalence potential' of P&D created points of tension around which managers were able to 'recontextualize' new concepts of CFM and teamwork.[7] It meant that managers at SutCo were able to create their own images of CFM and teamworking, framed by an evolving hybrid of P&D discourses and the particular (local) power dynamic within which they found themselves. Here, senior managers were shown to hold a pivotal position in framing operators' meanings and interpretations about CFM by drawing upon the metaphoric language of P&D to gloss over inherent tensions in work organizations and bring together competing concepts in such a way as to create an emotional and positive response to their plans for change.

Control over meaning construction was, however, shown to be fragile and preferred 'realities' created by senior managers soon became open to challenge 'from below'. As soon as plans were implemented there immediately began to emerge multiple interpretations about the meanings of terms, evident in the divergence in orientations across different levels and functions of management. Moreover, the constructions of 'empowered' workers emerging during training events around the ideal of an 'effective team' was perceived by the training manager to be a critical influence upon senior managers' interpretive frames. Consistent with a dialogic view of discourse, discursive responses of employees could not simply be 'managed from the top' at SutCo. While the power effects of language-use lead to the privileging and/or undermining of new discourses, dominant discourses are not hermetically sealed but always open to reconstruction and change (Deetz, 1996).

Secondly, and linked with the above, the perspective adopted here has provided me with a means to move beyond the either–or orientation that has characterized much debate about evolving philosophies and practices of P&D. Stewart and others call for more reflexive research designs that encourage us to analyse the relatively under-researched discourses of HRD, revealing dynamic tensions between opposing 'dualities' inherent in people management, often labelled in terms of 'hard' or 'soft' or 'performative' versus 'learning' (Evans, 1999; Keenoy, 1999; Legge, 1995; Kuchinke, 1998; Stewart and McGoldrick, 1996; Sambrook and Stewart, 2005). P&D inevitably reflects contradictory tendencies found in all management practice that requires a balance between the granting of autonomy/learning *and* the exercise of management control/performance.

My analysis of competing discourses at SutCo has provided rich examples of how P&D managers continuously looked for better ways to accommodate tensions arising between performative and humanist concerns, and this was particularly evident in the way HRD professionals sought to reconstruct HRD, from simply being a provider of training to being a strategic partner and at the same time focus more on workers' interests and development. The facilitation of collectively questioning managerially defined cell practices/relations during training sessions is consistent with the kind of 'emancipatory action learning' highlighted by Fenwick (2003, 2005a, b) and described as one of the hallmarks of a move towards a 'critical HRD foundation'.[8] Fenwick explains that small local projects can usefully combine pragmatic action and critical analysis by denaturalizing existing hierarchical conditions in ways that foster both employee and organizational well-being. Pointing to the dilemmas and complexities inherent in 'living out a critical orientation of HRD', she argues that it remains tenable as a field of study and approach to practice. Traps to avoid include 'representing managers as the unequivocal oppressors, slipping into naturalized illusions of unitary worker/manager interests, or presuming that dialogic spaces in workplaces are unproblematic' (2005a: 236).

Thirdly, the SutCo case illustrates how the 'mutation' of HRD was embedded in deeper social, political and economic discursive patterns that both enabled and constrained managerial agency; notably the corporate discourse of 'excellence' and 'grand discourse' of 'enterprise' (du Gay and Salaman, 1996, Alvesson and Karreman, 2000a, b). The constraining effects of these discourses became more evident as change unfolded within SutCo. While the concepts of enterprise and excellence highlighted processes of employee development, well-being and discretion, performative rationales appeared dominant as competition heightened in the health industry, giving primacy to notions of 'competitive advantage', the 'bottom-line' and tightening of managerial control.

This more instrumentally oriented view of people management and development became particularly evident in the corporate restructuring of production facilities within the company's European manufacturing businesses in 1993, leading to a number of plant closures. Moreover, eight years after this case study research was undertaken, in the spring of 2003, announcements were made at corporate level to close the SutCo plant just weeks after a visit from the centre, in which the SutCo executives were applauded for 'tremendous trends in cash flow, line item fill rate and cost control' which was attributed to the 'the unwavering commitment to quality' manifested by staff at the plant (Newspaper bulletin). The plant was closed down 'despite improvements of 2002 because work was duplicated elsewhere in the corporate group'. This dynamic clearly highlights the need for academics wishing to adopt a 'critical social science analysis' of P&D to carefully locate the choices managers are making about P&D practice within the 'context of material aspects of societal and global trends and... to issues of power at both "micro" and "macro" levels' (Watson, 2004: 457).

Finally, calls for more critical research of the kind suggested by theorists noted here suggest the need for academics to adopt more innovative ways of producing and disseminating critical work which effectively challenges assumptions underpinning the performance-focused model. This requires new media for encouraging dialogue between academics and P&D practitioners by promoting a collaborative effort of practicing and theorizing (Jacques, 1999), exemplified by Trehan and Rigg (2005), in their analysis of student experiences of critical education while undertaking a master's programme in HRD. They reflect on the potential impact of introducing critical reflection and the dissonance that may be generated amongst managers on such programmes and conclude that theoretical speculations on the hazards of critical reflection are, nevertheless, overly pessimistic.

A key task of HRD professionals in this context is to challenge dominant conceptions of management as doing/action rather than reflection and analysis. As Morgan observes: 'in a world dominated by practical considerations, there is often reluctance to get involved with issues of a theoretical concern. People tend to think that theory gets in the way of practice.' (Morgan, 1997: 376).

Morgan goes on to remind us that practice is never theory free and, especially at times of change, it is vital to be in touch with the assumptions and theories that guide our practice and to be able to shape and reshape them. As I note earlier, an increasing number of analysts are calling for the need to open up HRD theory to a broader array of critical perspectives to facilitate such questioning of assumptions/practices and associated language-use. While there has been an increasing amount of organizational research that is better placed than conventional survey designs in capturing the changing nature and scope of P&D, in-depth analysis tends to be restricted because of analysts' treatment of language as a transporter of meanings rather than a *creator* of meaning (Alvesson and Karreman, 2000a, b; Keenoy, 1999; Sambrook 2000).

My discourse analysis of the 'mutation' of HRD at SutCo, has focused on the action-oriented role of language in the construction of HRD and the nexus between this dynamic and other people-management policies and practices emerging as part of a planned change programme. As HRD professionals increasingly assume positions as 'strategic partners' in organizational change efforts (Ulrich and Brockbank, 2005), further research is required into the role that critical discourse analysis can play in shaping the practical and ethical dimensions of HRD in ways that lead to a greater focus on issues of employee well-being, development and the contested nature of learning at the workplace.

Notes

1 The concepts of knowledge management, knowledge workers and knowledge-intensive firms have become a central feature in management debate since the mid-1990s. Swart *et al.* (2003: 1) explain that knowledge-intensive firms gain their competitive advantage by converting their human capital (knowledge, skills and insights possessed by people) into intellectual capital in ways which create value in the marketplace and are difficult to imitate.
2 HRM has typically been classified into 'hard' and 'soft' versions (Storey, 2001; Legge, 1995). Hard HRM typically takes a business-strategy focus and places emphasis on the importance of close integration between HRM policies and practices with business strategy.

People are treated as a cost and resource to be managed in as 'rational' a way as any other factor of production. It is assumed that people can be managed in accordance with clearly defined organizational objectives with little or no recognition of any fundamental conflicts of interests and values between managers and employees.

The 'soft' approach to HRM also recognizes the need for integration of human resource and business policies and practices but shifts its focus from compliance and control to commitment and cooperation. Here, the language and practice of HRM play an important role in seeking alignment between the psychology of individuals to the goals of the business, and includes new phrases such as 'empowerment', 'teamworking' and 'competitive advantage' (Storey, 2001: 6; Keenoy, 1999).

3 Recontextualization involves a rearticulation of meaning that is not the same as found in the original context (Thomas, 2003: 793). The concept can be deployed to analyze how discourses change and are drawn upon by participants as a resource to shape their own or others' version of 'reality'. Such analysis rests on exploration of the 'intertextuality' of discursive events – the way in which texts are made up of snatches of other texts (Fairclough, 1992; see also Chouliaraki and Fairclough, 1999).

4 I eschew the tendency for some analysts to reduce social practice to discourse alone (Gergen, 1998; Hosking, 1999) and treat this a dynamic mix of abstract and material dimensions that are mutually dependent, including discourse, material conditions, institutionalized social relations and psychological processes (Chouliaraki and Fairclough, 1999; Fairclough, 1992, 1995; Morgan and Sturdy, 2000).

5 Operator tasks were distinguished according to three grades depending on their level of skill. The most highly paid were ' Class A needle attachers' responsible for particularly fine needle attachments.

6 Each cell comprised two or three shift groups, and the objective was to establish approximately 12 product cells, employing 80 per cent of production, within the next five years.

7 This term is applied where a word may be taken to have a combination of two or more senses, in contrast with 'ambiguity' where a word may be taken to have one sense *or* another (Fairclough, 1992: 113).

8 Informed by literatures in critical management studies and critical pedagogy, Fenwick argues that the precepts for critical HRD may include 'purposes of workplace reform aligned with equity, justice and organizational democracy; knowledge treated as contested, political and non-performative; inquiry focused on denaturalising organizational power and knowledge relations; and methods of reflexivity and critical challenge to prevailing conditions' (Fenwick, 2005a: 236).

Chapter 6

Shifting boundaries in work and learning: HRD and the case of corporate education

Jean Kellie

▉ Introduction

Business schools are increasingly expected to demonstrate 'corporateness' and 'relevance' through external partnerships, customized courses and through the production of 'applied' knowledge and research. In parallel, corporate clients are increasingly confident in influencing the curriculum and asserting their perspective on what is relevant and useful. These developments prompt a requirement to explore the pedagogical and epistemological issues raised by the shifting domains of management education and management development. This is brought into sharp relief with the emergence of 'corporate education' programmes where HRD practitioners find themselves at the intersection of educational and work-based learning initiatives. This chapter highlights the unfolding tensions concerning what constitutes appropriate 'learning' in corporate management education (Macfarlane and Lomas 1995, Mutch 2002). It also explores some of the implications of the shifting boundaries as educational institutions embrace corporate agendas as legitimate drivers of the curriculum (De Fillippi 2001, Keegan and Turner 2001, Garrick and Clegg 2001). Finally, it points to the responsibilities of HRD in maintaining sight of humanistic as well as instrumental goals in corporate education programmes.

For the purposes of the chapter, the definition of corporate education follows that cited by Prince and Stewart as: 'any award or non award-bearing programme of study that is developed and run by a university with the involvement of a company or companies' (2000: 207, adapted from Kennedy and Mason 1993:12). The discussion here draws on empirical research undertaken with two public sector organizations both of which developed and implemented award-bearing programmes (Post Graduate Certificate in Management and Diploma in Management Studies) with a UK university.

Management education and management development have grown significantly in importance and extent in the last two decades (Thomson *et al.*, 2001: 158). It is indicative, that in 1998 the DfEE noted that 40,000 managers were undertaking MBAs whereas four years previously it had been 18,000 (DfEE, 1998). Armstrong, citing AMBA (the Association of MBAs) data for 2004, reports that there are as many as 7000 part-time students and 5000 full-time students studying MBA programmes in the UK with considerable support from their sponsoring employers (2005: 229).

The context of the current upsurge in interest in management development can be traced to the critique of management education in the 1980s (Mangham and Silver 1986; Constable and McCormick 1987; Handy 1987). These reports revealed the lack of investment in management development and consequently the comparative disadvantage of UK managers in terms of training and development. Since then considerable attention and debate has focused on the need for educated managers and the development of management qualifications including more vocational qualifications (Thomson *et al.*, 2001). Furthermore, the last two decades have witnessed increasing evidence to suggest a positive relationship between investment in learning and the propensity for economic success. With regard to management education and development this is manifest in the government's rationale for establishing the Council for Excellence in Management and Leadership in 2000. From all sides there emerges a consensus 'that the quality of an organization's human resources represents a critical success factor' (Prince and Stewart, 2000: 207) and that HRD has a significant role to play in this (Garavan *et al.*, 2001).

Corporate management education has emerged as an important part of these trends; indeed Prince and Stewart go so far as to assert a 'sea change' in the extent of corporate education as it can be perceived as contributing to better organizational performance. 'Strategic education is seen by a growing number of organizations as a necessary major investment and a prerequisite for sustaining and developing competitive advantage' (Prince and Stewart, 2000: 210). Importantly, their research revealed that corporate clients engaging in corporate education demonstrated a growing sophistication with regard to their requirements from such programmes as well as their involvement in it. This extends variously to clients' expectations of participation in, or influence over, design, delivery, curriculum and assessment of courses and programmes. Clearly, these expectations challenge traditional assumptions about the exclusivity of the role of the academy in the determination and execution of educational provision. This challenge deepens as the boundaries between management *education* as academic process, and management *development* as an organizational process are increasingly blurred.

Management education and management development are not synonymous terms, nor do they necessarily refer to the same kinds of practices and interventions. They are however, both connected to that which is of central concern here relating as they do to the acquisition of knowledge, skills and attitudes of those individuals in organizations who have managerial roles and responsibilities.

Management development has traditionally been more closely associated with the world of the organization and the corporate enterprise. At best, it has aspired to contribute to the development of individual managers and to the managerial process itself by focusing on how organizational goals might best be met. Burgoyne and Jackson (1997) argue that this can be predominantly characterized as the 'institutionalisation of management learning' where organizational requirements, however constructed, dominate what is deemed to be appropriate management knowledge. HRD concerns in management development interventions take account of the developmental needs of individual managers but must necessarily foreground the contribution that such interventions can make to the organization and its articulated goals (Garavan *et al.*, 2001). Management development has often been designed, delivered or commissioned by HRD professionals. Management education, on the other hand, has been seen as the preserve of educational institutions that have had the power to set academic standards and award qualifications. Curriculum development, delivery and assessment are in the domain of the academy. Preoccupations in this domain centre on the ontological and epistemological problems of the nature of management and management knowledge (Anthony, 1986; Alvesson and Willmott, 1996; Chia, 1997), and pedagogy (Schön, 1987; Grey *et al.*, 1996; Vince, 1996; McGivern and Thompson, 2000).

Providers of management education have had to grapple with the competing demands of academic enquiry, with its emphasis on *question and critique*, and the expectations of the profession with its overtly instrumental orientation underpinned by a belief in a *tools and techniques* approach to the practice of management. This tension is succinctly summed up by Quinn's differentiation between 'know what and know why' (Quinn, 1992 cited by Fox, 1997: 21). The horns of this dilemma provide the departure point for much soul-searching in the profession of management educators. There is a vibrant debate in the academy about what constitutes an appropriate pedagogy (French and Grey, 1996; Burgoyne and Reynolds, 1997). What do radical teaching and learning interventions look like? How do we embrace experiential learning and what role does it play in the learning process? How might non-conventional texts and discourses facilitate innovation? How might the dichotomies of theory versus practice, conceptual versus relevant, abstract versus 'real world' be addressed? Management educators have increasingly striven to concern themselves with problematizing the nature of organizational and managerial practice and process.

It is not intended here to characterize management education as thoughtful and radical and management development as instrumentally organization focused. Such dualism would be false and simplistic. Management develop-ment also embraces a broad spectrum of traditions and interventions. As with management education, management development interventions may reinforce the rational, prescriptive, solution-based approaches to management. Alternatively they may offer opportunities for personal diagnosis, reflection, challenge and development. Management development might range from offering 'quick fixes' and technique 'tricks' to radical, innovative challenging programmes underpinned by pioneering behavioural techniques. Management education and management development have their origins in different tradi-tions and concerns. Despite the proposition that the two areas increasingly overlap they represent very divergent communities of practice (Fox, 1997).

Whilst the two domains remained relatively distinct the question of appro-priateness of the curriculum and what constitutes relevant learning has given rise to lively debates that have tended to preside *within* separate confines. Increasingly however, the rise of corporate education provides a contested arena in which corporate and educational agendas come into direct contact and in which the former 'expert' power of the academy is challenged by the 'legitimate' power of the HRD professionals.

There is certainly a growing confidence from professionals outside of acade-mia professing an equivalent or superior claim to knowing what constitutes 'relevance' in the context of management education and knowledge. David Clutterbuck puts it thus:

> 'a revolution is happening in the relationship between large companies and business schools. Traditionally, firms have taken a pick-and-mix approach (to management education and development), sending executives to a variety of schools or develop-ing a relationship with a few academics.

> 'But companies are proving less willing than they were to accept the traditional fodder offered by schools, much of which is more aimed at achieving dry, academic qualifications than appropriate learning. Many companies are now starting to demand more influence over the learning process.'

> (Clutterbuck, 2000: 40)

Clutterbuck applauds the break of the academy's grip as the guardian of the management education and identifies an emergent pattern. He ascribes this trend to the inappropriateness of the academic curriculum to organizational needs. He unquestioningly asserts the ascendancy of organizational needs in curriculum development in ways that might be confronting to educationalists from more liberal and humanistic traditions. More recently, the debate about the purpose and content of management education has received fresh impetus from Mintzberg's broad-ranging critique of 'conventional' MBA programmes in the US in which he argues strongly that the 'wrong people' are educated in the 'wrong ways' (2004: 5). Though directed at a particular genre of educational provision, he has nevertheless thrown down a gauntlet to management educators and stirred up much debate (see, for example, Nord 2005: 213; Feldman, 2005: 217; Tyson 2005).

It can be argued that to some extent these trends point to the vocationalization of management education. To some extent this has facilitated and accommodated employers' recognition of their own power in determining what constitutes appropriate knowledge in the context of management education and development. According to Usher *et al.* (1997) such workplace learning initiatives have emerged under a 'vocationalist pedagogy'. These are more likely to take a 'solution-orientated' approach to learning. This view is supported by Garrick (1998) and Garrick and Rhodes (2000) who are concerned that such an orientation closes down the opportunities for questioning assumptions and challenging the status quo given that the overriding preoccupation is instrumentalism.

This chapter provides the opportunity to explore the potential tension between key stakeholders in this process and the implications for perceptions of 'relevant' knowledge. The research on which it is based draws on the positions and perceptions of HR practitioners, participants and key providers.

■ HRD and the strategic imperative

HRD practitioners are increasingly drawn into the strategic arena and an emerging body of thought is beginning to address the theoretical implications of day-to-day organizational practice. The last decade or so has seen the rise of debates as to whether or not there has been a fundamental shift in the management of human resources and what this involves. Attention has also been focused on the extent to which any such shift has implications for the power relations between employers and employees. Organizations may be seen as increasingly unitarist through increased efforts to be more 'strategic' in their use of otherwise disparate aspects of HR practice. Thus, recruitment and selection, appraisal, payment systems, mentoring and employee development schemes can be seen in the context of attempts to integrate employee behaviour and attitude to organizational objectives, however these come to be constructed (Iles and Salaman, 1995; Townley, 1994; Beech and Brockbank, 1999). Such interventions can be analyzed in relation to the role they play in privileging of the interests of some groups, or individuals, more than others. They may also reveal the more subtle ways in which power is exercised in organizations.

Whatever the debates about 'reality and rhetoric', it is widely acknowledged both in academic literature and through organizational practice that effective management of the organization's human resources is central to organizational efficiency and success (Sisson and Storey, 2000; Boxall and Purcell, 2003).

Such assertions are underpinned by a growing acknowledgement of human capital theory which substantially make the 'business case' for training and development. In theory and in practice the management, and development, of human resources has come to be seen as a strategic as well as an operational matter. The linkage between individual and organizational performance is increasingly recognized as significant at the level of the organization as well as in national and global economic terms.

> 'Few issues are as central to the analysis, control and practice of HRM as skills and knowledge. Their possession and effective deployment can provide the basis for national and organizational competitiveness'.
>
> (Skills Task Force 1999 cited in Grugulis, 2003: 3)

There is a widespread consensus that skills are 'good things' and can benefit all participants in the employment relationship and most commentators 'assume the existence of a direct, positive relationship between skill formation and economic performance' (Heyes, 2000: 150 cited in Rainbird and Munro, 2003: 30).

Interest in HRD as a means to achieve corporate objectives is evident at all levels. Despite the earlier criticisms about the lack of investment in training and development for UK managers, the linear association of training and development with economic performance is prevalent (Keep and Mayhew, 1996). The Investors in People (IiP) kitemark officially acknowledges organizations that can demonstrate good practice in strategically focused employee development. Such developments have accentuated the role of HRD in organizational life. Pursuing national benchmarks, demonstrating the 'integration' of HRD policy and practice and addressing corporate objectives has served to raise the profile of the HRD function and practitioners. Equally HRD advocates (Garavan et al., 1995; O'Donnell and Garavan, 1997; McCarthy et al., 2003) have underlined the significance of the relationship between HRD's role and individual and organizational learning and effectiveness. Foregrounding learning as a key to economic performance has simultaneously focused attention on the role of HRD as a mediator of individual and organizational learning processes.

One consequence of these developments is a heightened awareness of the need to *show* that investment in training and development is demonstrably linked to corporate goals. Another consequence has been the acceptance of the legitimacy of the workplace as a site of educative development and that organizational requirements are legitimate educational goals. Insofar as corporate education programmes are concerned this might occur in a variety of ways through the design of the curriculum, programme discourses and work-based projects, etc. These issues are explored through a detailed discussion of two organizational case studies.

■ Methodology – background to the case studies

This section documents two local authority case studies. Both organizations developed and implemented award-bearing corporate education programmes between 2001 and 2003. Both programmes were accredited with postgraduate qualifications and started with cohorts of approximately 15 students. Mid-shire County Council (MC) began with a Postgraduate Certificate stage only, whilst Northern Council (NC) recruited cohorts at both Certificate and Diploma stages. The programmes were delivered over a 12–15 month time-frame. Each of the programmes have, at the time of writing, experienced a complete stage of study and were preparing to recruit further cohorts. The programmes were designed in partnership with the university and aligned to a campus-based, part-time MBA programme. The programmes were delivered exclusively by university staff, or university-approved staff, rather than by the internal members of the organization as is sometimes the case with corporate educational programmes. The NC programme takes place on the employer's premises whereas the MC programme is located at the university campus. Both programmes were developed by a process of negotiation in which the boundaries pertaining to learning outcomes were set by the university but which allowed some scope for flexibility in terms of curriculum content, modes of delivery and assessment. In both cases the project leaders in the client organizations had 'HRD' roles and both were responding to organizational drivers in pursuing the twin goals of establishing a management development programme for middle managers and securing university accreditation with recognizable qualifications. The data for the case studies is derived from a qualitative approach involving interviews and informal discussions with course participants, HRD personnel, and university academic staff including course leaders and the delivery teams.

NC is one of the region's largest employers with more than 4300 staff. It provides a wide range of public services spanning an eclectic range of professions from social or educational services to highways maintenance. The programme was open to supervisory and middle-management grades across the authority, subject to admissions criteria. MC is one of six directorates of the county council and employs approximately 1000 employees. Typically participants on the programme were middle managers in cultural services.

In different ways each of the organizational project leaders, HRD professionals, sought to influence not only the curriculum of the corporate education programme but also the 'ethos' of the programme. This occurred in both subtle and more obvious ways, thus shaping aspects of the provision and the narratives that surrounded it, as illustrated below.

Northern Council (NC) – case study one

NC approached the university in 2001 with a view to developing an in-company management development programme. The organization was facing substantial organizational change following the national agenda of reform and restructuring of local government. A key issue was 'change management' and the desire for more 'forward looking' management, able and confident in challenging perceived inertia. The council had a wider change management initiative and it was intended that the corporate education programme would be complementary to this. It was explicit in the introductory and subsequent meetings between the university and organizational representatives that the HR perspective was clearly linking the corporate education initiative to the 'change management' agenda and indeed this later became the basis upon which the programme was 'sold' to the prospective participants. It was evident from those early meetings that, from the organization's point of view, there needed to be a clear relationship between the corporate education programme and the wider strategic goals of the organization. In this respect, the development of the programme was framed by the perceived organizational objectives and thus followed a classically unitarist model of strategic HRD.

The council had already identified four principles which would guide action and be a focus for moving forward. These were:

- best value
- corporate governance
- the well-managed authority, and
- performance management.

These were broken down into further sub-headings which taken together became the basis for evaluating the 'relevance' of the curriculum of the management development programmes. The generic programme to which this in-company variant was aligned comprised a number of standard business and management modules, each with designated learning outcomes. In the development process for NC a complex mapping exercise was undertaken to match module content and learning outcomes to organizational requirements as specified by the 'four principles'. An abridged version of this was publicly available so that the relationship between the programme and the organizational objectives was made explicit in the public domain and some discussion of this took place at a programme launch with the senior management and prospective participants. The programme was launched in the following spring.

The mapping process identified that some modules/learning outcomes were perceived as less relevant than others and these were designed out of the programme. There was a desire for a more work-based project focus and this was included. What is of interest here is not so much what was included and what was not but rather the device by which these evaluations were made. NC's four principles and their concomitant subcategories act as both a gatekeeper of 'relevance' and as a benchmark framework against which educational and developmental evaluations are made. What is also significant in this case study is the extent to which it was deemed important for the corporate education programme to be seen to be linked to the corporate objectives. This was emphasized discursively in a variety of milieu, in the planning phase, at the launch, at the introductory meeting and in all course and promotional documentation. In this respect, for some stakeholders at least, the programme's legitimacy as a developmental vehicle is dependent on its perceived explicit relationship to stated organizational objectives.

Mid-Shires County Council (MC) – case study two

The development of the MC programme took place in a similar time-frame to the above and there were some very clear external drivers for the corporate education programme. MC had received an Investors in People report earlier in the year which, among other things, had identified a 'lack of appropriate development for managers'. The Investors in People agenda was very powerful and this was continually stressed throughout the development phase both verbally and in the notes of meetings of the development team. Senior management had already developed a management competency framework which had emerged from a combination of an internal competency model together with competencies derived from the Management Charter Initiative (MCI). The project leader from MC was clear that these were to form the basis for the management development programme. The competencies were:

- Strategic Planning
- People Management
- Developing Self and Others
- Communication
- Working with Others
- Personal Contribution and Achievement, and
- Managing Change.

The development of the corporate education programme was preceded by a training-needs analysis initiated by the training and development manager and was fed into this process. Again, a mapping exercise formed the basis for deciding what aspects of the university-based programmes sufficiently met the competency requirements and for identifying areas that were lacking. The relationship between the organizational agenda and the programme structure and content was publicly promoted through programme documentation and publicity. In some early promotional material the project leader made explicit the link between the Investors in People agenda and the corporate education programme:

'In line with its commitment to Investors in People the MC wishes to offer a range of development and training options for managers, which develops their management competence and helps them improve the performance of the organization, in a period of immense change.'

(HRD manager)

The programme was launched at an event involving the Directorate's senior management and the opening session had a strong 'personal development equates to organizational development' theme. Internal to the organization the objectives of the programme were promoted as:

- taking into account the expressed needs of managers;
- looking at the needs of the organization and local government;
- drafting management competencies which set the standards for a Cultural Services Manager;
- linking these into the university programme;
- utilizing cultural services vision;
- opportunities for participants to work together and with university tutors away from distractions;
- networking, sharing ideas, giving and receiving support;
- enabling managers to assess themselves against the competencies;
- reflecting on own development through a personal development journal;
- providing grounding in essential management skills;
- improving the service by work-based projects attaining a nationally recognized standard;
- supporting managers in the management of change.

MC's HRD project leader entitled the management development programme 'Developing People, Developing Services' thus reinforcing the link with corporate objectives. The competency agenda was an important one for MC. This was emphasized through the client's request to include a 360-degree appraisal process, based on the competencies, as an integral part of the programme. At the outset of the programme, participants were invited to solicit feedback against the competency framework using a 360-degree appraisal tool and to use this as the basis for the development of a learning action plan. The study modules and inputs in the programme would support the participants achieving development in the identified areas. Initially the client aspired to the assessment of the programme being tied into this process but it was subsequently agreed that it would be more meaningful as a parallel to assessment, not a substitute for it. It would in any case have been challenging for the university's assessment procedures at that time. Nevertheless the competency framework formed the basis for part of the evaluation process at the end of the programme.

Corporate objectives and competencies – epistemological and pedagogical issues

In both these case studies, corporate objectives and competency frameworks play an important role in providing a rationale for the development of the corporate education programmes. Both organizations required their managers to be developed in line with predetermined competencies and these influenced the curriculum and how it was packaged for internal consumption. It is evident in both cases that NC's 'four principles' and MC's competency framework operate as gatekeepers in what is considered to be 'relevant' knowledge. The organizational agenda, as interpreted by its representatives, is perceived to provide a sufficient framework on which to structure the curriculum. 'Useful knowledge' is that which is deemed to enhance individual performance as a primary consideration. This approach to knowledge is one of functional instrumentality. As Garrick and Rhodes (2000: 4) note:

> 'with the de-differentiation of disciplinary-based knowledge has come an emphasis on instrumental knowledge. This instrumentalism of knowledge is connected to whether knowledge is considered to be "useful", whether it can be applied to work contexts, and whether it can generate a competitive edge or profits.'

Such a view of knowledge locates its validity with 'purpose'; this for Lyotard (1984) is the distinction between modern and postmodern conditions of knowledge. In modernity, knowledge was justified on the basis of its contribution to truth or its qualities of liberty but the essentialism underpinning this perspective is in doubt in these post-modern times. In the post-modern context, 'the question (overt or implied) now asked by the professionalist student, the state or institutions of higher education is no longer "is it true?" but "what use is it?"' (Lyotard,1984: 51 cited in Garrick, 1998: 108). In the case studies there is a clear instrumentality in the way the curriculum was perceived and this impacted on its design and construction. This was evidenced though the mapping processes described above. In both cases the corporate objectives and competencies drove what might be seen as 'useful knowledge'. In the case of NC it was deemed desirable to put emphasis on some knowledge inputs at the expense of others, depending on what was considered to be necessary to enhance the 'change agenda' and the managerial capabilities to contribute to it. With MC a greater emphasis was attributed to the competency framework and the participants' achievements in relation to that. This is not to argue that the educational (university) and corporate agenda were at odds with each other as there was indeed a high degree of consensus about what constituted relevant knowledge. The point is rather that organizational discourse, in these cases concerning 'competencies' and a 'change initiative', have to be seen to be accommodated in order for the curriculum and subsequent learning to be seen as legitimate.

Garrick (1998), in his research on work-based learning, has examined the ways in which educational and industrial agendas are converging on the language of competencies and competency-based standards. These provide pre-defined sets of standards which provide an apparently 'objective' means by which performance can be evaluated 'at the same time they serve to disguise the way in which power operates in particular (contexts) and their implementation has some specific consequences for the ways practitioners operate. One consequence is that they can (pre)determine ways in which one sees others perform' (Garrick 1998: 103). This notion of performance and its measurement provides another area for tension; clearly the organization's perception of the success of the programme and of individuals might be tied in with the programme's *raison d'être*, however this is constructed, i.e. its propensity to develop required competencies or facilitate change. As a formal educational intervention, individual performance is linked to assessment strategies and learning outcomes. Naturally, where corporate objectives have impacted on curriculum priorities, educational and organizational performance become more closely intertwined. One such example might be work-based projects which explicitly address work-based issues. Course participants sometimes showed greater sensitivity to how their performance(s) might be perceived internally by their peers and managers than by their university assessors. So although course participants' performance was officially based on module assessment, unofficially performance was perceived to be evaluated by other criteria.

Another interesting example of these boundary tensions was the use of a 360-degree feedback instrument in a personal development module. The HRD project manager aspired for this instrument (which put peer feedback into the public domain), and progress against a related action plan, to be part of the module assessment. The feedback instrument was designed around the core competencies identified in the MC case study above. This is illustrative of the way in which the organizational priorities might be seen to migrate into both the vehicle, and the evaluation, of learning and raises thought-provoking dilemmas for educators and HRD professionals. In this example, the matter was resolved without the inclusion of the 360-degree appraisal forming part of the assessment but it illustrates the implications of recasting the boundaries of work performance and education: what learning is being assessed by whom and to what purpose?

Garrick (1998) has shown that the greater the role the workplace has in determining what is considered to be legitimate knowledge, the greater the propensity for performance (developmental and educational) to be prescribed exclusively by this.

Whilst Garrick's research centres on learning in the workplace where HRD practitioners were central to the development initiatives, in the case studies presented here there is an arena of negotiation and contestation about what constitutes appropriate knowledge and how it might be framed. An interesting, though not surprising, point pertains to the determination of the curriculum in NC and MC. The client organizations' means of determining and evaluating 'useful' knowledge did not always concur with a 'university' view. Both MC and NC had considerable power in the negotiation process by virtue of occupying a 'client' role in which the university faculty in question had a vested interest in being seen to be working with the 'local business community'. At the same time the university rules and procedures offered relatively fixed boundaries around what might be negotiated with regard to programme learning outcomes. These tensions are played out against a backdrop of the increasing legitimacy of the workplace as author and authenticator of educational and developmental outcomes.

Other tensions surfaced within the delivery team about the content and structure of the curriculum. Some tutors felt undermined that a particular module might not be included, or that they might be asked to customize modes of delivery or materials in line with the client organization's expectations. This was sometimes expressed as antipathy towards corporate educational programmes, questioning their legitimacy and credibility. Others called into question the client's influence in framing the mode of delivery or the delivery time: for example, in both case study organizations, block delivery was favoured above week-on-week delivery typical of the campus-based provision. These variations precipitated some disquiet about the 'equivalence' of the 'student experience'. Some of these responses might be understood as the responses of stressed-out academics struggling to become more flexible and addressing the needs of different client groups, often without proper development opportunities to do so. Nevertheless academic staff did experience a shift in the boundaries of influence and control in the curriculum and its delivery. Overall, the positive benefits of working with corporate client groups were widely acknowledged and valued. These included opportunities for research, developing case studies and professional updating. However, taking on the role of a 'service provider' for a client organization recasts the traditional academic/student relationship in ways not yet fully explored.

■ The impact of instrumentality on reframing the boundaries of learning

The foregrounding of organizational objectives and competencies also has implications for pedagogical issues to do with reflection and theorizing. Reflection is regarded by most learning theorists as central to the learning process. For Schön (1987) reflection is the key to learning. The terminology of the 'reflective practitioner' is emphasized as the vehicle through which learning takes place. His concept of 'reflection-in-action' presents a very 'here and now' element to the way in which individuals observe, process and evaluate experience. Kolb's (1976, 1984) model of the 'learning cycle' identifies reflection as crucial to making sense of our experience. In both cases reflection is taken to be an active process requiring a high level of skill and personal awareness. Notwithstanding this, these theorists and others are often marshalled as witness to the significance of 'learning by reflecting on experience *at work*'. In the languages of competence-based standards, lifelong learning, work-based learning and the like, 'reflection' has come to mean 'thinking about work issues' and 'how to solve them'. Neither Kolb nor Schön would regard as sufficient, definitions of reflection as merely being thoughtful about different courses of action. In the context of management development and learning, Reynolds has taken this a step further, arguing that reflection should contain the possibility of social critique and advocating the need for learning opportunities that challenge taken-for-granted assumptions (1998: 198):

> 'management and management education, like any other social domain, accumulate taken for granted beliefs and values reflecting the view of the majority or those in power so pervasively that they become unquestioned "common sense". The fundamental task of critical reflection is to identify, question and if necessary change those assumptions. It is a process of making evaluations, often moral ones and not simply exercising judgements of a practical, technical nature.'

Reynolds' views can be located in critical theory and with Habermas, who promulgates the view that the pursuit of reason through critical reflection is emancipatory because it frees us from the ideological constraints pertaining to existing power relationships. This resonates with Kolb's emphasis on 'abstract conceptualisation' as an aspect of learning and his notion that learning is about challenging existing truths (1984: 108):

> 'the development of knowledge, our sense of ideas about ourselves and the world around us, proceeds by a dynamic that in prospect is filled with surprising, unanticipated experiences and insights, and in retrospect makes our earlier earnest convictions about the nature of reality seem simplistic and dogmatic. As learners, engaged in this process of knowledge creation we are alternatively enticed into a dogmatic embrace of our current convictions and threatened with utter scepticism as what we thought were adamantine crystals of truth dissolve like fine sand between our grasping fingers.'

Learning and development, then, have a radical potential. A possibility to reframe reality and 'see' things as they really are, or at least to see things through alternative prisms and perspectives. The crux here is the relationship of theory and practice. Theorizing our own and others' experience, meanings and feelings enables us to see things differently, perhaps do things differently. The extent to which this radical possibility can be embraced within corporate education presents a challenge. The language of 'theorizing' is associated with the world of the educational academy not the world of the organization and is distrusted as being inevitably 'abstract', unconnected to the 'real world' and irrelevant to work-based problems. Theory becomes permissible only insofar as it can be seen to be commensurate with an instrumental agenda. Theories, concepts and analyses which are identified with understanding and resolving functional issues and problems of implementation are deemed to be more acceptable than those which address, or challenge, the social, political, ethical and philosophical bases of organizations and management. As Garrick and Clegg have noted, in work-based contexts some questions are 'out of bounds' (2001: 124).

Corporate education programmes might be argued as evidence of the breaking down of the boundaries between education and work with contradictory effects. Mutch has noted that on the one hand corporate education might draw in a range of participants who might otherwise not have participated in higher education (2002: 182) thus extending developmental and educational opportunities. Yet, on the other hand, it is this blurring of boundaries between education and work that makes possible the potential to pose 'work' as 'education' particularly from the perspective of the learners. This clearly challenges the liberal and humanist views of education and development.

In both case studies, programme participants as well as HRD project leaders articulated, albeit in different ways and for different reasons, the importance of workplace relevance and usefulness. Participants as well as HRD practitioners would be understandably keen on programme inputs that related directly to their sphere of work and critical of those that did not. In in-company programmes, the charge of 'not relevant to the job' assumes the status of powerful and legitimate criticism. In this context theorizing and critical reflection are filtered though a prism of instrumentalism. It is not possible to make the claim that programmes emerging under corporate parameters are exclusively instrumental in orientation, but it is possible to say that what constitutes 'relevant' knowledge is no longer the exclusive domain of the educator. It is more closely tied to the perceptions of the organizational stakeholders.

Management education and HRD are central to the challenge that this poses. The debates on the importance and possibility of a 'critical management education' are more pointed in the context of growing numbers of corporate education programmes. Meanwhile HRD in theory and practice struggles to resolve the tensions between the 'individual' and the 'organizational' and the implications for the role of HRD in this dualism. In the case studies here we have seen some of these tensions played out as we observe how organizational objectives might be embraced in the educational arena through the technologies of HRD. This is unsurprising given the importance HRD attributes to its contribution to organizational performance. However, it does point to a need for a level of responsibility and awareness about the implications of HRD practice and its possibilities and its limitations.

The emergence of HRD as a coherent body of knowledge and practice has flourished in parallel with the significance attached to learning as a key to organizational success. Interest in knowledge management, the learning organization, work-based learning and related developments positively correlate learning and performance. HRD undoubtedly has a role in facilitating this and much of the emerging HRD debates are about how this might happen and how important it is that it does. What we must not lose sight of in the hyperbole is that learning is an individual and a collective process that occurs in a social and political context. HRD practitioners and management educators are part of the process and the context in different ways representing different milieu and power relationships. Vince (2003: 559) has argued strongly that HRD must be more self-consciously alert to its role in contributing to organizing and understanding its political possibilities if it capitalizes on its current strategic impetus. This is reiterated from another perspective by Elliot and Turnbull who emphasize the moral and ethical aspects of HRD. They assert its role as 'critical educator and moral conscience raiser ' (2003: 469) whilst articulating a concern that such a role might be difficult to embrace. These perspectives encourage us to problematize the relationship between learning and performance with regard to the role of HRD and point to the need to look more enquiringly at learning interventions such as those described in this chapter.

■ Conclusions

The HRD role is frequently at the intersection of the shifting boundaries between management education and management development. This is especially so in the context of the emergence of award-bearing corporate education programmes which are increasingly thought to be a valid alternative to campus-based university provision. These developments blur the distinction between education and work and have implications for what learning might be considered legitimate. Furthermore, the role of HRD as a mediator of organizational objectives in relation to the development and implementation of corporate education programmes has been highlighted. So too have the potential tensions in the determination of the curriculum, modes of delivery and assessment. Related to this is the notion that the context of learning may privilege some forms of reflection over others thus constraining the more transformational potential of learning. Research on corporate education programmes is only just beginning to emerge and it is clear from the material in the case studies in this chapter that the HRD role in relation to forming and reforming the work/education boundaries will be context specific. Further research is needed to understand the dynamics and tensions of these processes together with the responsibilities of HRD in relation to learners and organizations.

Activities for Part Two

1 (a) Produce a personal statement on the role and purpose of HRD in the workplace.

   (b) Consider how your statement is or is not supported by the chapters in this part.

   (c) Discuss the results with colleagues. Attempt to reach a consensus on what constitutes legitimate purposes for HRD.

2 (a) Formulate a design for a work-based HRD intervention which meets one or more of the purposes agreed as a result of the first activity (above).

   (b) Present your design and supporting rationale to colleagues and seek their views.

   (c) Review the results of this activity to inform design of future interventions.

3 (a) Select one chapter from this part.

   (b) Produce a thorough analysis of the arguments presented in the chapter.

   (c) Present your analysis to colleagues to facilitate debate on the arguments.

   (d) Identify the implications of the results of this activity for workplace HRD practice.

Part Three

CONSTRAINTS IN THE CLASSROOM

Introduction to Part Three

This part is named 'Constraints in the classroom'. As with the previous part this is an arbitrary category to distinguish it from Part Two. The main focus is what happens when HRD practitioners are directly interacting with participants. This focus encompasses both face-to-face interaction and the work that happens in preparing for those face-to-face interactions. The latter includes design decisions on content and process as well as the preparation of specific teaching/training materials for particular and individual encounters in the classroom. In addition, it also includes decisions which all HRD practitioners face as their practice occurs: for example, how to respond to the responses and reactions of participants to the prepared materials, which of course cannot be predicted: they can only be 'managed' as and when they happen. The chapters tend to assume and so focus on the university or academic classroom. However, the arguments are of relevance not only to those who perform their practice in that context, for two reasons. Firstly, and as argued earlier, education-based interventions form part of the practice of HRD practitioners in work organizations since such practitioners are involved in decision-making on whether and for whom university programmes will be used. This may be in the context of corporate programmes, such as those described in Chapter 6 by Jean Kellie, or perhaps more commonly their involvement may be in approving funding for individual employees or perhaps deciding whether to include qualification/university programmes for groups of employees such as technical or professional staff. Secondly, face-to-face programmes form part of the practice of most if not all HRD professionals. There may be particular and unique characteristics associated with university programmes and therefore need to be taken into account by academics in their HRD role. However, HRD professionals in work organizations, just like their academic counterparts, have to make design decisions on content and process, and also have to prepare materials for specific and particular sessions. They also have to react and respond to participants in real time. The impact of the particular context of university programmes will not make a significant difference to the commonality of those areas of practice. So, the issues and arguments presented in the chapters in this part have as much relevance to the workplace as they do the academy. This illustrates the arbitrary nature of the category. That said, it does have value in emphasizing what might be termed this 'micro' area of practice.

HRD work 'in the classroom', whatever the context, can and does bring into sharp relief the challenges and difficulties of applying a critical approach. Whatever that concept might mean to the particular practitioner it inherently implies that traditional, established or 'normal' paradigms and approaches are not being applied. The challenges and difficulties arise in part because a critical or 'different' approach itself will not usually meet the expectations of participants. That in turn will mean potential conflict between practitioners and participants. It will also raise the possibility of dissent both within groups of participants and between those groups and HRD professionals. It might be thought that 'managing expectations' is the answer and that this can be achieved by involvement of stakeholders in design decisions and by appropriate description, explanation and promotion of the particular programme. This though is a simplistic view which does not take sufficient account of the shift in mindset required in embracing a critical approach. Paradigms and approaches which are based on alternative assumptions to those which normally go unstated, let alone questioned or challenged, are not easily or quickly understood. Indeed, it may be the primary or even exclusive purpose of a programme to achieve the clear expression of previously unstated assumptions and so that is not achievable in descriptions or explanations. The process of surfacing such assumptions is itself difficult and challenging for participants and thus for the HRD professional to facilitate. It also usually means an examination of long and firmly held beliefs, and examination of personal values. This can be an emotional and uncomfortable experience, and one which many participants may question on the basis of relevance and benefit. This is an additional reason why practitioners have difficulty with initiating and sustaining a critical approach.

There are at least two additional reasons for these difficulties. The first will be fairly obvious from the previous part of this book. It is simply that established economic and political interests are often challenged through the application of critical approaches. This is the case whether the context is the workplace or the academic classroom. The second reason is the application of the same analysis to the relationship between HRD practitioner and participants. There are a-priori factors at play which work to establish particular power relationships between the two and these present difficult challenges for practitioners. We have to be willing to question our own assumptions and established practice. This means that it is not only the expectations of participants that will be unmet but also those of the practitioner who moves to adopt a critical approach. So, critical HRD practice is constrained by HRD practice and practitioners as well as by the social context in which each operates.

The first chapter in this part, by Lisa Anderson and Richard Thorpe, tackles most of the issues mentioned above. Their focus on action learning crosses the workplace/academic divide since this is a method utilized in both contexts.

Anderson and Thorpe's analysis also encompasses a number of possible interpretations of 'critical' in examining their relevance and value in action learning. The examination reveals many of the tensions for all involved in applying 'critical' ideas and concepts in practice, tensions which arise from factors in both the macro- and micro-contexts. What emerges is the significance of questioning and challenging to learning and development, and so the importance of the very ideas and concepts which give rise to the tensions, but which also facilitate the required questioning and challenge to established ways of thinking and viewing the world if development is to occur. The second chapter by Claire Valentin examines the impact of the macro environment on higher education and highlights the associated instrumental emphasis on 'performance' and results. The chapter in a sense applies ideas from critical management to the management of universities as a way of analyzing and understanding the difficulties of utilizing those same ideas in the classroom as part of the content and process of the curriculum of management programmes. Thus a link between the macro- and micro-environment is established. Claire Valentin begins to raise the issues that will confront practitioners in the classroom. The final chapter by Brendon Harvey takes us more directly into that setting. Here the focus is on one teaching, or training, method which has direct connections with critical approaches. Drawing on a range of literature and concepts associated with critical management and critical management learning in support of the method, Harvey identifies and examines the constraints, from both institutional and individual factors, that confront the practitioner in applying critical methods in face-to-face interactions. The argued constraints are supported by analysis of critical incidents in teaching practice. While this practice is in the context of a professional qualification delivered in an educational context, Harvey shows that similar factors in the workplace can and do operate with similar impact.

The main themes in this section are the following:

- the similarities and differences in educational and non-educational work settings;
- the role, influence and impact of macro-level factors on the micro-practice of HRD;
- the challenges and difficulties of incorporating a critical HRD approach in designing the content and process of HRD programmes and interventions;
- reconciling the necessity of questioning and challenging established thinking with the expectations of both HRD professionals and their clients;
- overcoming contextual factors in applying and using methods appropriate to a critical approach.

As with previous parts this list should not be seen as definitive but as suggestions to stimulate and support debate.

Chapter 7

Putting the 'C' in HRD

Lisa Anderson and Richard Thorpe

Introduction

Critical HRD is a term that has been coined in an attempt to fuse the ideas that stem from recent managerialist pressures and perspectives (HRD and the associated HRM/performance agenda) with those from the critical management studies movement. Here, notions of power, politics and a move towards emancipation of employees within organizations are dominant themes. Combining two such radically different philosophies make the field a difficult one to both conceptualize and put into practice, given the obvious contradictions of the management and neo-Marxist viewpoints managers are encouraged to adopt. Fenwick (2005b) proposes that one of the purposes of HRD could be to work towards workplace reform by challenging theories such as human capital. Knowledge in critical HRD should also be contested and inquiry should be multi-faceted, focusing on issues such as power. Fenwick (2005) also argues that critical HRD methods should challenge prevailing ideologies and promote reflexivity.

For many, critical reflection is the cornerstone of critical learning and perhaps also, we suggest, of critical HRD. Schön (1983) indicates reflection is an intuitive process and he characterizes it as 'individual cognition'. Marsick and Watkins (1990) move away from a solely individual focus and emphasize the value of collective learning and Reynolds and Vince move further suggesting that reflection is best understood as 'a socially situated, relational, political and collective process' (2004: 5).

There have been many approaches suggested to promote reflection by managers – one such approach, action learning, has had enduring and popular appeal. Action learning has been suggested as having the necessary components to engender collective critical reflection (Willmott, 1994, 1997;

McLaughlin and Thorpe, 1993; Alvesson and Willmott, 1996; Rigg and Trehan, 2003; Fenwick, 2005b). Notwithstanding these endorsements, as Perriton (2004) identifies, there are precious few accounts of the practice of critical action learning. Furthermore, those attempting to develop managers' critical qualities are most usually management developers as opposed to management academics. In this chapter, we provide an account of the experience of management academics attempting to adopt critical action learning to promote critical reflection within the context of management development. The chapter describes the content and the workings of a qualification programme designed for practising managers. The majority of the participants on the programme were HRD managers working on issues identified by them from within their own organizations. In the chapter, we describe how theory and practice were integrated within a qualification (part-time MSc programme) to encourage HRD managers to be more critically reflective of their work and their workplace, and to use this reflection to inform action.

■ Action learning – a pedagogy to engender critical reflection

'Action learning' as a term is used to define a wide variety of management development practice. For some, its use is synonymous with approaches that might be appropriately used to describe 'active learning'; for others, when it is the method that is emphasized the focus moves to stress self-managed learning; and for yet others, action learning cannot be action learning unless a *Revansesque* or 'Scientific' (Marsick and O'Neil, 1999) approach is followed. In any of its guises, however, action learning is essentially based on the premise that through a process learning can be promoted. This process involves individuals being helped to reflect on the attitudes and actions they adopt when solving real organizational problems (McGill and Beaty, 1996). The forum for reflection and discussion is in most cases seen as a 'set' (a small group of like-minded individuals) facilitated by a set adviser. In 'traditional' action learning, an equal emphasis is normally placed on personal learning and development, and on the solution of a real (and important) organizational problem. So, as McLaughlin and Thorpe (1993) observed, the method offered a new paradigm for management development, one that embraced the individual and their development within the context of organizational development. This approach challenged established approaches to management education and development in a number of ways. The usefulness of learning was tested through practice and application and reframed as a consequence of action and reflection. In some ways, the process is akin to action research and the method, with knowledge being tested through practice, has a 'mode 2' component, that is, knowledge which is created in the context of its application and is transdisciplinary in nature, as opposed to 'mode 1' knowledge which is created within disciplinary bound-aries, usually by academics (Gibbons *et al.*, 1994). Pedler (1991) offers the following definition:

> 'Action Learning is an approach to the development of people in organizations which takes the task as the vehicle for learning. It is based on the premise that there is no learning without action and no sober and deliberate action without learning... The method... has three main components – people, who accept responsibility for taking action on a particular issue; problems, or the tasks that people set themselves; and a set of six or so colleagues who support and challenge each other to make progress on problems'.

Revans (1971) himself recognized that what needed to be brought into the practice of action learning were some of the perspectives and rigour that are the hallmarks of postgraduate management education and one of the most important qualities for students working at Master's level is the development of a critical perspective.

From teaching to learning

Willmott (1997) stated that critical management pedagogy is important as it represents an attempt to counter the growth of positivist, technicist approaches to teaching and learning about management in UK universities. This sentiment is one that has gained recent currency in the debate about the value of business schools and the pedagogy of the MBA in particular (Bennis and O'Toole, 2005; Mintzberg, 2004; Pfeffer and Fong, 2002). The critical management studies movement claim that a 'management by numbers' approach forces out approaches that allow individuals and collectives from making insightful contri-butions and questioning current orthodoxies and received wisdoms. Action learning is one of a number of approaches that serves to challenge the practice of management and management education. Post-Fordist restructuring and the associated rise of new or repackaged management thinking (e.g. HRM, TQM and corporate culture) has brought about this need for change (Willmott, 1994). In effect, the point Willmott is making is that management is taught rather than learned; students are asked to largely accept the views of tutors and textbooks and not to question. The dangers of such an approach, particularly within a context of higher education, are that the education of managers within universities prepares them to solve problems using methods of analysis against a set of formulae as opposed to giving them an ability to 'read' a situation and to make their own judgements. The critical management studies movement also deplores the fact that in the teaching of management the management process is depoliticized so that the inherent conflict that exists between, for example, organization and employee, manager and managed, goes largely ignored. This is not to say that there are no difficulties associated with introducing critical management pedagogy. Management is an applied discipline (some say more like a design science) that requires a strong focus on practice and an eye to relevance; few study management for its intrinsic value. Similarly, most do so with a fair degree of instrumentality, usually linked to the objective of commanding higher salaries in the marketplace. We believe this is certainly the case for many part-time masters students who see a Master's degree in management as one route to promotion. Yet Master's education within a university needs to stretch participants academically and help them develop appropriate conceptual frameworks as well as critical faculties that will enable them to frame appropriate questions and challenge conventional wisdom. Action learning with its questioning approach seems to be ideal for developing this kind of criticality at Master's level yet able to retain its applied context.

Willmott (1997) explained how critical action learning can contribute to critical management practice:

> 'Critical action learning explores how the comparatively abstract ideas of critical theory can be mobilized and applied in the process of understanding and changing interpersonal and institutional practices. By combining a pedagogy that focuses on management as a lived experience with theory that debunks conventional wisdom, managers can be enabled to develop habits of critical thinking… that prepare them for responsible citizenship and personally and socially rewarding lives and careers.'

Although action learning is advocated by many as an extremely useful and accessible way of bringing a critical focus to management education, it does have detractors. Fenwick (2005b) has argued that action learning was originally formulated as a way of serving organizational purposes – to assist in raising the levels of performance and productivity. As such the process may promote little more than an illusion of worker participation. Instead she advocates 'emancipatory' or non-elitist action learning, a process whereby real changes to systems of control and power relations come about. Another criticism, gleaned from anecdotal evidence, is that action learning attracts learners with a strong personal or spiritual focus on their own development and that the evangelism this often engenders may have a disproportionate influence on the rest of the group leading to a marginalizing effect on overall performance.

We believe that action learning works best when there is a focus on individual and organizational development, where knowledge is produced through the dialogue created in the process of problematization and questioning, and where the context for learning is the workplace. Of course the development trajectory of individuals will to some extent relate to the circumstances of the organization. Critical action learning will, however, allow individuals to reflect on their current role in the organization, their future development and to see that through this process they actually do have choices. In critical HRD, therefore, individuals make choices informed by a wider perspective of the political implications of current and future actions as well as in the context of the power relationships which exist.

From reflection to critical reflection

Reynolds (1998) argues that through the process of critically reflecting, managers become aware of a much wider environment in which they operate and begin to realize the social power relationships of the organization and their own networks. The characteristics which distinguish critical reflection from other versions of reflection are (1998: 189–90):

- It is concerned with questioning assumptions.
- Its focus is social rather than individual.
- It pays particular attention to the analysis of power relations.
- It is concerned with emancipation.

So far there may appear little to differentiate critical reflection from mainstream critical pedagogy. The crucial distinction we propose is that in a critical pedagogy there is concern for the curriculum *and* critical reflection within the learning process itself. This follows the distinction Giroux (1992) makes between 'content focused radicals', who advocate a more politicized curriculum, and 'strategy based radicals' who adopt a humanistic approach to teaching and learning by employing techniques such as experiential learning or action learning (Reynolds, 1998). We recognize that some tutors may not always be in a position to choose between the two approaches. For example, tutors who want to offer critical perspectives may find difficulty when faced with a group of 150 undergraduates. Here the potential for interaction may not make it possible to employ techniques that would engender debate such as small group working and high tutor contact. Similarly, even with small groups of postgraduate students where there is extensive experience of organizations and where they value a pragmatic orientation they may not take kindly to being subjected to what some might construe as overly politicized points of view.

What these students so often fail to appreciate is that the development of a critical capacity may in itself contribute directly to enhanced managerial skill. It may, for example, help develop their judgement; this includes the skills of judging what information is important, how and when to obtain it, and how best to communicate results. It may also strengthen their independence but, perhaps most important of all, it will develop their critical facilities so that they become more conscious of what they count as knowledge and what they might already know. This is important as it helps in a manager's self-knowledge; to know the assumptions they are making and how such assumptions were formed as a prelude to considering how they might be changed as well as the implications of this for future actions. This kind of understanding and the ability to critique the assumptions being used by others develops in students a valuable 'meta-competence' – one that we believe is extremely important. This contribution is the distinctive outcome of study at Master's level.

Perriton (2004), in her critique of reflection and critical reflection, argues that whilst critical management academics enthusiastically embrace student-centred techniques, as educators they should question their own motives and underpinning beliefs. She also suggests that what she calls the 'shifting nature of criticality' should be examined and that critical reflection, although widely acclaimed as a pedagogical practice, has in fact to date been adopted by few educators and practitioners.

■ Learning to be critically reflective at Master's level

One of the regular questions asked by students is exactly what the characteristics of study at Master's level are. To answer this question many academics highlight the links between academia and ecclesiastical practice. Thus the BSc offers the knowledge to sit in the congregation of a church and understand the sermon. The MSc, on the other hand, offers the knowledge of the scriptures to be able to choose between the passages of the Bible to give the sermon.

Master's level work self-evidently is about mastery. It can be likened to an apprentice craftsperson who on the conclusion of their apprenticeship has to produce a 'masterpiece' (a complete object that integrates all the skills of their chosen trade). So the Master's student should be able to demonstrate their command of the subject of management and integrate, as appropriate, different perspectives and understandings, and show competence in collecting, analyzing and interpreting information within a variety of domains of knowledge. Some of these within a critically reflective process need to move beyond the application of management knowledge and understanding on to the implications that this knowledge has for a wide variety of stakeholder groups.

■ Scholarship

Whatever the particular pedagogy adopted, all Master's level study could be said to have a number of features in common and although little has been written that defines it there is some agreement that Master's level work needs to be scholarship. Boyer (1997) reminds us that to be a scholar means often that we must consider activities wider than simply what is known from research. He argues, for example, that knowledge is not only acquired through research activity, but also through synthesis, through practice and through teaching. Porter and McKibben (1988) identify four types of scholarship:

1 the scholarship of discovery (of research);
2 the scholarship of integration (what do the findings of research mean when weighed against previous research and ideas?);
3 the scholarship of application (how can the knowledge be applied to problems of consequence?) – implicit in this is that the process of application might lead to new intellectual understandings; and finally
4 the scholarship of teaching (which implies that academic work might only become consequential if it is understood by others).

In a similar way, Mauch and Birch (1983) have suggested that scholarship needs to be understood in a number of different ways and that whilst they suggest that those examining higher degrees would not necessarily expect work to exhibit every single characteristic, students should be able to demonstrate a significant number of them. Brown, (1996, 2006) has used this work to suggest the characteristics indicated in Table 7.1.

Table 7.1 Master's level scholarship characteristics

- Someone who believes and supports findings of a careful investigation without becoming a partisan or biased advocate.

- Someone who is willing to entertain the possibility that errors might occur in 'their' work and acceptance that their propositions might be challenged.

- That part or the whole of the work should be capable of being published in a recognized journal or in a book form, and in the field of specialization appropriate to the work.

- That the work should be brought into the public domain for debate and criticism, and be able to withstand criticism.

- The work should demonstrate that the writer is familiar with the field of literature in which they wish to be taken seriously. When their ideas depart from this in new directions the author should present the rationale for such a departure.

- The work should be both *critically reflexive and analytical*. Critical in the sense that it critiques others' literatures and explains the limitations of the research process and the theories generated in such a way that it allows others to make judgements. Analytical in the sense it provides explanations not simply description.

- The work should demonstrate to others that the author has become an 'expert in the field' – someone who really understands the theories and concepts in the field, and as such their work should be useful to other writers as they begin their own research, as well as being seen as a reference point to others as they begin their own work.

- Their work should not be toned down in case it may be unpopular with any political or organizational body.

Source: Brown, R. (1996, 2006) based on Mauch and Birch (1983)

The concept of level three learning

Bateson's (1972) taxonomy of levels of learning (paraphrased and explained by Vince, 1996) also provides a useful way of conceptualizing the differences between final year undergraduate thinking ('Learning 2') and Master's level thinking ('Learning 3'). Learning at Level 2 suggests that students become conscious of new ways of approaching problems that are 'transferable' and useful to them in the future. Level 3 learning however challenges the whole way they conceive of situations and problems, and often leads to what Engestrom (2001) refers to as expansive learning. This is where individuals begin to gain completely new insights into problems and situations, and embrace new possibilities. Table 7.2 outlines these three levels of learning.

Table 7.2 Bateson's levels of learning

Levels	Implications
Zero Learning	Zero Learning is based on predictable or specific responses which are not subject to trial and error. Zero learning does not signify the capacity to reflect in any way to enable change. It is simply about response. Even the recognition of a wrong response would not contribute to any future skill.
Learning 1	Learning 1 implies a change as a result of trial and error, within a set of alternatives. Correction does therefore have an implication for future action. In other words, this level has moved from stimulus/response to stimulus/response/reinforcement. Learning 1 is therefore about a process of habituation.
Learning 2	Learning 2 implies some flexibility in the potential to act as opposed to reinforcement of action. It is therefore a change in the set of alternatives from which choice is made. Learning 2 implies a capacity to 'learn how to learn': in other words, a shift of frameworks from which choices are made.
Learning 3	Learning 3 is a shift in the underlying premises and belief systems that form frameworks. Level 3 learning involves a capacity to 'make a corrective change in the system of sets of alternatives from which choice is made': in other words, the capacity to examine the paradigm or regime within which action is based.

Source: Vince (1996) based on Bateson (1972)

Although academics refer to these levels, what is often not addressed is how these learning levels can be developed and how they can be linked and embedded within management Master's education.

Social constructionist/critical approaches to HRD

Schön (1983) emphasized that problem definitions are not objective facts, but rather social constructions – a perspective that is particularly well written up in

Messing About in Problems (Eden *et al.*, 1983). As Schön (1983: 40) argued: 'in real-world practice, problems do not present themselves to the practitioner as given. They must be constructed from the materials of problematic situations which are troubling and uncertain' – all these ideas are concepts central to action-learning situations. This emphasis on the subjectivity of the practising manager in constructing an understanding of problematic managerial situations resonates with the work of Shotter (1995) on practical authorship. Shotter, however, adds an emphasis and a caveat to the social-organizational context, and the norms of social accountability placed upon managers within such a context, which he calls conditioning (enabling and restraining) *socially* constructed world-views. As Alvesson (1990) argues, in many instances the perspectives managers present (as depictions of managerial problems and situations) are 'settled' upon by specifying them in a form that requires subsequent interpretation. A number of approaches have been developed which may help managers argue for their different positions, explain their own views and insights, and generally redefine issues in ways relevant to their interests.

Dealing with complexity – using images and visual media

Images, and the visual media through which they are produced, can be seen to play a pivotal role in such managerial sense-making activities (see Weick, 1995), not only because of their vividness, depth and clarity (enhancing the interpretability which in turn strengthens a manager's grasp of key concepts) but also because of their inherent ambiguity and the way they are able to convey different meanings for different people (Astley and Zammuto, 1992). In this sense, visual media and the meanings that they evoke can enable managers to participate in the managerial language game with the purpose of facilitating practical action. In such a language game, managers espouse their own constructed or authored theories-in-use about the way they see how the 'world works' and the conceptual language they use to do this establishes a context within which organizational life is constructed and reconstructed (see Astley and Zammuto, 1992; Shotter, 1995). As in Shotter's (1995) notion of practical authorship, the role of management, consequently, becomes one of using words and ideas as a mediating device to shape conceptions of organizational life (Thorpe and Cornelissen, 2003). The types of visual media that can be useful include the use of cognitive maps and projective tests although we recognize that right across the domains of knowledge that encompass management, writers have advanced a vast array of what might be referred to as 'tools for thinking' (Pidd, 2003). We believe that by using such devices the complexity and ambiguity of organizationally related problems can be better understood and reduced.

Concept mapping and cognitive mapping

Eden *et al.* (1983) have shown how personal construct theory can be used for exploring difficult problems within organizations. One method described by Eden and Jones (1984) is called *dominoes*, in which play, messing around and having fun are encouraged. In dominoes, constructs derived from previous interviews are written on cards. Managers are then asked to put them together to produce a construct system in the form of a pictorial map. They are asked why they have chosen that arrangement and why they see the problem in that way. It is their comments and the ensuing discussion which prove useful as managers are able to explore one another's understanding of a problem. A more sophisticated extension of dominoes is the process called 'cognitive mapping' (Eden, 1988). Based on personal construct theory, cognitive maps are another way of representing the relationships between constructs, and one of its most successful applications has been in the support of strategy formulation. Composite maps, it has been argued, can be constructed by merging individual maps (Mackaness and Clarke, 2001).

What is important, however, in cognitive mapping is not just the map and its subsequent analysis, but the process by which it was formed and the actions that are taken from discussions based around it. A balance between content and process is therefore essential in cognitive mapping in order to yield maximum benefit. A focus on content allows a complex organizational issue to be displayed as each individual group member sees it. The process enables those taking part to challenge the views and perspectives of others, and it is often the realization of difference between individuals and the ensuing discussion which proves most useful (Ackerman and Belton, 1994).

Storytelling and argument analysis

Gold *et al.* (2002) take a different route but also make the case for developing the critical capacity of managers so as to enable them to better interpret and understand their practice within both a local and organizational context, as well as within the broader socio-cultural context as Burgoyne and Reynolds (1997) advocate. Through the use of stories they outline their own attempts to develop explicitly the critical aspects of reflection in managers by helping them to use a method which involves storytelling and argument analysis. They employ Toulmin's (1958) approach to argumentation as a way of enhancing the critical abilities of managers with some considerable success.

Morgan (1986: 131), a strong advocate of the use of metaphors in management, suggests that organizational reality 'exists as much in the heads and minds of its members as it does in a set of rules and regulations'. As such, as with the use of cognitive maps in strategy, there is a recognition that this reality is continually in the making, emerging (Mintzberg, 1973), reformulating and being created (Pettigrew, 1979).

The importance of examining the recent history of an organization (the metaphor of biography) has been argued by a number of authors as being particularly useful (Salama, 1992; Pedler, 1992). Several writers have gone further by advocating the advantages of a group approach to its development (Simpson, 1995; Burgoyne, 1994). Uncovering biographies in a group allows, according to Steyaert and Bouwen (1994), the opportunity to hear different voices on the same history at the same time. In a typical exercise members of a group would be invited to examine the recent history of their organization.

In yet another use of this technique (Simpson and Thorpe, 1996) participant managers were asked to work with a series of metaphors which included viewing the organization as a parent and visually drawing the organization as it appeared to them now, contrasting this image with a description of the same 'person' ten years hence. In addition, the group was asked to construct a biography of the organization over the past ten years through their recollections of key events or through stories which were illustrative of the period, and individuals were asked to present a personal view of the organization's mission which they then shared with the group. A final exercise involved drafting a character reference for the organization.

So far this chapter has offered an explanation of critical reflection in the context of HRD practices and has examined various approaches, most notably action learning, which may promote critical reflection and lead to a change in mindset and ultimately in management practice. The remainder of this chapter goes on to explain how critical reflection was encouraged on an MSc in People and Organizational Development programme – one that focused on assessment and the 'tools for thinking' (McLaughlin and Thorpe, 1993) which were adopted and offered to students as part of an overall process of action learning.

■ Action learning and HRD

Background to the programme

This MSc in People and Organizational Development has been offered at the University of Salford for 12 years, attracting HRD managers from a range of organizations. There is a strong focus on both personal and academic development on the programme; students are encouraged to view the process as a learning journey and to identify clearly where they want to be, personally and professionally, at the end of the three years of part-time study, and to consider how their development of their own staff might benefit from the adoption of similar approaches. Many former students cite the programme as one of the most significant learning experiences of their life and a good proportion make bold career choices on achieving the qualification. Most students build sound networks and friendships. Drop-outs are rare; a real community feeling is engendered on the programme – students are often supported through crises by tutors and peers. However, prior to a rethink of the programme a few years ago, despite the fact that students were gaining a great deal from the experience, it seemed that much of this could have been attained by attending networking sessions with peers from other organizations. The balance of learning was tipped in favour of personal development. A decision was taken to examine the nature of Master's education and to focus on developing higher levels of critical reflection as the 'hallmark' of Master's level thinking. In addition to this, much stricter guidelines were introduced regarding completion of the degree within three years in order to ensure a 'level playing field'. The aim was to achieve a balance between intellectual and personal development, and to ensure that students who preferred to focus on the latter met minimum standards in their 'academic' work. The inherent danger was in taking away the distinctiveness of the programme by making it just like any other Master's degree. The continued inclusion of the action learning approach has ensured that this has not happened.

Action learning in practice

This type of management development experience enables participants to work on problems in their organizational context within the 'set' which models the openness required for organizational change. Specifically, they work with the perspective, cognitive style and *weltanschaung* of their fellow 'set' members and have the opportunity to reflect on their own views, values and styles as a prelude to change. What is important in the method is that managers learn to solve their problems or surmount their difficulties by working with a group of other experienced managers drawn from either within or outside the organization. (Revans (1971) suggests that if the managers come from outside with very different experiences, then the level of questioning and challenge is that much greater.) The value of 'set' work, it is argued by protagonists, cannot be overstated in the learning process as it is thought essential that the understanding of the problem they are trying to solve and their approach as to how change might be complemented, is seen to be drawn from colleagues' current 'theories-in-use', rather than simply provided by an expert or drawn from the literature. As most managers achieve what they do both through the contribution and by the persuasion of others, the sets positively help managers create increased certainty around situations in the way they provide a safe environment to try out ideas and to negotiate and communicate with other set members: as they do, they rehearse their arguments and they learn.

Groups on the programme consist of six to eight members so that interaction can be maximized and are facilitated by a set adviser. They meet once a month as a set and follow the normal process of 'checking-in' (giving a brief résumé of what has happened professionally and personally since the last meeting), deciding on priorities for that meeting (in effect, 'carving up' the four-hour time slot) followed by individuals 'presenting' their issue (usually their assignment topic) and other members asking questions about it in order to help that individual's learning. At the end of each student's slot, they are invited to reflect, honestly, on their learning from the session and to set objectives based on this. At this surface level, the process appears to follow the 'experiential' model of action learning (Marsick and O'Neil, 1999) based on Kolb's experiential learning cycle (1984) enabling learning at each stage of the cycle: action, reflection, theory and practice (Bunning, 1992; McGill and Beaty, 1992). However, this programme goes further by explicitly incorporating a social constructionist perspective and in particular focusing on the use of language as an important mediating device that can be mobilized to shape conceptions of organizational life (Shotter, 1993).

Raising consciousness of language use

Marsick and O'Neil (1999) cite two alternative ways by which critical reflection may be encouraged through the process of action learning:

1 Weinstein (1995) proposes that participants discuss their beliefs and values and how these may be changing and in so doing, become more insightful.
2 Marsick (1990) suggests discussing real issues and subjecting them to scrutiny from a number of perspectives, allowing learners to question underlying norms and perceptions.

The approach adopted on this MSc programme has a similar approach to the second of these but goes one step further in encouraging students to consider the contribution that three critical epistemologies offer as a basis for insightful questioning, namely critical social theory, postmodernism and critical realism. Many students, understandably, struggle with the vocabulary of epistemology and often feel uncomfortable about using the terms associated with these new ideas. The ideas are introduced in a tutor-led session during a residential that takes place one month following the start of the programme and tutors ensure that the discussions are continued in subsequent set meetings. Despite initial awkwardness, evidence suggests that, by the dissertation stage of the programme, students have become much more confident in using and understanding this language. So whilst the critical approach is seen as an underpinning element of learning and teaching on the programme, it is not something that can be introduced as a 'once and for all' but rather it involves students 'mastering' concepts and new shared language over the whole of the three years. The rationale behind the early introduction of this discussion of critical epistemology is to promote a heightened consciousness of the language they are using. In this case, students are offered a new vocabulary which they can deploy to co-construct fresh meanings and solutions. They are encouraged to use and explore the meaning of this 'research' language. The 'strangeness' (Thorpe, 1992) or 'discomfort' (Cunliffe, 2002) of using unfamiliar words, phrases and ideas is intended to promote learning. Set advisers help learners to explore questions and problems using two seemingly incompatible speech genres (Bakhtin, 1986): that of their everyday management practice and that of the management academic. As we indicated earlier we consider students on a Master's degree programme in management should be developing as management academics; adopting the language is a rite of passage so long as we believe we can demonstrate that this new knowledge and understanding adds value to a manager's practice. When students enquire about the programme, they are often surprised that learning outcomes are not clearly defined and that a problem-centred, learner-centred approach means that 'chunks of knowledge' are tailored to individual needs. What managers find they are offered instead is a chance to adopt a new way of thinking ('Master's level' thinking) which predominantly manifests itself in a new way of talking and it offers them a new 'learning to learn' competence.

The definition and explanation of these three critical epistemologies has been a factor in enabling students to become more confident and skilled in giving useful feedback to other members of their set during the peer assessment process. 'Critical thinking' no longer constitutes the ability to criticize per se but involves the discussion of issues which were previously taken for granted and the questioning of underlying assumptions. This may involve questions of power, gender, race and language. Students are encouraged to write from a whole range of perspectives rather than simply adopting the management stance to which they are accustomed in their workplace. If other points of view are not considered in a written piece of work, peers will pick up on this and use it as a source of questions and/or feedback.

◼ Conclusion

What is found to be extremely important about this approach is the manager's *reflection* on the outcomes. Within the process of action learning, critical reflection has a number of benefits. Managers reflect on the results of the practical problem-solving situations thrown up by their projects and, at the same time, on their learning processes and personal development as managers. They become more conscious of their theories in use, how they were formed and how they might be changed. What is achieved is not just learning a new fact – what Bateson (1972) referred to as Level 1 learning or the transfer of learnt experience from one situation to another (Level 2) – but a more general revitalizing of the manager's *weltanschaung*. Managers, by the process of critical reflection on practice and on how their underlying assumptions are formed and changed, achieve what Bateson calls Level 3 learning.

Above all, through a process of action learning, learners gain a heightened consciousness of the language they use as managers, and the effect this has on the understanding and actions of others. Most importantly they 'learn how to learn' at a level beyond instrumental techniques, procedural frameworks, or even theories. The examples given here describe a process whereby managers learn to adopt a new and more complicated language than they would normally use in their day-to-day practice. This is offered as a way of making them more conscious of language use and, in doing so, promotes a deeper level of reflection. However, by using this language they are also becoming members of a particular community of practice (Lave and Wenger, 1991): in this case, the academic community. The technique is one which could be transferred to organizational management development or HRD practice by encouraging managers, through the process of action learning, to adopt, for example, a language that is more business-focused or alternatively to substitute organizational jargon for words which customers may find more readily understandable. A long-term result may be a change in the way that managers engage with the various communities in which they practise.

Critical action learning is often cited as an ideal vehicle for implementing critical HRD. However, there have been few examples of how the theories of both action learning and critical management can be applied in practice. In this chapter, we have suggested that a heightened focus on language in set meetings is one way of achieving this. However, this practice of critical facilitation aimed at promoting collective and individual critical reflection has a wider application than in action learning and need not necessarily be underpinned by a focus on language. Action learning is not a panacea for an organization's ills and its overuse may lead to introspection, overload and a general disillusionment with it as a method of development. HRD within organizations takes many guises, from formal approaches, such as training courses, and particularly the increasing use of methods such as coaching, counselling and mentoring to incidental and haphazard learning experiences which are then formalized by the use of learning logs and diaries. All of these experiences require some kind of reflection and facilitation. We recognize that the critical questioning approach of action learning could well be replicated in other circumstances in order to promote the ethical, egalitarian and emancipatory principles of critical HRD.

Chapter 8

How can I teach critical management in this place? A critical pedagogy for HRD: possibilities, contradictions and compromises

Claire Valentin

▌ Introduction

This paper explores the development of a critical curriculum for postgraduate teaching of HRD. Critical management studies argue that management education focuses on the conveyance of instrumental rather than questioning knowledge. Techniques are taught with little regard for the ends that organizations serve. But the mechanistic application of formulae is inadequate to address the complex issues and problems that managers face. Managers require 'complicated understanding' to deal with the uncertainty, uniqueness and value conflicts in business (Dehler *et al.*, 2001). Students of management face contradictions between their experiences of theory and of organizational reality, and the unintended ways in which today's solutions generate tomorrow's problems (Roberts, 1996). A critical perspective argues that the purpose of management education must not simply be about how to '*do* management', but also about the study '*of* management'. Management is not simply a technical function, it is social practice. Management knowledge is political; it does not represent disinterested truth, but 'its theory legitimates some practices while it marginalizes others' (Clegg and Palmer, 1996: 3).

Whilst there is an emerging critical literature in HRD, there has been little systematic research into HRD programmes (Kuchinke, 2001). Critical management studies (CMS) have devoted considerable attention to the study of management education programmes such as the MBA (see French and Grey, 1996). This chapter examines the significance of these observations for the teaching of HRD, drawing on research into critical management education (CME), exploring the epistemological and pedagogical issues in developing a critical approach to HRD education. The discussion draws on my experience as Programme Leader for a Master's programme in HRD, the Diploma/MSc in the

169

Management of Training and Development. The programme includes a full-time route with an international cohort and a part-time route for practitioners. It is accredited by the Chartered Institute for Personnel and Development (CIPD), the UK professional body for people working in the fields of human resource management (HRM) and HRD. I have previously had experience of trying to develop critical approaches to teaching on professionally validated programmes in adult and community education; I also draw on my own experience as a business school student studying for an MBA. Our programme is unique in some respects in that it is situated in a school of education rather than a management school and the experience of members of the course team, as well as covering management, HRD, training and organizational development, also encompasses social work education, teacher training, counselling training and arts management. Whilst as a team we have not specifically set out to develop a critical curriculum, elements are reflected in our practice.

This chapter largely reflects upon my own practice. The discussion reflects work-in-progress as my interest in critical HRD has developed. As such, it raises as many questions as it answers. I reflect upon the literature on CME; upon the attempt to develop a critical curriculum within the bounds of a professionally validated programme; on the impact of context; and on matters of teaching and learning. The first part of this chapter looks at critical perspectives on management and HRD and how these are reflected in CME. I then explore features of a critical HRD education, exploring approaches to teaching and learning, and the processes of critical teaching.

■ The dominant paradigm in management and HRD education

In this section, I examine critiques of management education and reflect upon their significance for postgraduate teaching of HRD. A curriculum is more than the selection of content, methods of delivery and evaluation. These are all influenced by the context; they will reflect underpinning values, beliefs and assumptions (Armitage *et al.*, 1999). What we teach, where we draw our materials from, how we teach and where our teaching takes place all serve to reinforce a particular paradigm of HRD. The knowledge taught will be selected from a wide basis of possible knowledge:

> 'It is a form of cultural capital that comes from somewhere, that often reflects the perspectives and beliefs of powerful segments of our social collectivity. In its very production and dissemination... it is repeatedly filtered through ideological and economic commitments. Social and economic values, hence, are already embedded in the design of the institutions we work in, in the "formal corpus of school knowledge" we preserve in our curricula, in our modes of teaching, and in our principles, standards, and forms of evaluation.'
>
> (Apple, 1979: 8–9)

Apple was commenting on schooling 25 years ago, but his argument illustrates how management and HRD education is not simply about the conveyance of 'neutral' knowledge, but also about the promotion of cultural capital, which reinforces particular values and assumptions. CMS argue that the dominant paradigm in management education represents management as an objective, impartial activity, simply concerned with techniques, a 'technical rationalist' perspective which focuses on the means to help organizations to achieve their goals, rather than any questioning of ends. It privileges the interests of shareholders and managers, and marginalizes the interests of workers and communities, and environmental concerns. The role and power of managers and the functional divisions in organizations are assumed to be necessary and natural (Alvesson and Willmott, 1996). The management science school seeks a single management paradigm that can be universally applied (Fulop, 2002). Conflicts, debates, tensions and uncertainties in the disciplines that management theory draws on are not explored. There is no questioning of cultural values or ideological beliefs; no view of management as a social and political activity, complex, ambiguous, contradictory and uncertain (McGivern and Thomson, 2000; Dehler *et al.*, 2001).

Fulop and Rifkin (2004) distinguish between an *instrumental orientation*, where education is to provide knowledge to solve particular problems or result in some action or end result; and *conceptual orientation*, which seeks to help better understand management across many settings. An instrumental perspective dominates management teaching. Even though areas such as business ethics form part of most management curricula, it is justified in terms of the threats and opportunities to corporate self-interest (Nason, 2000). This provides 'an ethically neutral blanket wherein technical efficiency can be examined independently of any moral or political context' (Currie and Knights, 2003: 44).

Whilst HRD teaching and theory may be more humanistically informed than the conventional MBA, and possibly employ a wider variety of modes of delivery, HRD shares many of the assumptions of conventional management. The strategic turn in HRD urges practitioners to become more business literate; HRD supports the development of knowledge and learning to sustain competitive advantage. Texts urge organizations to abandon old 'command and control' styles of management and traditional hierarchies, in favour of a new vision of the organization as a learning community. 'Empowered' staff engage in self-development and self-directed learning in partnership. The learning organization, it is argued, generates mutual benefits for employer and employee (Holden and Hamblett, 1998). But this view of HRD sits firmly within the dominant management discourse. The business model portrayed in the standard management textbook does not usually question the underlying rationales of management theory.

A critical approach to HRD education will study HRD as a social, political and moral practice, rather than as a set of techniques or skills, recipes to be learned and subsequently applied. Thus the study should not be simply about how to *do HRD*, but also to *reflect upon* HRD. There should be a commitment to questioning the assumptions and 'taken-for-granteds' that are embodied in theory and practice, recognizing that there are no simple answers. 'Management, by its very nature, focuses on many issues and practices that are dynamic, ambiguous, contradictory, often political in nature, highly gendered and deeply embedded in specific situations and contexts' (Fulop and Rifkin, 2004: 19).

One might assume that the examination of competing discourses, and the encouragement to think critically, should form part of any study at postgraduate level. Whilst this is true (although not always reflected in practice), there are specific themes in the approach of a critical HRD. This involves the examination of the ideological assumptions underpinning theory and practice; stimulating questioning of social, organizational and political processes within organizations; raising moral questions about HRD; relating practice to broader economic, political, historical and social contexts. Themes such as examining how institutional structures, procedures and practices serve to reinforce power inequalities, and the impact of factors such as class, race, age and gender are developed; there is a social rather than simply an individual focus. A key theme is the study of power and how it is inscribed in everyday reasoning and actions (Perriton and Reynolds, 2004; Grey and French, 1996; Wilmott, 1997). Hegemony – 'the way that people learn to accept as natural and in their own best interests an unjust social order' – is challenged (Brookfield, 2005: 43).

CMS are not anti-management, but they counter the pro-management bias of the conventional management discourse. CMS have an 'emancipatory intent', the realization of a more equal society based on democracy and which gives voice to minority groups (Perriton and Reynolds, 2004). The aim of education is to develop students as critical, reflective practitioners, who can reflect upon their own experience and behaviour as managers, generating alternative ways of thinking (McGivern and Thomson, 2000). The development of insight and critique will seek to generate 'transformative redefinition', to 'develop critical, managerially relevant knowledge and practical understandings that enable change and provide skills for new ways of operating' (Alvesson and Deetz, 2000: 19).

In developing a curriculum for critical HRD it would be anathema to think of it as simply a matter of applying a new formula, the 'techniques of critical management'. CME describes an approach rather than a set of specific activities. There is no single blueprint: rather, an opening-up to a range of possibilities. But there are methods and approaches which one can draw on. In the following sections, I explore the feature of a critical approach to management education and discuss how these can be considered in developing a curriculum for HRD. I examine issues around teaching and learning, and highlight some key features of a CME process: dialogue, critical pedagogy and critique.

A critical curriculum for HRD: content, process and context

A key element influencing the construction of the curriculum in much HRD education in the UK is the CIPD Professional Standards. These map out what are seen to be the required knowledge and operational skills for the work of a 'People Management and Development professional', and form the basis to which all validated programmes must adhere. They provide a detailed prescription of the competencies required for the HRD role and list the required learning outcomes. The aim of HRD is 'to advance continuously the management and development of people to the benefit of individuals, employers and the community at large' (CIPD, 2004: 5). Practitioners are exhorted to 'uphold the highest ideals in the management and development of people' (CIPD: 5). However, there is an assumption that such an aim is unproblematic and uncontested, with no suggestion that there may be inherent contradictions and conflicts of interest in the role.

The challenge for critical HRD is to develop a coherent curriculum, one that maps the terrain of HRD and provides critical insights: the study *of* HRD and study *about* HRD. It must neither assume an uncritical pragmatism focusing solely on 'practice', nor be so theoretical that no connection can be made with practice. However, students need a base of knowledge from which to develop. You cannot develop a critique of 'conventional' management theory if you have never read any of it. Students need to gain familiarity with the concepts and theories in the field, to distinguish between different literatures: popular management books, policy documents, reviews and evaluations of practice, the array of scholarly literature such as textbooks and journal articles.

The material offered in the standard management textbook is an insufficient basis for a critical HRD curriculum. Fulop notes how 'the bestseller lists worldwide continue to be dominated by US management academics, with specific management titles, and the POLC (plan, organize, lead, control) model is still implicit in many of their publications' (Fulop, 2002: 431). However, the emerging discipline that constitutes HRD draws on a range of disciplines, including organization studies, organization development, education, psychology, economics, sociology, politics, philosophy, cultural anthropology and feminist theory (Swanson, 2001). A multidisciplinary subject such as HRD poses a particular challenge. The knowledge base is so wide that little depth of understanding may be developed. Thomas and Anthony see in this epistemological richness ' the growing fashion for eclecticism'; drawing from 'distant academic disciplines' means that the need for scholarly knowledge is avoided, and 'they do not occupy the foreign field long enough to risk argument or refutation' (1996: 29).

There is also the danger that, in a postmodern spirit of relativism, in the effort to ensure that no knowledges are excluded, all are considered equally valid, and there is little critique. But as Brookfield argues, 'to teach informed by critical theory is, by implication, to teach with a specific social and political intent' (2005: 353). Through providing alternative frameworks for understanding management practices, the emancipatory intent of critical theory sees 'a vision of a qualitatively different form of management; one that is more democratically accountable to those whose lives are affected in so many ways by management decisions' (Alvesson and Willmott, 1996: 40).

But putting these ideas into practice all seems rather daunting in the face of our need for the curriculum to conform to the CIPD Professional Standards and to meet the needs of our students and their sponsors, who tend to want 'working knowledge'. We already have more than enough to cover in our curriculum. Perhaps the appropriate way to include such ideas into the curriculum would be to develop an optional module in 'Critical HRD'? For the remainder of the programme we can teach to the CIPD Professional Standards. I considered the prospect of such a module as an exciting development, which would enable me to peruse texts by writers such as Foucault, Habermas, etc. in the company of enthusiastic students. But transformation of the curriculum cannot simply occur through one module.

A more radical approach might be to abandon the CIPD Standards altogether, to develop a new programme in critical HRD, unfettered by the conventional discourse. But whilst such a development might be stimulating, we have spent several years working up to our professional validation, which we feel provides our students with a professional return for all the time and money that they put into their studies. Our experience with other programmes suggests that the 'market for critical HRD' may be limited, as students unfamiliar with the ideas will not see their relevance. We might lose our core market of practitioners and professionals who want to develop or further a career in the profession, and the organizations that sponsor many of them. Academics, even critical ones, are as subject to the vagaries of the market as any 'practitioner'.

More importantly, I feel that critical HRD is not an esoteric academic discipline of interest to a few, but has something vital to offer to HRD theory and practice in general. The challenge is also to consider its relevance to professional practice as well as theory, and to see if it can be infused throughout the whole programme. In the introduction to the CIPD Professional Standards, 'personnel management and development professionals' are endorsed to 'understand and critique the objectives and methodologies of their business colleagues'. An invitation to critical HRD? But increased class sizes, greater demands for monitoring and control, increased academic workloads and the requirements of professional bodies do restrict the room for manoeuvre to develop a more critical curriculum. In a Foucauldian analysis of management education, Boje likens the context of management education, including the influence of professional validating bodies, to a 'panoptic network' of audit, monitoring and control, and examinations. Together, these represent a network of many subtle mechanisms of discipline:

> 'Management education is part of a larger disciplinary machine: the modernist university which maintains many juridical and penal apparatuses that pertain to a set of rules and offences against them... We are increasingly dominated by a power that is not our own... the network of power of the institutional discourses that produce the disciplined student and professor bodies.'

> (Boje, 1996: 177)

But Alvesson and Willmott's (1996) use of the ideas of Foucault highlights the 'complex and precarious dynamics' of social organization. Power is not single, unified or unshakeable. 'Within systems of power and control there are invariably contradictions and "loopholes" that can be exposed and exploited for purposes of critical reflection and emancipatory transformation' (1996: 171). We might teach around the CIPD Standards, but there is still scope for interpretation in content and method. Furthermore, is it really necessary to reinvent the wheel every time you devise a new curriculum? Surely something that has emerged from the HRD profession deserves consideration – must we assume that there is no common knowledge and skills required for the study of HRD? A position as a critical scholar of HRD should not be one of disdainful distance from the messy pragmatism of practice. Academics are, of course, practitioners themselves – negotiating, compromising, juggling priorities. Our position is rather one of standing alongside HRD practitioners, considering how critical ideas are reflected in both the micro-practice of daily work and the bigger picture of HRD. Surely it is possible to develop a 'critical reading' of the CIPD Standards?

The Professional Standards are prescriptive and detailed, and limit the space for creativity. Undeterred, however, a colleague considered how her successful option course, Human Dynamics in the Workplace, which draws on students' own experiences in small group teaching, might form part of our CIPD curriculum. Management Development seemed the most appropriate Standard to map the course onto. She reconfigured the course to incorporate the required elements, but maintained the process of teaching, and the theoretical underpinnings which included drawing on psychodynamic psychology.

CMS pose a challenge to the development of a programme of professional education such as our MSc, since they are strong on theory but weak on the application of theoretical principles to practice. As we have seen, CMS are rather dismissive of the idea of the teaching of management skills, seeing such an approach as 'instrumentalist', 'technical rationalist', 'performative' (Edwards and Usher, 2000), 'fostering a "technocratic consciousness" ' (Roberts, 1996); a 'vocationalist pedagogy', resulting in a 'conformist professionalizing discourse' (Collins, 1995: 81). For the CIPD, the 'reflective practitioner' becomes the 'thinking performer.' Barnett (2000) reflects upon the arguments that 'working knowledge' and 'knowledge at work' is seen to be more useful for the practice of management than more academic theory. Barnett contends that this 'new knowledge' is (2000: 28):

> 'saturated by pragmatic interests, improvement is simply what the market or the shareholders will bear, or which will assist in projecting the company's profile... It is a domain in which, far from there being an open debate in which a wide range of people can join (as with propositional knowledge) the forces of commerce and politics can wield undue power and control.'

However, French and Grey (1996) rather grudgingly suggest that there is some place for enabling managers to learn the techniques of the 'new management', such as culture management and quality management. I would argue that skills must form part of a programme of professional education; whilst it is insufficient to teach skills unreflectively, a critical practitioner is not an unskilled practitioner.

But it takes time to develop knowledge and understanding of the literatures and consideration of the theory and practice. Even for the students who are experienced practitioners of management, the richness of interpretations in a critical HRD perspectives may seem bewildering. Students may find this kind of uncertainty difficult to accept and to cope with:

> 'They tend to want to know what is "right": not for them the beauty of debate, the tolerance of ambiguity, the pleasures of the text that requires yet more resolution. They want prescription. They want to know which way to go on; they want to know not only the best way but also the most foolproof recipe. To be told there is not one "best way", when what you want is an answer, is not immediately helpful even while it may be illuminating.'
>
> (Clegg and Palmer, 1996: 11)

This was reflected in the observation of a visiting tutor on our programme, an HRD practitioner, who commented that students appeared to have difficulty in applying theoretical concepts to the consideration of a case study, preferring to respond anecdotally. What approaches might help students to move beyond this?

In my eagerness to open up students to a more critical view of HRD, in my course HRD Theory and Practice, I presented a range of theoretical perspectives and extracts from critical literature, alongside more conventional HRD texts. However, in the course feedback some students commented that my lectures were somewhat difficult to follow, that I did not sum up key points, which made subsequent application difficult. In my desire to open up and expose students to new ideas, I had found difficulty in following through with helping them in their own sense-making. How should a critical educational practitioner respond to this? My immediate response was a rather positivist desire to solve the problem, be a good teacher who shows students the way forward. Perhaps, however, I should take a postmodern perspective, persevere with the same approach, tell the students that ideas are unsettling, and try to help them to live with the troubling of their certainties? Perhaps I should summarize a response from critical theory, pointing out the correct interpretation?

Some argue that there is a danger that in seeking to make sense of the multi-disciplinary complexity of understandings that a critical approach requires, students will be tempted simply to take on board the received wisdoms of 'critical' authorities without engaging with the debates themselves. Teachers may also find difficulty in escaping the authoritative nature of their discourse. 'The process often remains one in which control of the class and students is based on the authority and expertise of the teacher, or established texts, as the arbiter of what is "right" or "wrong"' (Currie and Knights, 2003: 32).

> 'There is a risk that Critical Theorists "know best" and establish themselves as "Authorities", thereby silencing a dialogue that they profess to promote... Even something that begins by opening up understanding or facilitating reflection can end by locking people into fixed, unreflective thinking.'
>
> (Alvesson and Willmott, 1996: 175)

It is true that some students may initially view the teacher as the main source of wisdom, particularly those coming from some more authoritarian and didactic educational experiences. However, if attention is paid to expressing ideas in a dialogical manner, students gain in confidence to challenge the authority of the teacher and of the texts. Experienced professionals may express discontent initially that the teacher is not authoritative enough. It requires confidence to live with this discomfort and challenge. Critical pedagogy is not an easy option for the teacher; critique develops as the result of an intellectual struggle on behalf of both students and tutor. In the words of Paulo Freire:

> 'Knowing demands discipline. Knowing is something which demands many things from you, which makes you tired in spite of being happy. It is not something which just happens. Knowing, I repeat, is not a weekend on a tropical beach.'
>
> (Freire and Shor, 1987, in Kirkwood, 1991: 53)

I realize that I need to pay more attention to the process of teaching. The tutor has to gain the respect and support of students, in order, as Freire observes, to 'struggle to transform a situation of a transfer of information into a real *act of knowing*' (in Kirkwood, 1991: 43).

Brookfield provides a helpful suggestion of four contrasting methodological emphases in critical teaching (2005: 357):

1 'The importance of teaching a structuralised worldview which analyses private problems and personal dilemmas as structurally produced.
2 The need for abstract, conceptual reasoning, considering broad questions, not only focusing on the particular.
3 The need for adults to step back from the demands and patterns of everyday life to allow them to view society in a newly critical way.
4 Dialogic discussion – fully participatory, inclusive conversation.'

Whilst my teaching may have been stronger on point two, it is the linking of private troubles to personal issues which is an important part of a critical education, through helping students develop a structural analysis, and to use theory to reflect upon practice. Reflection on personal experience forms a starting point in critical pedagogy. Students bring their own conceptions and experience of management, gained not only through academic study but also through their experiences as managers, workers, students, pupils and consumers. For example, students may be engaged in work to fund their studies, work that is often unskilled or semi-skilled, in fast-food outlets, bars, shops or hospitals. These provide a starting point to help identify the competing interests and contradictions inherent in organizational life and how they are portrayed in management literature. But unlike traditional humanistic approaches, the focus is not simply on individualized 'self-awareness', but also a starting point from which to problematize management knowledge (Grey *et al.*, 1996).

In my HRD course, a video depicting the management guru Tom Peters always provoked a strong reaction from students. However, I have found difficulty in moving from this reaction to a deeper analysis. Fenwick (2005b) found management students particularly receptive in two areas of critical analysis based on their experiences. These involved the analysis of 'management guru' texts, and discussion on oppressive discourses and practices in their own organizations. Students welcomed tools of critical cultural analysis. Individual stories were analyzed beyond the micro-terms of individual personalities or simple internal organizational relations. Organizational structures and practices were examined along with larger cultural discourses such as globalization, change and the knowledge economy. 'The pedagogy combines students' story-telling with critical analytic tools (critical discourse analysis, historical analysis of normalized practices, exclusions, and implicit ideologies)' (Fenwick, 2005b: 40). Focusing on personal issues is not unproblematic, and can generate embarrassment and discomfort. Fenwick (2005b) suggests the use of short written texts, such as newspaper editorials, business magazine articles and excerpts from popular management texts, to focus away from personal experience if this becomes difficult. This distance can help students to reflect anew upon personal experiences and the wider historical, political and social forces operating in the situation under review.

A key aspect of critical pedagogy is the process of critique. As Welton observes, whilst 'educators, social scientists, literary critics and philosophers all use the word "critical" '; it is by no means clear that we are all talking the same language' (Welton, 1995: 13). Mingers (2000 after Habermas) highlights four dimensions of questioning in CMS:

■ 'Critical thinking – the critique of rhetoric.
■ Being sceptical of conventional wisdom – the critique of tradition.
■ Being sceptical of one dominant view – the critique of authority.
■ Being sceptical of information and knowledge – the critique of objectivity.'

This now brings us to consideration of the process of critical teaching. Grey *et al.* (1996) argue that to teach critical management in a conventional mode of pedagogy is a contradiction in terms; it requires a critical pedagogy. We may put students into groups to discuss things, but simply getting into a group does not imply that any particular critical thinking will develop. Shor (1992) suggests that the key to presenting any sort of theme adopted is the problem-posing method. The teacher does not seek to transfer knowledge but poses it as a critical problem relevant to students' perceptions. The process of discussion centres on the problematization of knowledge, ways of seeing and purposes of different ways of seeing.

This requires that learning takes place through dialogue in small groups and plenary. Brookfield sounds a cautious note on the trend for group work in teaching. Cohorts can readily generate 'automaton conformity', a tyranny of the majority and uncritical reproduction of dominant ideology (Brookfield, 2005: 357). Fenwick notes that 'there are always voices, sometimes very loud or aggressive ones, espousing dominant epistemologies or even discriminatory sentiments' (Fenwick, 2005b: 40). Creating dialogue calls for an active role on behalf of the tutor: mediation, posing problems, encouraging participation. In our programme, our experience and feedback from students suggest considerable time be spent early on in the programme, working with students on issues around group processes and the dynamics of group work. We are also experimenting with putting students into action learning sets to help develop a more sustained process of group dialogue.

Conclusion

I felt somewhat apprehensive embarking on this chapter, believing that we had only gone a little way along the road of developing a critical curriculum. And as there is no blueprint to follow, how would we know when we had got there? A critical approach encourages greater reflexivity on behalf of the teacher, reflexivity which is stimulating but challenging. I now see that there are a number of dimensions to a critical approach. It is not simply about what literatures one draws on, although this is an important element. There are a growing number of more critically oriented HRD texts (e.g. Elliot and Turnbull, 2005), which provide more resources with a specific HRD focus to draw on.

Critical pedagogy also argues for transformed relationships between teacher and student. The authority of the tutor comes from knowledge of content and process; they must seek to divest themselves of the authority of status and see themselves as partners with students in a process of enquiry. There are both personal and institutional factors to consider. Being open to questioning, admitting that there is much that you do not know, can raise feelings of vulnerability on behalf of the teacher. It would have been easy for me to respond to the students' concerns for more guidance by simply being more prescriptive. It is more difficult to suggest that there are many ways of seeing things; that there are no truths, only propositions; that learning can be uncomfortable, unsettling and not provide answers to problems; to suggest readings of authors who make seemingly 'simple' problems difficult.

The focus for change to the curriculum cannot come simply at the level of the individual teacher or course. Critical pedagogy emphasizes the importance of teaching. But the university context is one of increasing demands on staff to produce more with less, increased administration, increased audit and monitoring. Whilst universities profess the desire to become ever more student (client)-centred, and publish teaching and learning strategies, contradictions are exposed. And the role of universities must not simply be one of equipping individual students to succeed, but also a public one of studying social practices and developing new knowledge. If HRD is not simply to be a strategic tool focusing on organizational rationales, it needs to question and debate HRD and management knowledge. A critical pedagogy can help to take the debate beyond the conferences and academic journals, and into the lives of students and practitioners.

Chapter 9

Chuck out the chintz? 'Stripped floor' writing and the catalogue of convention: alternative perspectives on management inquiry

Brendon Harvey

■ Introducion

Writing, for managers, researchers and students, is often a means to an end – to complete a report, to write a dissertation, to fulfil the requirements of the quality review. Script is often crammed in within tight deadlines, delivered and the author moves on to the next task. Such forms of writing rarely move outside certain conventions of what is regarded as 'academic' or 'business-like'. However, this chapter seeks to explore an alternative view: that the conventions of writing about management inquiry limit the choices for creativity and engagement with wider audiences, in constructing and representing the results of such endeavour. Moreover, writing can be seen as a pedagogical tool as well as a source of reflection on the workplace, for both students/practitioners and their teachers. Examples will be taken from teaching and research to explore different forms of writing that offer the potential for alternative ways of sense-making.

The chapter begins with reflection on my practice as a lecturer endeavouring to challenge the accepted notion of what many students, and some lecturers, regarded as traditional HR pedagogy for professional students. Through exploration of a critical incident two key insights emerge that lead to a further section of inquiry. This is characterized by inquiring how the students experience inconsistencies between empowerment rhetoric and how they experience it in practice. This section of the chapter explores the organizational backcloth to their studies, which seemingly, emphasizes 'sameness' and consistency, rather than experimentation and difference. This leads to a discussion of the significance of mess and uncertainty, which counters the rational, predictive and instrumental management practices of the organizational backcloth. The contention is that reality is co-created by the interaction of different agents, they themselves being influenced by the system of which they are a part. Therefore, in seeking to control and emphasizing individual agency, organizations are missing the opportunities to act in alternative ways, founded on emergence and sense-making. The chapter contends that the student experience of their professional study is no different. It concludes by suggesting that considering the different uses of writing beyond the summative or rational, write-up of the dissertation can involve students, inviting them to explore critically their experiences alongside others. It is not demeaning the importance of such forms that transport the successful student towards professional qualifications, more that alternative forms have to be considered that counter the instrumentality of the former.

The work with the student group highlighted in the chapter was an integrative part of doctorate research utilizing a particular action research methodology (Weil, 1998, 1999). At the heart of this approach is a series of research cycles, driven by critical questioning of both participants and myself, that seeks to unravel complexities and puzzles of so-called empowered environments, and then identify choices for research participants within such environments. Therefore, the chapter seeks to reflect critically on how contact with the student group connected with previous research experiences with other participants by identifying similar themes, or whether new questions emerged.

■ A balancing act

I teach on a course for the Chartered Institute of Personnel and Development (CIPD) Post Graduate Diploma. One element of this programme seeks to explore ways in which individuals learn and the concept of the 'learning organization'. The critical incident outlined below relates to a particular session with a part-time student group discussing such concepts.

The part-time group itself was made up of human resource (HR) employees with varying degrees of responsibility in their organizations: a rich source of stories concerning organizational life across differing sectors and sizes of organization. At least half of this group worked in the motor industry, either for car manufacturers or their first-tier component suppliers. I rarely 'lecture' solely to this group but try to enable learning through workshop format, group work and discussion, taking advantage of their rich experience. Yet there is always an underlying tension, the balancing act, generated by the requirements of the professional syllabus, the course content and their anxiety over assessment. Moreover, their workplaces seemed increasingly under pressure as these particular students, due to their HR responsibilities, were often at the forefront of reorganization plans, procedures and consequent fall-out – redundancy, closure or relocation.

What I am seeking to emphasize here is that when they arrive at the university their time seems incredibly compressed. Therefore, they often seek the quickest route to success. For an increasing number, I sense, this means 'just getting through', 'doing enough' to satisfy the requirements of the course. This is not meant to be a criticism of their strategy, more a reflection of the impact of their working lives on tackling the demands of professional study. Consequently, the exams loomed large in their thinking, discussion with each other and myself. Success in essay writing and performing in the examinations may be critical in moving forward in their career. I noticed therefore, an increasing pressure on me to 'teach to the exam' and reward particular forms of rational, well-argued, often very formulaic pieces of writing. Attempting to 'do something different' with this group, to move away from a lecture–discussion format of our meetings by attempting more experiential modes of learning, was fraught with difficulty and risk. Nevertheless, I refused to be hidebound by the straitjacket of the examination whilst at the same time being sensitive to their need to pass. An interesting balancing act! The university rhetoric encouraged staff to experiment but common practice with postgraduate groups, particularly those studying for external awarding bodies, was to impart pre-packaged knowledge tightly lashed to the set text. For many the examinations loomed large, yet I became increasingly frustrated with participants doubting the relevance of their own experience and reluctance to move outside the safety of the textbook.

I therefore set up a session whereby we would seek to determine the different ways in which they learnt about how to do the job they were now doing. But I did not want them to write about this in a conventional sense but to individually reflect and then draw the results of that reflection on flipchart paper using whatever images or words that came to mind. I explained the task and then facilitated the varying groups around the room. Some immediately set to draw quite startling images with accompanying captions – phrases, company rhetoric, emotional reactions – of workplaces and individuals within them, others of amalgam of influences emphasizing complexity in learning. One student remained stuck in front of a blank sheet, pens untouched. The student was often an active member of the group and I just enquired whether it was the drawing aspect of the task that was proving a bit of a block. She turned to me and said, 'No, but... [she paused]... is this in the exam?'

After all of them had finished we then looked at the task elements of the exercise and what this had to say about influences on learning and the varying forms these took. The 'process' of how we had gone about it was intriguing and I was interested to find out what they had thought of working with image rather than the usual written forms of collecting their data. Their responses to my probes were startling. Some had initially believed it would be 'a waste of time' but were willing to 'go along with it'. Some echoed the member of the group who had the blank sheet by saying that unless tasks seemed to be mirroring how they were going to be assessed in the future they could not really see the point. The dominant comment concerned the 'different' nature of the task. Many spoke of just how strange it seemed to be working in this way, talking about it with others and sharing pictures (and having to take the generally good-natured comments about their artistic ability!) but once they 'got into it' many stated that they 'really enjoyed it' and 'got something out of it'.

This led to a productive exploration of what stops them working in different ways in different situations and how this related to being creative in their own organizations. All of them agreed that this was an increasing requirement in how they carried out their work, particularly those within 'continuous improvement' environments of the motor industry, at car plants or first-tier suppliers.

For me, I was struck by the rich brew that this task had created and the following are two key insights provoked by the critical incident:

1 It had vividly displayed some of the issues facing individuals wanting/having to be different in their working lives. It showed that creativity and empowerment discourses were part of their workplaces and helped shape many of their working practices, for example, being part of a continuous improvement team or designing a coaching and mentoring scheme. They wanted to involve others and wished to be involved themselves in improving their own practices. For many in the group, such actions were built into their performance review; they were *expected* to be like this.

2 Moreover, the task was being carried out within the context of professional awards influencing a form of pedagogy that does not always prompt these forms of behaviour. It seemed that at the interface is the tutor working with both of these elements. On the one hand, the CIPD emphasizes skill development over pure knowledge transmission of facts or concepts but the course is still weighted towards traditional assessment forms. The university providers have limited contact time with part-time students who arrive at the class after a full day's work. When time is limited, a more prescriptive pedagogy becomes a pragmatic option, particularly with larger numbers in student groups. The 'active' lecturer and 'passive' student relationship becomes embedded as learning practice.

The following section of the chapter illustrates the transition from the critical incident above to further research inquiry. The research question then becomes: what does the student/employee 'do' faced with the contradiction illustrated above?

The latter is characterized by an exploration of tensions and puzzles in working in different ways within their work environments, whilst being confined by expectations and assumptions of practitioners and other bodies.

Further sections offer insights into how these may be worked with given the current UK higher education (HE) environment. For such a question could also be posed to the representatives from their higher education establishments hosting their programmes bounded by the professional award, conformity and a pragmatic pedagogy.

■ Methodology

The ways in which the 15 students and employees were engaged with for this study were heavily influenced by the work of Kemmis (1993) and his view of action research and critical social science. Here the aim was to create a form of collaborative learning engaging with both the 'here and now of the student experience' linked to 'wider webs of interaction which structure social life in discourses in work'. Importantly, following Kemmis, this study was critical, in the sense that it was trying to understand how creativity was perceived by students who were also employees and how it could be better exercised within the classroom and the workplace.

This research has at its heart the 'critically reflective' approach to action research, especially the Critically Reflexive Action Research (CRAR) model proposed by Weil (1998), but also by others (Lather, 1991; Reason and Rowan, 1981). Here, learning is seen as engaging with contradictions and dilemmas, through reflection in, and on, action.

The cyclical nature of the CRAR model was helpful in guiding me, and other participants, to inquire into my practice, as well as guiding managers in similar quests with significant others, as part of the wider context of my doctorate research. Therefore, the participants in this inquiry, the 15 CIPD students, were part of a longer-term cyclical research process. Their work was informed by previous research cycles in two companies and the insights generated by them informed further cycles of inquiry with other participants outside of the HE setting. Above all, it is a practical process which, when engaged in, rigorously leads participants into further cycles of inquiry. The CRAR model highlights a series of steps:

1 *Appreciating starting problems/dilemmas*: Initially, awareness of the contradictions and dilemmas experienced by myself and other participants. These could include some of the starting assumptions of what employees understood by 'empowerment'. For example, the inquiry may focus on experiences of being so-called 'empowered' or disempowered' within work settings or outside of work, or could explore some of the history of initiatives that had sought to develop such 'attitudes' or 'practices'/'competences' within the three companies of this study. It was important to focus on the participants' own constructions so these could be captured and then played

back to highlight the limitations and potential of existing understandings and processes.

2 *Focusing and framing inquiry cycle in context*: The second step then is to focus and frame the inquiry cycle whilst engaged in it. I interpreted this step in my own inquiry as facilitating both individuals and groups to plan and enact more insightful choices through playing back the issues identified, particular recurring patterns and concerns. The intention being to focus on whether these are critical in understanding what is being experienced in the workplace, as well as to recognize alternatives.

3 *Use of critical incidents and revealing stories*: The third step leads to an intended deepening of understanding of the key questions of the inquiry. This inquiry contains a number of revealing narratives where individuals relate critical incidents. My intent was to explore these with them, document and playback to participants my reactions and interpretations of what I had heard.

4 *Planning for insightful actions – individual, group, cross group, organizational*: Again my intent was to enable the individuals and groups to put the conjunctions and disjunctions that had been brought to the surface into perspective. What different choices could be made in such circumstances? What actions might be generated as a result?

5 *Critical reflection in/on action*: Surrounding each of these is the 'cloak' of critical reflection. By this I mean that action, wherever present, is scrutinized and challenged. This is in both self and others. In particular I was respectful of the difficulty of changing behaviour in so-called 'empowered environments'. This became more evident as the differing cycles progressed outside of this particular HE context and I became more aware of the corrosive effects of the continuous improvement environment that had been nourished and embedded.

This particular model of conducting inquiry served me well. It constantly focused on the analysis of the situations that were presented by participants and helped them address better the issues faced by them.

Moreover, when applied to myself moving through the different groups of participants (of which this HE group was one) it also served as a guide to how I could engage and then reengage with particular issues that seemed to be reoccurring, so, highlighting particular narratives that spoke within and beyond context.

The question arises as to how we can move beyond mere 'representation' of differing disjunctions and choices of action within organizations where empowerment rhetorics dominate. The themes and stories that form this discourse are inconsistent with the representation of managers and employees engaged in some form of technical activity or in a series of specified functions. The 'social relations through which managerial work is accomplished and upon which it ultimately depends' (Whittington, 1992: 696) are the bases for a critical analysis of the rhetoric of empowerment as encountered by employees. Alvesson and Willmott (1998) contend that although critical theory can provide 'a process of critical self-reflection and struggle [and that] people can become freed from diverse forms of domination, its analysis is highly abstract and esoteric'. Nevertheless, critical theory is important because it does not regard empowerment as something to be 'bestowed' upon employees: 'substantial forms of emancipatory change must involve a continuing process of critical self-reflection' (Alvesson and Willmott, 1998: 163). Later, the chapter will determine the role of different forms of writing in fostering such inquiry within the students' own professional study.

■ The organizational backcloth

The following outlines the particular characteristics of organizations that seem, according to students within this group, to espouse notions of creativity but at the same time stifle such initiative, so for the employee the experience of such notions is very different in reality. What follows was derived from student statements and my explanation, when listening to them, of the links to previous research work I had been conducting with other participants from other organizations as part of my doctorate.

This work beyond the CIPD group had generated the concepts of the 'strategic straightjacket' – the increasing pressure to produce sleeker structures – and its relevance to 'organizational mess' – as well as the tendency towards a 'lean management' practice that followed from the strategy being adopted. These notions of contemporary organizations will be used as a counterpoint to the issues surrounding pedagogy and the professional demands made on such students and their notions of being 'successful' in their studies.

Three students in the group spoke of their experience of working in so-called 'empowered environments' within the motor industry. Company literature and training programmes they had experienced stressed the importance of fostering such environments. Here 'empowerment' means (Whittington, 1992: 42):

> 'getting it across to individuals that if something is in the way of meeting customer requirements then, regardless of rank, they are empowered to shift it or, if it is beyond their control, to kick and shout until it is shifted.'
>
> (DTI, 1991)

This understanding of empowerment was from a case study of the major British computer company, ICL, promoted as 'best practice' in a DTI publication from its 'Managing into the 90s' programme, and highlights the tenor of the messages being received by managers at this time. This quote was presented to the IPD group to determine whether their company's interpretation of empowerment was similar and how it was experienced in practice. The following group members responded:

Chris: *Yes I do think there are real pressures on me to be more creative, especially from senior managers. They are constantly looking for cost-savings and to be seen by customers to be more competitive. Training programmes I have been on encourage us to 'think differently', bring about ' process control improvements' and come up with 'novel ideas'. Yet I get a real sense that this is all within pretty strict parameters. A number of us have got an ear-bashing because we went a 'bit far' in some of the things we did, not checking for authorization or leaving work to go to a customer's premises to sort a problem out when we were thought to be needed here, that sort of thing.*

Jenny: *At work we always seem to be entering a 'step-change arena', what I mean is that we do not seem to have a gradual improvement but constant movement to produce novel reports from our new systems and change managers' views and opinions on different issues. All of this is incredibly wearing and stressful. When it comes down to it we just do not have the time to engage in all of it.*

Susan: *There are lots of things that stop me being more creative. I get a feeling that if I do something different I am going to be criticized by others if it does not go right. Also, there is a real pressure to get things done quickly so we tend to stick to what we have done before. It gets things done.*

Here the students do not lack the motivation to be different. There are a number of strategic pressures that require them to be so. Yet there are also powerful pressures not to be different. Capra and Flattau (1996) have referred to this contradiction as 'sameness and otherness'. They contend that with 'the development of scientific management theories, up to and including present-day managerial programs like Total Quality, Human Resource Management and Business Process Re-engineering, there has been an almost extensive focus on the business organization's ability to produce "sameness".' The thrust of these initiatives, or 'strategies', has been to design structures that bring about identical products or services – a toaster, car or tax return. This, they contend, has been reinforced in recent years by the goal of new 'sleeker' structures, with no excess waste and so 'no room for either redundancy or chance'. This uniformity has become such a feature of both of our working (and some of our social) lives that we have become used to gaining the benefits from such structures so we do not spend a great deal of time thinking about them.

Yet there is a price to be paid for the reliance on these 'designed structures'. We can identify it in the employee's remarks above – stability does not easily allow for novelty. 'Sameness' becomes a drug, employees becoming increasingly dependent and unwilling to reject it for alternatives when the need arises. To kick the habit and do something different, the 'otherness', is challenging in such environments. Similarly, it will be contended, the practice of teaching and learning is subject to such forces – pulling towards conventional pragmatic practice and away from experimentation and creativity. How to do something different is the continuing theme of this chapter.

Organizational mess

The above notion of the 'strategic straitjacket', this goal of sleeker structures, appears a powerful limiter of the students' creativity at work and it is compounded by the 'mess' they had to deal with day to day. The 'messiness' of the students' working lives was epitomized by the combinations of organizational structures, changing competitive conditions, constant reorganization and the individual relationships that form their social world of work. All of this was perceived by the employees to limit choices and engage in the 'knee-jerk' reactions. Stacey *et al.* (1998) have remarked on how different voices in the management literature have dealt with this mess and uncertainty. They contend that those that concentrate on control and individual agency are 'more appropriate for articulating contexts close to certainty and agreement'. These tend to be the most dominant voices and so dominate managers' understanding.

Referring to the usefulness of the social constructionist position epitomized by the work of Shotter (1993), Stacey *et al.* (1998) argue that social reality is not predetermined but constantly being created and emerging out of what people say and do in their working lives. For this author, Stacey *et al.* relate much more closely to the reality of the managers as described above (1998: 323):

> 'when groups of managers in organisations engage in their everyday conversations they are doing much more than applying theories, building teams or fostering positive motivational attitudes – they are constructing the nature of their work. Conversations at this ordinary, everyday level do not unfold according to anyone's intention and they cannot be modelled in advance... it is also difficult to see how anyone could identify levers in such conversations that they might then use to control its direction.'

This 'web' of everyday conversations and interaction can be immensely powerful in impacting on the working lives of people in the organization and potentially changing them. The challenge for working with this system therefore becomes one of accepting its nature but not seeking to control it: respecting that life in organizations is often intangible, that the complex cannot always be rendered simple and tucked into convenient categories. Moreover, we need to engage in sense-making, a seeking of a sense of coherence, what's meaningful, recognizing the emergence of new patterns of order out of disorganized activity. Here is one manager from my own doctorate research encountering the formal and informal within her own working life:

> 'The place is formally team-based but they are all very large... this is not conducive to team spirit... we are constantly being told to "get out there and do the business". And also subtle messages of what your job should involve... what you are "being paid for"... its constant stress... all these messages seem to be reinforced on a daily basis... if teams do have someone who is not performing then they tend to get passed around other teams like a "bad apple". No one will bite the bullet and act and try and engage in any sort of conversation with this person and see what it is that's stopping them doing well.'

Here the manager is expected to get into 'action mode' and 'come up with the goods' with this employee. Agency is seen as individual with intentional control through 'performance management', so dominates management thinking. What is not being taken into account is the reality co-created by the interaction of different agents, they themselves being influenced by the system of which they are a part. The manager still felt it was necessary to act alone, to 'do something about it'. Nevertheless, there was pressure that it might not go 'right', that her approaches would be construed as 'misguided, misdirected, and not conforming to the norm'.

Is this so far away from the student who asked, 'Is this in the exam?' There the student, like the manager, recognizes that there are alternative ways of depicting learning. In the case presented above in the classroom, this was through engaging in a group process around a visual object, yet the pressures of conforming to the norm possibly cut the student off from considering alternatives to learning. This might encompass alternative forms of pedagogy beyond the purely instrumental tools of tutor input, then revision of notes, followed by an examination. Here, learning, as in the discussion of work above, cannot always be tucked into neat categories and 'performance managed' but can be spontaneous, unpredictable, slow burning or just for fun. The latter did not feature in many of the students' conversations of their experience at work, or university for that matter.

So, to reiterate: how can such powerful facets of organizational life – 'sameness and otherness' and organizational mess – be worked with within the classroom environment and reflected on so as to impact on working practice? Further, is the tutor free of such pressures themselves that they can simply step back and scope such activities?

Different ways of knowing and doing

However, not all managers encountered had such limited choices. What seems to allow the more successful managers to cope with a complex environment is an ability to deal with the messiness of their working lives and the impact this has on them outside of the workplace. One of the chapter's main themes needs reiterating: that when the employees are coping with the pressure they are not 'straitjacketed' into acceptable ways of behaving but have an ability to 'go' with the mess and uncertainty.

An example of this was explained to me recently by a young manager of an advertising agency office:

> 'you end up having knee-jerk behaviours based on particular thought patterns of "situation… my response… this is what I do". I began to look at this differently and recognized that the thought pattern was just like a train coming into the station. I did not have to get on it. If I did, I knew where it would take me. Just that feeling of not being an automaton but having a choice of how I thought about situations and courses of action was something really different and liberating. I have used this with my staff and we have a real laugh about trains coming into stations in the office. But it works.'

Not only do they have an ability to do this themselves *but they also participate with others and take them with them*. Here, I believe, is the link between the managers who are successful and how they deal with the pressures. They do not display arrogance about their work – 'that this is the only way to do things and if only others follow this lead then all problems will be solved'; the manager and her staff are doing something different by using the metaphor. They recognize the surreal nature of it to their context and that, for all their attempts to not 'hop aboard', sometimes the patterns of response, so beloved of their culture, pop up from time to time and reassert their power over individuals and their relationships.

So how does exploration of such responses illicit meaning for the IPD group and my own work as a tutor? It is the contention of this chapter that such reflection aids sense-making of my own experience as a tutor and how the students reacted. Moreover, do barriers similarly exist in the institutions that seek to work with these students, in other words the professional bodies and HE institutions? Consequently, when the students have the opportunity for being creative, different, taking risks, exploring new ways of being and doing, do these institutions serve them well? Moreover, what are the vehicles for illuminating critical pedagogy and could different forms of writing aid this process?

We have already considered two factors that I believe stop such alternatives being considered, these being the 'strategic straitjacket' and how individuals, and the organizations of which they are a part, deal with mess and uncertainty. However, a third powerful factor prevents creativity and different ways of knowing and being. Trends identified through my own work and others, (Weil, 1998, 1999; Wildermeersch and Vandevabeele, 1998; Lather, 1991; Shaw, 1992) will now be identified that are preventing such notions of participation and creative ways of working being enabled in organizational life.

Lean management

What I observed through my doctorate research was the way in which the rhetoric of the 'empowered' organization was placing demands on individuals to find their own way through this mess. It was often coupled with a ruthless search for perfection and 'lean' methods of managing, incorporating the 'right ways' of doing things.

The manufacturing sector, which predominantly the CIPD group was drawn from in this example, was influenced by the whole plethora of Japanese production and management techniques of the 1980s and 1990s – *kaizen*, just-in-time, lean production. The central thrust of these developments, when introduced into modern plants, was to ensure that products were of quality and able to be manufactured 'right first time', so eliminating waste and ensuring the most efficient means of production. Similarly, my own doctorate research has demonstrated that 'lean management' leads to a paring down of behaviours in employees. What characterizes such practice? This is a phenomenon so apparent in the fast-food 'have a nice day' cultures of responding to customers or the call-centres with the operatives almost responding in harmony, like well-drilled backing singers, slick and together but potentially antiseptic and soulless. Moreover it is being reinforced by the trends for the development and then measurement of competences that employees are to abide by (Meldrum and Atkinson, 1998). Such a system is thus reinforcing as work practices become centred on demonstration of these and employees are rated on their ability to accomplish them. Funds for training initiatives become 'focused' on the competences, as do endless meetings which need to be set up to try and manage it all (Hirsch and Strebler, 1994).

This has two main consequences. Firstly, energy and funding is sucked into an exercise that reduces the capacity of the organization to take a more critical look at what employees require – the 'competence framework' becomes an industry in itself (Fletcher, 1991). Secondly, managers themselves are discouraged from considering alternative perspectives of their work as they are urged to conform to this common doctrine. It is not surprising, therefore, the student in the critical incident at the beginning of this paper reacted to the exercise in the way she did. Is it not naive to believe that these notions of a 'common doctrine' are left in the faculty car park as the student leaves the workplace and enters the HE domain? Here, I would contend, scope does still exist, in part, for working in different ways, yet it is often presented alongside the conformity of professional body regulations, syllabus, writing outputs of essays, case study responses and the exam script, assessment and the potential impact on student career of 'not getting through'. Such a catalogue of convention.

Weil (1998) comments that 'we make a difference by placing real-life dilemmas at the heart of collaborative inquiry and not confining students to traditional faculty or disciplinary boxes'. In my experience, the CIPD professional awards reinforce this notion of separate disciplines, which bear no resemblance to the reality of HR, which is becoming increasingly more complex in its activities. This is signified by the student conversations of real-life dilemmas that they face day to day. So, given the powerful pressures on managers and the CIPD group discussed above, how can the 'catalogue of convention' be challenged? Could writing be the vehicle for illuminating critical pedagogy? First, it is important that the constraints of the HE environment for both student and staff are outlined.

■ What we are capable of rather than what I do: the role of critical inquiry

I have found strategies identified by Bookfield (1987) particularly useful in my own work. He argues that to learn to think critically is one of the most significant activities of our adult lives. We can do this by identifying and challenging assumptions, being contextually aware, imagining and exploring alternatives, as well as being sceptical of universal truths. Yet this also places a responsibility on HE institutions and professional bodies to create the climate for this to happen.

This quest for the creation of a critical environment is fraught with difficulty because the trends so described by the students and employees above are, in my experience, increasingly prevalent in the HE sector. For example, from the students' point of view it is important to recognize how, within the lean environments they inhabit, they can obtain their award, 'clear the hurdle' of the exam as cleanly and quickly as possible, and move on in their career. Pragmatism such as this is not confined to the student. Teaching staff are also suitably motivated within their HE environment to obtain the 'outputs', gather the 'centre of excellence' tag, capture extra funding and prestige, which leads to further recruitment, higher numbers, more income... Such forces shape therefore the relationship between student and tutor and the wider relationship with funding/awarding bodies. This instrumentality does not lend itself well to critical study.

Alvesson and Deetz (2000: 209) have called for both 'closeness' and 'distance' in researching social phenomena. *Closeness* in the sense of 'being able to be familiar with the site under study. To sensitively listen to the considerations of the situation, and not rejecting immediately the viewpoints of management'; and *distance* 'which ideologies are at play that frame these situations... what are the institutionalized doctrines that play behind the backs of actors... just how can we reform such tasks so to reduce the contradiction between emancipation and instrumental values... how can we interpret social reality in a really novel light?'

There are real constraints, therefore, on a tutor with a large group of students trying to balance work and the pressures it imposes on them. In the short term, in finding the time and energy to just getting to classes on time and with enough spare enthusiasm to engage with others (students not staff!); or in the long term, to satisfy examiners in giving them a suitable award that is so necessary to advance their careers. Yet here is a tutor trying to suggest that knowledge is not pre-packaged like a frozen dinner ready to be warmed up and served on a plate. That meaning may be contested and the process highlighted to gather alternative sense-making and alternatives to powerful discourses. These are the 'institutionalised doctrines playing behind backs' of both tutor and student, and to the forefront in the case detailed earlier in the chapter. Therefore, what is the 'novel light' that can be directed on this situation?

So the challenge for the organizations of which they are a part of, as well as the institutions offering professional development is, are we engaging with our students in a way that facilitates this critical process, or are we purely reinforcing and colluding with the conforming tendency of the strategic straitjacket (Kemmis and McTaggart, 2000)?

The challenge for ourselves and others is how we can work *with* these dilemmas rather than *on* them. Alternative forms of writing are therefore explored to determine their role in fostering such participation within a professional course.

■ New forms of writing: individual and collective minds

If the quest for fostering inquiry and engagement in different learning practices is at the heart of pedagogy, then how participants connect with this is critical. Conversation and facilitated discussion may be one way in which this can be accomplished. Nevertheless, I would contend that, in light of the importance of the examination structure for CIPD that is still heavily biased towards traditional forms of assessment, focusing on developing new forms of writing has real advantages. Namely, that it counters the instrumental, but quite necessary, rational structures of the assignment, dissertation or exam script.

Writing, I would contend in the traditional sense, is often seen as still 'writing-up' thoughts and ideas. We encourage our students to engage in the learning process by being open about experience, sharing and analyzing this through workshop dialogue and plenary sessions, hoping at the same time that they have this same sort of enquiring 'conversation' with themselves as they read selected text. The resulting writing then is sanitized into a rational model of writing conforming to the requirements of the examination or assessment module. As Richardson points out 'how we are expected to write affects what we can write about' (2000: 927). Such traditional forms of writing reinforce the metanarrative of scientific objectivity and mutes the situated speaker engaged in inquiring about the world as they see it.

If the effects of lean management practices are to be countered in the HE environment then I believe a new convention of writing needs to be adhered to. This is much closer to the work of Richardson (1992, 2000) and Ely *et al.* (1999). Here writing is seen as central to a method of inquiry, it is *part of a process* rather than purely the *product of a process*. The part it plays is to be both creative and analytic, both of which can co-exist as so many different forms, or 'species' as Richardson terms them, are now available (2000: 930). These representative forms *invite in* rather than exclude, encouraging others, (as well as ourselves) to seek clarity or shed fresh light on their own situation. Here writing is seen as *not complete or right* but as a means of engaging with others to try and make sense of complex phenomena. For example, the group described at the beginning of this paper used writing as a means to explore the experience of graphically representing their ways of learning about their job, in the classroom at that time. These were then shared, feedback or additional comment gleaned from other members, and then discussed as a whole group. Our insights were not complete but emerged out of the process of thought–writing–discussion.

Traditional writing forms are not to be excluded: as stated earlier the success of the students in my earlier example depend on them, but they should be not seen as the accepted and other forms, as 'alternative' (Denzin, 1994). By promoting this view practitioners are undermining what I believe are the real opportunities given to educators by the postmodernist critique: in that the quest for particular unspecified assumptions hindering sense-making, and the search for different practices that work, should not be thwarted.

◼ Summary

In summary, this paper has sought to identify similar trends in both the narratives of the HR group members, managers from my own research and my reflection on teaching within the HE environment. These are characterized by what have been termed the pressure for conformity and the difficulty of creative enterprise brought about by the strategic straitjacket and processes of lean management. These conventions, however, were challenged by a different view of organizations that identified the messiness of working lives and the critical role of inquiry. The tutor and participant are caught in the middle of two conflicting discourses, which the critical incident vividly illustrated. First, the empowerment discourse, whereby the student is encouraged to develop new avenues of knowledge and critically reflect on practice. Second, the student at the same time is being exposed to a different discourse, of rational instrumental means emerging from the requirements of their course and its assessment. For the tutor, a more prescriptive pedagogy becomes a pragmatic option, for they are also subject to similar influences within a performance culture of UK higher education that is so concerned with recording outcomes rather than dialogue around the means, the pedagogy, that produces them. Therefore working differently becomes a challenge and the use of writing becomes central to meeting it. Traditional forms are often the culmination of thought and a collection of ideas. Here writing is seen as central to encourage engagement with others and to develop means to explore complex phenomena alongside them. Different forms of writing were therefore seen as important to foster the process of inquiry rather than purely as the sculpted outcome of thought, 'stripped down' and 'in the exam'.

Activities for Part Three

1 (a) Consider the role of education and qualification-based programmes and the extent to which they offer the opportunity for a critical approach to HRD practice.

(b) Assess the chapters in this section and the value of their arguments for justifying a critical approach in HRD practice.

(c) Discuss the results of (a) and (b) with colleagues.

2 (a) Select a current problem or opportunity facing your organization.

(b) Consider how appropriate critical action learning will be to your selected situation.

(c) Produce a proposal for a HRD intervention which incorporates the use of critical action learning.

(d) Formulate and present to colleagues an implementation plan for your intervention.

3 (a) Produce a list of criteria for critical practice in 'classroom'-based HRD.

(b) Assess the extent to which your criteria reflect common practice.

(c) Present the results to colleagues for discussion.

(d) Review existing practice and identify desired changes.

Part Four

CRITIQUE OF CRITICAL ORTHODOXIES

Introduction to Part Four

This final part entitled 'Critique of critical orthodoxies', brings the book to a close. What might this mean? There is a fairly simple answer to that question which really reflects the title and theme of the book as a whole. It is simply that today's radical critique can easily become tomorrow's tradition. History suggests that change is a continuous process, perhaps also punctuated by periods of more significant and speedy change, sometimes referred to as revolutionary change. Such processes can also apply to the history of ideas so that what was once a marginal and radical idea becomes the accepted way of thinking about the world or a particular part of it. For 'accepted' we can substitute the word 'orthodox'. So, the orthodoxy is the dominant idea which pervades the thinking about and analyses of a given phenomenon. The danger for us is that what are currently defined as 'critical' ideas themselves become orthodoxies. It will be clear from earlier chapters that in some ways ideas referred to as critical are defined as such because of their challenge to established, or currently orthodox, ideas. Depending on success in that challenge, the critical ideas may become established as dominant and established and so lose their power to question and challenge. Or, and more likely, become incorporated into established ideas in ways which have a similar effect. For that reason it is important that critical approaches have their precepts applied to themselves. In other words, the questioning and challenge inherent in critical approaches is not ignored when examining those same approaches. This process is a feature of what is referred to as reflexivity. What we are suggesting in this part then is that critical HRD needs to be reflexive.

The notion of reflexivity can be applied at a number of levels. One level can be a particular idea or a range of ideas. Another can be the application of the idea or ideas in professional practice. A third can be practice itself, as and when it occurs. All of these and any other potential level is important in its own right and each can inform and stimulate thinking about any or all of the others. Reflexivity in and on practice is perhaps the most difficult to apply, but it is also the level that could be argued to be the most significant since it will have more direct impact on those being influenced by critical HRD practice. In addition, it is the level where institutional policies and processes such as continuing professional development intersect with critical HRD. We are personally persuaded that without reflexivity the potential for change and outcomes of value to society, organizations and individuals from critical HRD become less likely. For that reason this part seeks to make the case for critical HRD to question continuously its own ideas. This is not necessarily achieved by a direct or exclusive focus on those ideas. It is rather achieved by chapters which examine ideas that are generally incorporated into both critical and established approaches. The chapters also apply reflexivity at a range of the levels suggested earlier.

The first chapter in the section by Valerie Owen-Pugh is concerned with a recent innovation in HRD and that is the idea of communities of practice. This idea is, of course, based on an alternative understanding of learning. Building on the basic assumptions of this idea, and utilizing an additional concept from group theory, Valerie Owen-Pugh makes the argument that all approaches to HRD have the potential for oppressive as well as emancipatory outcomes. This comes not necessarily from the HRD approach or practice itself but from the inherent nature of social groups and processes. The argument is of key significance for critical HRD since emancipation of work and employment is often the normative rationale for such approaches. The following chapter by Len Holmes is also concerned with learning theory. These two chapters are highly significant since our understanding of learning is at the heart of HRD, whether traditional or critical. Len Holmes subjects both traditional and more recent understandings of learning to a radical critique which draws on philosophy and, in particular, ideas associated with the 'linguistic turn'. His chapter highlights the ideological purposes and effects of language and, in doing so, in common with Valerie Owen-Pugh, questions the supposed and claimed emancipatory achievements of HRD. The chapter has direct relevance to most of the levels of reflexivity suggested above.

The final chapter of the part, and of the book as a whole, is a contribution from the editors. The chapter seeks to identify and highlight tensions in critical HRD which arise not so much from its challenge to 'the establishment' as from potential contradictions in its own ideas and practice. An example of this is the potential impact of emotion in critical management learning to be disempowering as well as serving the purposes of emancipation. The example has primary application to and relevance for the level of practice in action. The chapter though does not ignore other levels and questions the 'real' and lasting impact of critical HRD on and for organizations. An interesting and additional argument is that 'performance' is not to be ignored or always denigrated as a less than desirable purpose or outcome. In that respect the chapter reinforces the case for reflexivity at all levels, including that of ideas.

It seems ambitious to offer key themes for this part. This is partly because they may be seen as themes for the book as whole. Within that context, the following themes are offered not as a summary of the book but as some significant ideas from the following three chapters:

- the status and reliability of our understanding of learning;
- the centrality of ideology and power in HRD and so in critical HRD;
- the difficulty of maintaining declared beliefs and values in day-to-day behaviour;
- the contradictions and potential for unexpected outcomes in applying and utilizing critical HRD approaches;
- the importance and significance of reflexivity in critical HRD.

As already indicated, these themes relate primarily to the final part. That said, the part as a whole does have resonance with the title and major themes of the book as a whole and so the list above is of relevance for that purpose. As editors we are happy to leave readers to identify additional generic themes and their significance for and application in the theory and practice of HRD, if such a distinction can be accepted. The list is also our last word as editors except to say we hope readers gain as much from the book as we have in compiling it.

Chapter 10

Acknowledging conflict in 'communities of practice': a figurational perspective on learning and innovating in the workplace

Valerie Owen-Pugh

Introduction

Lave and Wenger's theorizing of the 'community of practice' (COP) (e.g. Lave and Wenger, 1991; Wenger, 1998) portrays learning as the social construction of identity. These two authors have made a significant contribution to our understanding of learning through work by showing how knowledge and understanding can emerge in free-flowing ways as individuals engage with one another in the resolution of work problems. The application of COP theory (COPT) to organizations has largely been explored within two parallel streams of academic literature. The first of these, most obviously relevant to the concerns of HRD, is the literature on workplace learning, illustrated, for example, by the work of writers such as Fuller *et al.* (2005), Hodkinson and Hodkinson (2004) and Billett (2001) who have drawn on Lave and Wenger's ideas in exploring the ways in which workplaces support the induction of new employees and their development of occupational and professional skills. Within this stream, emphasis tends to be placed on the ways in which individuals master the established practices of their colleagues and forbears: that is to say, on the ways in which workplace communities reproduce themselves through making a commitment to keeping existing skills alive. The second stream, linked primarily with organizational development, is the literature on organizational learning and the 'learning organization'. Here, many current debates on knowledge management have their origins in Brown and Duguid's (1991) portrayal of organizations as 'communities-of-communities-of-practice' (Ibid.: 53) and their suggestion that the deliberate fostering of COPs within workplaces might facilitate innovation (e.g. Brown and Duguid, 2001; Swann *et al.*, 2002). Meanwhile, Wenger's promotion of 'cultivated' COPs as a knowledge management solution (e.g. Wenger, 1998, 2000; Wenger and Snyder, 2000; Wenger *et al.*, 2002) may be contributing to an uncritical stance within organizational studies, as a result of which COPs are acquiring idealistic connotations of employee empowerment. For example, the aspirational principle of 'free exchange in, across and between communities of practice' now plays a significant role in 'learning organization' discourse (Snell, 2001: 320), while mainstream management texts frequently portray COPs as collegial and productive (e.g. Davenport, 1999). This popularized view of COPs may also be impacting on critical academic debates (Contu and Willmott, 2003). The present discussion will aim to counter such idealism by exploring their conflictive dimensions.

This aim will be pursued by highlighting two recognized limitations of Lave and Wenger's theorizing, namely, its limited capacity to acknowledge both the self-conscious subjectivities of community members (Elkjaer, 1999) and the asymmetries of power that shape both the internal relations of COPs and their dealings with their wider social worlds (Fox, 2000; Contu and Willmott, 2003; Owen-Pugh, 2005). It will be argued that these limitations make it difficult for COPT to acknowledge the ways in which learning though work can cause individuals and groups to find themselves in opposition to one another. These include, for example: the ways in which individuals can come to dis-identify with practice communities and can become marginalized within them (Hodges, 1998; Fuller *et al.*, 2005; see also Rigg and Trehan, 1999); the ways in which such communities can resist the aims of their parent organizations (Korcynski, 2003); and the ways in which intended learning outcomes can become distorted by such things as lack of trust between colleagues (Billett, 2001; Wasko and Faraj, 2000; Ardichvili *et al.*, 2003) and the manoeuvring of organizational power holders (Ciborra and Patriotta, 1998). It will be suggested that this problem is caused by Lave and Wenger's prioritizing of collective agency, which leaves COPT with no satisfactory means of acknowledging the oppositional stances of community members. To explore such conflictive relations, it would seem necessary to locate Lave and Wenger's theory within a broader conceptual framework. For this purpose, the present critique will seek to make links between COPT and the 'process' theorizing of Norbert Elias (e.g. Elias, 1991a, 2000) which, though comparatively unknown within organizational studies, offers a means of linking power with subjectivity through its use of the 'figuration', a relational construct reflecting individuals' functional interdependencies. Eliasian theory can be used to make links between global social processes and the forms and outcomes of work practice (Newton, 2001; Dopson, 2001; van Iterson *et al.*, 2002), and therefore appears to offer a valuable counterpoint to popularized interpretations of COPT.

This discussion will also touch briefly on the design of workplaces as social learning environments. Such development initiatives might include, for example, not only the formal construction of groups working for knowledge creation, such as Wenger's 'cultivated' COPs, but also programmes designed to promote the development of occupational skill, such as Billett's (2001) 'workplace curriculum'. In designing, managing and supporting such ventures, organizations must resolve critical questions, such as: whether such initiatives should be seeking to promote the continuity of existing practice or to identify and develop innovative ideas; to what extent direct intervention by managers may benefit or detract from individuals' learning; whether or not individuals' learning goals can be reconciled with those of their learning community; and how readily a community's goals might be reconciled with those of its parent organization. Such questions create many philosophical and practical dilemmas for HRD managers. In particular, they are likely to find themselves charged with meeting the needs of individuals, collectives and organizations, and consequently have to reconcile the interests of all three groups in pursuing their work role (Swann et al., 2002; Slotte et al., 2004; Short and Yorks, 2002). While such dilemmas have no ready solutions, it will be argued that they cannot be addressed theoretically from within the conceptual model offered by COPT. However, here too, a solution may be found by reappraising Lave and Wenger's theory in Eliasian terms.

The discussion will be structured in the following way. Firstly, it will remind readers of key insights offered by Lave and Wenger's work and clarify their position with regard to the theorizing of subjectivity, power and agency. It will then aim to locate COPT within the wider organizational literature, as a means of highlighting current problems in its acknowledgment of conflictive relations. It will subsequently show how the work of Elias, and the recent contributions of writers such as Dalal and Stacey, might enhance our understanding of conflictive relations within and beyond COPs. Finally, it will seek to draw these various threads together by considering the ways in which a synthesis of COPT and Eliasian theory might enhance our understanding of learning through work.

■ Theorizing subjectivity, power and agency within communities of practice

Lave and Wenger's first published account of COPT (Lave and Wenger, 1991) expanded on several critical arguments that were first put forward in Lave's studies of 'everyday cognition' (Lave et al., 1984; Lave, 1988). It was in these earlier studies that she first sought to critique individualistic assumptions in education by proposing that social relations, rather than individual minds, form the primary medium through which knowledge, as lived meaning, is created and sustained. In developing this argument, she adopted a structuralist perspective, portraying the social settings in which individuals live, work and learn as a 'locus of articulation', or point of connection, effectively acting as an interface between the structuring of individuals' actions and the structuring of their wider social worlds (Lave *et al.*, 1984: 75). She also adopted a broadly Marxian stance, criticizing the ways in which the commercial privileging of abstract, but functionally valueless, forms of knowledge were leading to the alienation of many learners in schools and workplaces. These ideas are taken further in her subsequent collaboration with Wenger. For example, the co-authored (1991) text extends her earlier critique of educational practice by demonstrating how 'communities' of working practitioners, such as Liberian tailors and Mexican traditional midwives, can devise effective ways of developing the skills of their members without reference to pedagogy. It also offers a stringent critique of the ways in which workplace learning can become distorted by the imperative to meet commercial goals, showing how well-structured practice communities can work to counter such pressures. Lave and Wenger (1991) argue that this takes place when COPs offer their members authentic opportunities to acquire identities of mastery, a developmental process they term 'legitimate peripheral participation'. Here they prioritize the enabling role played by a community's 'structuring affordances', that is to say, the learning opportunities and resources it offers its members, over the agentic roles of its apprentices (or 'newcomers') and masters (or 'old-timers').

However, in emphasizing the enabling role of the collective, Lave and Wenger seem to understate the problems caused by conflictive peer-group relations. That is to say, they make few references to the ways in which conflictive relations between newcomers might influence learning outcomes. Their acknowledgement of inter-community conflict is restricted to the 'continuity-displacement contradiction', a generational struggle representing the different 'ways in which old-timers and newcomers establish and maintain identities' (Ibid.: 115).

Lave and Wenger suggest that this struggle is bound up with the tension between social continuity and social change, and that its resolution determines whether communities continue to promote existing practices or seek to develop new ones. They explain (Ibid.: 115):

> 'The different ways in which old-timers and newcomers establish and maintain identities conflict and generate competing viewpoints on the practice and its development. Newcomers are caught in a dilemma. On the one hand, they need to engage in the existing practice... On the other hand they have a stake in its development as they begin to establish their own identity.'

Here, they are seeking to distinguish between the vested interests of a community's established power holders, whose identities are invested in maintaining existing forms of practice, and those of its future power holders, whose identities are invested in change. However, this interpretation may be overly simplistic, as we will see shortly when we come to consider Elias' theory.

Wenger's subsequent (1998) text sought to develop COPT further in two significant ways. He offered an expanded theoretical account of learning, couched in abstract terms as a series of dualities, or 'macro processes' (Stacey, 2003: 355), in which he portrays social practice as the medium through which individuals negotiate personal meaning and construct identity. He also explored the ways in which this abstract theorizing might inform the design of learning settings within organizations. Significantly, while the collective struggles highlighted in the earlier text are largely unacknowledged in this later one, it does acknowledge the potentially conflictive dimensions of practice communities. For example, Wenger portrays the development of identity as a process of continual negotiation and tells us that 'participation... is not tantamount to collaboration. It can involve all kinds of relations, conflictual as well as harmonious, intimate as well as political, competitive as well as cooperative' (Ibid.: 56). Even so, the collective influence of COPs on such disputes is portrayed as broadly benign. For example, we learn that a COP: '1) provides resolutions to institutionally generated conflicts... 2) supports a communal memory... 3) helps newcomers join... 4) generates perspectives... 5) makes a job habitable' (Ibid.: 46). This paints a somewhat 'sanitized' picture of community relations that glosses over the effects that such conflict can have on individuals. For example, the ways in which conflictive relations might shape individuals' evaluations of themselves, lead to their marginalization by, or their departure from, communities, and so shape their future lives, are acknowledged but remain unexplored. To compound the problem, Wenger's later publications (Wenger, 2000; Wenger and Snyder, 2000; Wenger et al., 2002) have adopted an increasingly prescriptive tone and lay stress on the empowering qualities of COPs. For example, Wenger and Snyder (2000: 140) tell us that: 'Inevitably... people in communities of practice share their experiences and knowledge in free-flowing, creative ways that foster new approaches to problems.' His contribution to the literature therefore appears to depart significantly from the ethical positioning of the Lave and Wenger (1991) text, a stance that has been criticized (Fox, 2000; Contu and Willmott, 2003).

At this point, it would be useful to take a closer look at the treatment of agency, power and subjectivity within COPT. While Lave and Wenger's (1991) discussion makes reference to the relations between community members, their primary concern is to portray the collective agency of COPs in terms of the structural affordances they offer to members. In this text, the power relations of practice are interpreted in terms of two forms of collective struggle, economic and generational, and the ways in which individual members' subjectivities and actions might impact on their own and others' learning are not explored in any depth. On all of these points, Wenger's later contribution is less clear-cut. Although he makes reference to field research in his (1998) text, his abstract theorizing effectively prioritizes the negotiation of meaning and identity over the concrete relations of individuals, creating the sense of a representational, rather than a human, agency. While he acknowledges individual agency, his promotion of COPs as a structural form of intervention effectively reinforces the messages of collective empowerment offered in the Lave and Wenger (1991) text. His abstract theorizing certainly offers a very detailed structural map of human subjectivity and, despite his failure to explore issues of hegemony and resistance, he does acknowledge the power relations between individuals, which he defines as their ability to negotiate identity. However, neither version of COPT offers any theoretical mechanism for acknowledging the self-conscious manoeuvring of individuals, and therefore for exploring their conflictive relations. This means that Lave and Wenger are effectively unable to theorize: the ways in which individuals might come into conflict over practice; the conditions under which communities might collectively choose to maintain existing forms of practice or seek to develop new ones; the extent to which the learning of community members might be compromised by an organization's power holders; and the conditions under which such hegemony might be resisted.

The place of COPT within organizational studies

Both forms of COPT have had a significant influence on organizational studies. Indeed, the widely differing ways in which writers have drawn on Lave and Wenger's theory arguably bears testament to its versatility. For example, many writers have drawn inspiration from the (1991) text, offering studies grounded in field observations and exploring, on the one hand, the emergence of shared understandings through everyday work relations (e.g. Pálsson, 1994; Gherardi and Nicolini, 2002) and, on the other, the structuring affordances of workplaces as settings for learning (e.g. Billett, 2001; Hodkinson and Hodkinson, 2004). Other writers have drawn on Wenger's expanded theory, and his structural approach to intervention, to debate issues such as the management and circulation of knowledge and designing for learning and innovation (e.g. Brown and Duguid, 2001; Snell, 2001; Swann et al., 2002). However, despite the critical contributions offered by such wide-ranging studies the academic literature has tended to emphasize the empowering qualities of COPs, while the conflictive dimensions of learning are overlooked (Contu and Willmott, 2003). This popularizing tendency requires some explanation, since it runs counter to our intuitive understanding that, in organizations, 'conflict, contradictions, and recurring problematic behaviors are the norm, rather than the exception' (Kersten, 2001: 452). As will be shown, it also runs counter to a sizeable literature that acknowledges the emotional dimensions of organizations. The popularizing of COPT will be revisited later in the discussion. At this point, since studies of organizational emotion offer a contrasting perspective on conflict to Lave and Wenger's structuralist approach, their implications for COPT will be briefly explored.

Studies of organizational emotion can broadly be differentiated by the relative weight they place on causal factors, with social constructionist writers such as Fineman (2000, 2003) placing primary emphasis on the ways in which identity is shaped by the social world, while the psychodynamic perspective prioritizes processes 'internal' to the individual (Hirshhorn, 1988; Hoggett, 1992; Obholzer and Roberts, 1994; Beech et al., 2002). Social constructionist writers view conflict as a normative dimension of learning and acknowledge the ways in which experiences of learning create conflicts of identity within, as well as between, individuals, frequently triggered by fear of failure (e.g. Short and Yorks, 2002; Rigg and Trehan, 1999). In contrast, writers of the psychodynamic school draw largely on the psychoanalysis of Freud in emphasizing the individual's need to maintain an idealized identity. These writers tend to pathologize conflictive relations and assume that the influences of the social are mediated by internal processes rooted in early childhood development. Despite its predominantly individualistic stance, psychodynamic theorizing also acknowledges collective conflict, interpreted as clashes between 'social defences', such as when groups work to maintain secure identities by denigrating and devaluing one another (Hirschhorn, 1988; Beech et al., 2002; Hoggett, 1992: 144). From this perspective, barriers to learning are assumed to have their origins in individuals' subjective perceptions of threat. For example, fear of failure is thought to cause individuals to revert to less appropriate, but more 'secure', forms of identity, that may not only impair their own learning but also interfere with the learning of their colleagues (e.g. Beech et al., 2002).

Viewed from either of these perspectives, COPT in its current form appears to offer an insufficient account of learning in organizations. For example, both schools of thought would portray COPs as uncomfortable settings, characterized by clashes between constructed identities that may go too deep within the psyche to be readily resolved. They would imply, for example, that knowledge sharing will be influenced by members' reflexive evaluations of self and other, in particular: that knowledge might be withheld from others in the absence of trust; that such problems might be exacerbated by rivalries between communities; and that individuals may work to maintain secure identities regardless of the cost to their colleagues. While this portrayal might appear cynical, evidence of such problematic learning is not difficult to find. For example, studies confirm that individuals can be reluctant to share their knowledge with others out of fear for their own interests (Andrews and Delahaye, 2000; Billett, 2001) and have to negotiate learning opportunities with power holders (Driver, 2002). Their confidence in their ability may be deliberately eroded by both peers and superiors (Duffy et al., 2002). Learning within peer groups can lead, not only to the mastery of practice, but also to individuals' dis-identification with community aims and to experiences of marginalization (Humphreys and Brown, 2002; Hodges, 1998; Fuller *et al.*, 2005; Rigg and Trehan, 1999). And the outcomes of OD initiatives are likely to be determined as much by tensions between organizational powerholders as by the intervention of experts (Harrisson *et al.*, 2001; Vince, 2001; Owenby, 2002; Dopson, 2001). Furthermore, several recent studies of 'cultivated' COPs suggest that their functioning can sometimes be problematic. For example: members' felt obligations to share knowledge with one another can be countered by lack of trust and fear of criticism (Wasko and Faraj, 2000; Ardichvili *et al.*, 2003); it seems that knowledge can circulate more smoothly within their boundaries than between them (Brown and Duguid, 2001; Swann *et al.*, 2002); and their effectiveness as a tool for promoting innovation is likely to be impaired by conflicting disciplinary perspectives (Brown and Duguid, 2001) and the working of organizational power hierarchies (Ciborra and Patriotta, 1998; Swann *et al.*, 2002).

These findings pose problems for theorizing the design of constructed learning environments such as COPs since they make it very difficult to predict, in any particular instance, how specific forms of management intervention might influence learning outcomes. Translated into the terminology of systems theory, it becomes impossible to sustain the assumption that designed 'inputs' will lead logically to desired 'outputs'. Stacey and his co-workers (Stacey, 2003; Griffin *et al.*, 1998) suggest that, under conditions of high uncertainty, there are advantages in abandoning systems thinking and turning instead to process theory, and they stress the advantages of process thinking for exploring innovation. The difference between these two forms of theory can be illustrated by making use of Gherardi's (1999) distinction between 'problem-driven' learning, privileging 'results and consequences …, boundaries and divisions …, hierarchy and order' (Ibid.: 110–11) and 'learning in the face of mystery', privileging the 'incomplete, continuous, ambiguous, unfulfilled, partial and precarious' (Ibid.: 109). For Stacey, the advantages of process thinking for organizational development arise from its assumption that learning emerges unpredictably from misunderstanding and its consequent ability to acknowledge the emergence of truly novel forms of meaning through human dialogue. This brings us to the process theory offered by Elias. After discussing Elias' ideas, we will return to Stacey's views on innovation.

■ Introducing a figurational perspective

Critically, Eliasian theory shares with COPT the assumption that mind and society are reflexively and mutually constituted. However, since it takes as its starting point a focus on the functional interdependencies between individuals, it is able to acknowledge both collective and individual forms of agency

(Griffin *et al.*, 1998) and, as will be shown, to make connections between global social processes, the power relations of practice and individuals' self-conscious subjectivities. Since Elias was at pains to maintain a theoretical focus on the concrete relations of practice, while avoiding 'untestable' 'high level generalized abstractions' (Elias, 1974: xvi), his theory also avoids some of the problems posed by Wenger's abstract theorizing. A summary of Elias' ideas will now be offered. Readers wishing to become more fully acquainted with his work may find Mennell's (1992) introduction helpful.

Elias used his construct of the 'figuration' to represent the networks of constraint created by individuals' obligations to meet one another's social needs. In Eliasian theory, such networks of constraint are deemed to be in a permanent state of dynamic tension, and it becomes possible to view human development as emerging continually from the resolution of such tension, reflected in processes of social alignment, absorption, differentiation and conflict, as individuals and groups manoeuvre to promote their power opportunities (Elias, 1978, 1991a). From a figurational perspective, social change is therefore assumed to be driven by the 'interweaving of countless individual interests and intentions' (Elias, 2000: 312) and, while apparently orderly, its outcomes are deemed to be inherently unpredictable or 'blind', since they are likely to be other than intended by any particular individual. Since figurational changes are driven by individuals' reflexive social evaluations, social development becomes bound up with changes in human subjectivity. And, since it is shaped by the agential manoeuvring of individuals and collectives, social practice, including the use of 'symbol' through language, knowledge, and thought (Elias, 1991b), is therefore politicized. In this way, figurational theory can be used to make connections between macro-processes, such as the marginalization of groups within wider society, and micro-processes, such as learning within peer groups, and to explore the development of practice over both long and short time-frames. Writers such as Dalal (1998, 2002), van Iterson *et al.* (2002), Newton (1996), and Stokvis (2000) offer useful examples of the breadth of analysis that becomes possible when Elias' ideas are applied to HRD issues.

Elias explored the connections between practice, power and subjectivity primarily through his theory of the 'civilizing process' (Elias, 2000; see also Elias, 1974, 1987, 1991a) which draws on historical accounts of 'manners' and 'courtly' etiquette in Western Europe at the time of the Renaissance. He proposed that the increasing interdependency of global societies, combined with the reduction of power differentials between ruling groups, are currently giving rise to integrative figurational changes, that is to say, the chains of interdependency binding individuals to one another are gradually becoming longer and more complex. Elias set out to prove that, if sustained over long periods of time, such integrative figurational changes would lead to significant changes in the social meanings attached to practice, and also in individuals' appraisal and use of emotion. He suggested that, initially, such changes would lead to increased pressures on individuals caught up in complex figurations, such as the members of royal courts, to form strategic alliances rather than resolving disputes through conflict, and that such alliances could often be most safely pursued through the adoption of practices espoused by perceived powerholders. This would lead to pressures on groups to work to maintain such 'exemplary' forms of behaviour among their members and to identify and marginalize members who departed from accepted standards. Elias went on to argue that, over many generations, the policing of such practices would increasingly be carried out through individuals' self-scrutiny, motivated by a need to avoid private feelings of shame, rather than through the scrutiny of the group. In this way, practice would acquire value-laden connotations linked with social approval and so become integral to the construction of human identity. For example, some forms of practice might come to be seen as shameful and so be hidden from public gaze, while others might be promoted publicly as a sign of social status. Elias suggested that such practices would survive within societies long after their origin had been forgotten, creating bodies of shared understanding, or 'social habitus' (Elias' use of this term, as Mennell (1992: 30) notes, appears to predate that of Bourdieu). He also argued that these changes would be associated with other developmental trends, that is to say: individuals' collective or 'we' identity would gradually give way to a heightened sense of individuality or 'I' identity; there would be a corresponding historical shift from an unreflective and emotional stance of 'involvement' to an empathetic and intellectual stance of 'detachment'; individuals' work functions would become increasingly specialized; and old forms of community would begin to break down, leading to the development of specialized communities serving particular social purposes, including communities for residence, leisure and work purposes.

Figurational theory predicts that many social practices would be espoused by powerful or 'established' individuals primarily to create distance between themselves and less powerful, but potentially threatening, 'outsiders'. Since such outsiders would be likely to try to conform to the practices of the powerful, these practices would need to be progressively refined over time, so that the powerful might be enabled to maintain their social advantage. In addition, groups would continually need to find ways of repelling newcomers who tried to gain entry. This exclusion process is explored in Elias' theory of 'established-outsiders relations' (Elias and Scotson, 1994), which shows how established communities might police the practice of their members, and at the same time protect the interests of their power hierarchies, through the use of discursive strategies such as polarized 'praise' and 'blame' gossip, reflecting the social evaluations attached to practice. Even so, given time to organize themselves, it might be expected that outsider groups may eventually 'coalesce' around alternative sources of power and so effectively present further and more problematic challenges to the power of the established. Established-outsiders theory therefore offers a useful means of exploring the conflictive relations of engagement within small groups such as COPs. It has recently been taken further by Dalal (1998, 2002) and Stacey (2001, 2003), whose ideas will now be briefly explored.

Dalal's ideas

Dalal's contribution has been to theorize the building of collective identities, and the ways they come into opposition with one another, by synthesizing the work of Elias with Foulkes' ideas on group relations and Matte-Blanco's analysis of thought processes. He argues that emotions serve to guide individuals towards safety and away from danger, and therefore also to guide individuals towards and away from one another, consequently creating emotional dilemmas linked with attachment. It follows that the categories that individuals construct for themselves to impose order on their social worlds possess emotional valency and, since in Eliasian theory all thought is politicized, such categorizations mirror the ideologies of the powerful. These politicized categorizations are expressed, as 'hidden evaluations', in individuals' use of symbol and so shape their constructed identities. As a result, they are inclined to accept the evaluations of denigration and idealization passed on them by powerful others. Dalal goes on to argue that individuals will try to maintain their subjective sense of charisma by projecting the 'badness' that they do not wish to acknowledge in themselves onto out-group members. However, while powerful members of idealized groups can safely project the 'bad' outside, members of 'outsider' groups find themselves inclined to accept their stigmatization by the powerful. This creates a dilemma for outsiders that they may need to resolve by projecting the 'good' outside and retaining the 'bad' for themselves. Dalal's work would add further weight to the view that in organizations, as elsewhere, subjectively experienced identities are likely to be fragile constructions, in constant need of defence and reassertion. It also shows how individuals' constructed identities can become forms of constraint that shape their subjective interpretation of events, the value they place on one another and the social practices they promote.

Stacey's ideas

In contrast, Stacey's (2001, 2003) contribution has been to explore the ways in which organizational dialogue processes are shaped by their power relations. To do this, he has drawn on the writings of Elias and the symbolic interactionist, G.H. Mead, and also on complexity theory, to explore the ways in which such processes might shape the emergence of practice and therefore lead to outcomes of continuity or change. He argues that the source of innovative practice lies in the diversity of individuals' subjective stances and the consequent ambiguity of all human communication. Novel ideas are therefore deemed to arise from individuals' misunderstanding of one another in the course of everyday conversation. In line with process thinking, Stacey (2003) stresses the unpredictable outcomes of personal development, conceptualizing organizations as self-organized 'complex responsive processes of relating' (Ibid.: 363). He argues that much of an organization's 'evolving relational pattern of meaning and feeling' (Griffin et al., 1998: 331) remains hidden from 'official' scrutiny because established power relations, often reinforced by the reified systems and conventions of organizational practice, do not allow it to be expressed legitimately. However, such 'shadow themes' still find covert expression in organizational dialogue processes, where they will work both to reinforce and undermine 'legitimate' dialogue. Their value for organization development is that they offer alternative forms of meaning that enhance an organization's potential for innovative change and can be drawn on when power relations change sufficiently to allow them to be expressed openly. Stacey and his colleagues recommend the use of facilitated 'free-flowing conversation' (e.g. Griffin et al., 1998; Shaw, 2002) as a means of bringing such ideas to the surface.

■ Discussion

There are obvious similarities between COPT and figurational theory. For example: both privilege the unintended outcomes of learning; both also emphasize the learner's drive to construct a positively referenced identity; both recognize the desire of learners for mutual recognition through the mastery of practice; and both acknowledge the ways in which peer groups can empower and direct learning. However, figurational theory goes beyond Lave and Wenger's account of learning in the depth and breadth of its analysis. In particular, as has been demonstrated here, its capacity to acknowledge both individual and collective agency, and to explore individual's self-conscious subjectivities, makes it well suited to exploring the conflictive dimensions of learning. Consequently, whilst it would acknowledge the value of designed learning environments, such as COPs, as settings for knowledge sharing and innovation, it also allows us to acknowledge and explore conflictive subjectivities both within and beyond their boundaries. While COPT possesses some systemic features (Stacey, 2003), it appears that both forms of theory are sufficiently similar to allow us to use one as a framework for the other. Consequently it becomes possible to offer a figurational analysis of COPs.

When we do this, however, we find that Eliasian theory stresses, not the structural characteristics of practice communities portrayed by COPT, but their fluid and dynamic qualities, as will now be shown.

In Eliasian terms, groups defined by a specific shared practice, such as organizations, professions and COPs, would be regarded as examples of functionally specialized communities. Such communities may serve an obvious utilitarian purpose recognized by their wider society (examples would be formal organizations and professions), or they may have come into being primarily to maintain their members' habitus (hobby groups would fall into this category). They are likely to serve both purposes. For example, organizations with obvious commercial functions will also have implicit 'standards' or 'conventions' of conduct such as 'dress' codes and codes for the conduction of meetings that have developed over many years (Newton, 1996; van Vree, 1999), as well as more explicit conventions that have emerged during the recent life of the community, such as the ways in which staff socialize out of working hours. So far, this account of practice communities has much in common with Lave and Wenger's analysis. However, an Eliasian analysis would also emphasize the ways in which such collectives are bound to one another through complex figurational bonds, and so effectively become inseparable from their wider social world. Consequently, the boundaries of such communities become reifications, serving to keep their 'legitimate' members apart from 'outsiders'.

Elias' interpretation of established-outsiders relations makes it possible to explore the conflictive dimensions of COPs. Figurational theory would predict that such tensions would be present within all identifiable communities, creating pressures for opposition and alliance as their members work to maintain in-group charisma and stigmatize outsiders. Within COPs, such pressures could lead to the marginalizing of some community members and to subjective decisions on the part of others to dis-identify with espoused practices. If power relations permit, they may also lead to the formation of covert, or even overt, sub-groups for whom resistance to the wider collective has become their primary purpose. In a similar way, workplace COPs might come to resist their parent organizations. Here we have a means of explaining the conflictive struggles acknowledged by COPT in ways that are not limited to accounts of economic hegemony. For example, figurational analyses can show how the marginalizing processes of small groups mirror similar tensions in their wider social worlds, as in Dalal's (1998, 2002) studies of racism.

Established-outsiders theory can also be used to acknowledge the tension between continuity and change in ways that go beyond COPT. Eliasian theory would support Lave and Wenger's view that a community's powerholders are likely to have their identities invested in maintaining its established practices.

However, it would suggest that newcomers, too, would seek to identify with such practices, since this would allow them to form alliances with powerholders and demonstrate their eligibility for membership. From an Eliasian perspective, the impetus to change practices would therefore be more likely to come, not from a community's newcomers, as Lave and Wenger suggest, but from its powerholders, who might seek to distinguish themselves from newcomers as a way of upholding their personal charisma. However, though they might wish to make changes, powerholders themselves will be subject to constraint. For example, as Stacey (2003) shows, the figurational tensions within an organization, which would include pressures emanating from beyond its boundaries, and its reified systems and procedures, as well as the opportunistic manoeuvring of managers, would make it difficult for even high-ranking powerholders to support radical changes in practice. Figurational theory therefore offers support for writers such as Swann *et al.* (2002) who suggest that 'cultivated' COPs are likely to be more successful in promoting incremental, rather than radical, changes.

To what extent can the struggles within and between COPs, and other forms of designed learning environment, be controlled and directed by organizations? Dalal (1998) argues that individuals' subjective evaluations of others are largely beyond conscious awareness and therefore become resistant to change. In addition, as the present discussion has shown, an organization's power relations will constrain the ways in which its staff relate to one another. Consequently HRD managers, and others charged with supporting and developing learning communities, are likely to find themselves caught up in complex figurational tensions emanating from all levels of an organization. However, even when organizations work to minimize such struggles, such communities may function in unpredictable and (from an organization's point of view) potentially 'undesirable' ways, since the outcomes of learning are always uncertain. In any event, given Stacey's proposition that opportunities for change lie in misunderstanding, there would seem to be advantages in acknowledging individuals' differing perspectives, and accepting the subjective feelings of discomfort that this causes. This raises the question of how cohesive COPs and other designed learning settings should be permitted to be if they are to work effectively. Allowing members to select themselves, as Wenger recommends (Wenger and Snyder, 2000) would ensure comfortable work relations but, from a figurational perspective, might also reinforce existing power relations and so exclude those individuals most willing and able to invest themselves in change. Structuring such communities in non-hierarchical ways may make it easier for them to work towards change, but a figurational analysis would recognize that asymmetries of power are not confined to formal hierarchies.

And how can HRD managers best approach the task of balancing the demands of the organization with the needs of its employees? Many will instinctively make strategic assessments of the figurational tensions they have to deal with and look for compromise solutions. But figurational theory also has more formal solutions to offer, including structural forms of intervention. For example, Mastenbroek (1991, 1993) offers guidance on organizational design that takes account of figurational uncertainties. Drawing on Lawrence and Lorsch's distinction between 'autonomy' and 'alignment', he explores systemic ways of reconciling individuals' quests for independence with their moves to form alliances with powerholders. Alternatively, as Stacey and his co-workers have shown (Stacey, 2003; Griffin et al., 1998; Shaw, 2002), barriers to change can be countered in some ways through the use of managed dialogue. In their 'free-flowing conversations', consultants act as facilitators to foster safe settings in which individuals' diverse perspectives can be acknowledged and supported, and innovative ideas are allowed to emerge. However, these authors acknowledge that the fostering of such open dialogue must be expected to lead to subjective feelings of discomfort, not only on the part of participants, but also on the part of facilitators. As Griffin et al. (1998: 336) note, the facilitator is not likely to avoid 'a sense of confusion and turbulence'.

Finally, bearing in mind that Lave and Wenger have always acknowledged the conflictive side of practice communities, we need to ask why so much of the academic literature has emphasized the collegial qualities of COPs. Contu and Willmott (2003) argue that this popularization of their ideas can be traced back to Brown and Duguid's (1991) paper, which offers only a selective account of COPT. But there are also other considerations. Firstly, Lave and Wenger's structuralist perspective makes it difficult for them to explore human agency at anything other than a collective level. Secondly, it would seem that their use of the emotive term, 'community', with its lay connotations of harmony and support, will have inevitably encouraged an uncritical response from some sections of the management literature. Perhaps their work would have received a more cautious reception if they had avoided the term altogether and Lave's earlier references to 'settings' of practice had been maintained in their co-authored (1991) text. Thirdly, it is arguable that the literature is simply reflecting the reluctance of much organizational discourse to focus on human 'irrationalities' (Fineman, 2003; Domagalski, 1999). Certainly, figurational theory would suggest that modern human subjectivities, including those of contributors to organizational studies, are likely to be constrained by distaste for 'involvement' and a preference for 'detachment'. The present discussion has attempted to counter this apparent preference for the 'rational' by stressing the value, for both organizations and individuals, of acknowledging and exploring the conflictive dimensions of learning communities.

However, if we are obliged to acknowledge the enabling qualities of conflict, we also need to consider the extent to which ethical values should be used to guide organizational interventions (Snell, 2001; Owenby, 2002). In Miller's words, 'If learning can be sustained only through change, do I not have to risk taking a *moral stance* in relation to possible changes?' (Hoggett, 1992: 136). Hoggett (Ibid.: 166) stresses 'the need for the creative group or movement to contain the capacity to keep questioning itself', and collectively to 'challenge its establishment – its myths, its lies, and its propaganda'. However, it is also necessary to acknowledge the personal risks associated with 'speaking truth to power'. An Eliasian perspective implies that we cannot relinquish our personal responsibility for effecting change, even though debates about values will always carry some personal risk.

■ Summary and conclusions

This discussion has attempted to reintroduce struggle into COPT in ways that go beyond Lave and Wenger's original portrayal of economic and generational tensions. It has been argued here that, by reappraising Lave and Wenger's COPs in figurational terms, it becomes possible both to acknowledge the conflictive subjectivities and agency of their membership, and explore the ways in which wider societal pressures impact on learning. From an Eliasian perspective, the value of promoting collective learning lies in its capacity to capitalize on diversity. Figurational theory also advises us that interventions by organizations, whether designed to maintain existing forms of practice or to identify new ones, must take account of individuals' subjectively-directed pursuit of power opportunities. Such tensions are likely to be present at all levels of an organization's power hierarchy, but it is at the top, and not within their structured learning communities, that the greatest opportunities to promote radical change are likely to lie. Innovation therefore emerges from this discussion as a contested process, dependent on individuals' willingness to depart from the established practices in which their secure identities are invested.

In offering this argument, the discourse of collegiality underpinning much COP literature has been brought into question. From an Eliasian perspective, such collegiality is likely to reflect the diligent policing of practice by its established membership, while subjective experiences of cohesiveness may be expected to mask fear of change. We therefore have to recognize the potentially conflictive qualities of practice communities and the ways in which they serve the purposes of their powerholders. Learning and innovation are not necessarily comfortable for individuals or organizations. However, the discomfort of change needs to be borne, not only by the members of an organization's learning communities, but by its powerholders.

Chapter 11

The learning turn in education and training: liberatory paradigm or oppressive ideology?

Leonard Holmes

▇ Introduction

Over the past couple of decades the discourses of education and training (including the discourse of HRD) whether relating to theory, policy or practice, have been characterized by what we may term the 'learning turn'. In policy documents emanating from government departments and agencies, in practitioner-oriented texts and in academic debates, the use of the terms 'learning' and 'learner' now seems to be *de rigeur*, along with references to 'learning society' and 'lifelong learning'. The use of these terms and related phrases contrasts with the earlier vocabulary: those who were previously referred to as 'trainees', 'students', 'participants' and so on, are now called 'learners'. Whereas formerly reference would be made to 'educational aims', 'training objectives' and so on, such terms have been replaced by the term 'learning outcomes'. Courses are now 'programmes of learning' and libraries are 'learning centres'. Trainers, teachers and lecturers are encouraged to see themselves as 'learning facilitators', who 'manage the learning process'. There has been a pervasive change in the language of education and training, one that has received little critical comment. This chapter aims to engage in a critical examination of this change, this 'learning turn'.

It might be argued that these new terms merely reflect changing style and there is no need to engage in critical examination. However, as we shall see, proponents of what might be viewed as a 'strong' version of the learning turn, what I shall term 'learnerism', clearly view the change of terminology as indicating something more than stylistic. Rather, they argue, a 'new model' (Jessup, 1991), 'new paradigm' (Barr and Tagg, 1995; Field, 2000) has been created, one that is superior to the 'old' model or paradigm. The focus now is not on teaching and training but upon the 'learning process': students/trainees are now referred to as 'learners' and they are to be placed at the centre of the education or training. According to this new model/paradigm, learners naturally know best what they need to learn and how best they can learn; but under the traditional paradigm, that 'natural' ability to learn has been blocked. So, it is argued, teachers, trainers, etc. should concern themselves with 'facilitating' learning, especially by helping learners 'learn how to learn'. Some proponents of this strong version of the learning turn would regard this as a 'critical' approach, whereby learners are 'liberated' from the authoritarianism of 'traditional' teaching and training. This chapter will argue that such ideas are based on faulty reasoning; moreover, far from liberating, they may tend to be oppressive.

It is possible to note a less strong version of the learning turn, in which 'learning' is used as a more convenient term than 'education and training', 'education or training', 'teaching and training' and various other composite phrases. Often, it seems, the term 'learning' is used in such a manner for convenience. Perhaps we are making too much of the change of terminology? However, taking such a view would be to ignore the extent to which language, thought and human action are intertwined. The twentieth century saw significant developments in the study of the nature of language, particularly in philosophy and the social sciences. What was termed 'linguistic philosophy' developed not so much as a *branch* of philosophy (alongside moral philosophy, philosophy of science, metaphysics and so on), as an approach or method of *doing* philosophy. In this approach, close attention was paid to the *use* of language in the way that philosophical problems were presented: by doing so, it was argued, such problems can be solved or, as some would say, dissolved, i.e. rendered as non-problems (Rorty, 1967: 3). As Wittgenstein said in his *Philosophical Investigations* (1953: para. 109):

> 'Philosophy is a battle against the bewitchment of our intelligence by means of language.'

Two key principles of linguistic philosophy will be deployed in this chapter to examine the language of the learning turn, to show how it tends to confuse us, or 'bewitch our intelligence' to use Wittgenstein's evocative phrase. The first principle is to recognize that words or phrases ('learning', etc. in our case here) may have different (although possibly related) meanings in different contexts of use; the second is that such different meanings may be different *types* of concepts such that the logical connections between them may be complex or that no such connection can be validly made.

Within the social sciences, there has been a variety of strands to the increasing focus on language. The sociologist Andreski (1972: 61) warns that 'constant attention to the meaning of terms is indispensable in the study of human affairs, because in this field powerful social forces operate which continuously create verbal confusion.'

But it was not merely 'verbal confusion' that we need beware: there are social consequences from the way that language is used. As feminist and other scholarship from the late 1960s onwards has shown, the way that we use certain forms of language, for example, using 'man' and masculine pronouns when referring to *any* human person, results in certain social forms being taken as normal and any variations being taken as 'deviation'. The insights from a variety of areas of scholarship, including linguistics, literary theory and philosophy, have been taken up by social scientists to engage in new modes of analysis, based on the recognition that the social world is actively produced by human persons through their communicative practices. However, it is argued, such communicative practices do not arise within a 'vacuum', but makes use of 'bodies of already formulated meanings'(Shotter, 1993): that is, in order to communicate with others we have to do so within an existing set of meanings expressed in an existing set of linguistic (or other symbolic) forms. To emphasize the dynamic nature of language-use as a social practice, the term 'discourse' tends to be used by scholars working with such ideas, in various fields of enquiry including psychology (see, for example, Shotter and Gergen, 1989; Edwards and Potter, 1992; Harré and Stearns, 1995) and organization and management theory (see, for example, Grant *et al.*, 1998; Czarniawska, 1998; Thorpe and Holman, 2002; Tietze *et al.*, 2003).

The whole area of discourse theory and approaches to analysis based on such notion of discourse (discourse analysis) is varied and complex. In this chapter, two key ideas will be applied to the discourse of the learning turn. *Interdiscursivity* is the term used to recognize, and make use of, the relationships between forms of discourse: we can make sense of a particular discourse only by drawing upon and relating it to what Shotter (1993) calls 'bodies of already formulated meaning'. The second key idea is that discourses construct and reproduce positions that are both imposed on and taken up by human persons: their *identities* or *subjectivities*. These concern what *kind* of person they are, or are taken to be, with expectations about how they should conduct themselves, what rights they are to be accorded, and their relationships with and to others.

These two separate but related areas of scholarship concerned with language/discourse will be used to sketch a twin critique of certain aspects of the way that the discourse of education and training has developed from the learning turn. Firstly, using the principles of linguistic philosophy indicated above, the discourse of the learning turn will be examined as *rational discourse*, i.e. its logical and conceptual validity will be critically examined. Considered in this

223

way, the 'learning paradigm' will be shown to have serious conceptual problems, such that its claim to rationality must be rejected. Secondly, using the discourse analytical ideas outlined above, we shall examine the discourse as *ideological* in character, that is, as part of the social practices by which language constructs and reproduces reality. Such socially constructed and reproduced reality includes identities and social relations. Analyzing in these terms, it will be argued, leads us to the conclusion that, far from being emancipatory, as its proponents would claim, the discourse of the learning turn has oppressive tendencies.

■ Learning: the new paradigm?

The ways in which the learning turn is expressed may be viewed on a continuum. At one end, the 'weak' form of the learning turn may be seen in discourse adopting the vocabulary of learning merely as a change of style and fashion: the single word 'learning' used in place of more cumbersome phraseology such as 'education and training', or 'education, training and development'. A 'stronger' form is that where the learning turn is presented as a new model (Jessup, 1991) or new paradigm of education and training (Barr and Tagg, 1995; Field, 2000), and/or assertively engaged in a 'campaign for learning' (RSA, 1996). Discussing 'the new educational order' Field (2000) states that

> 'a paradigm shift is taking place, away from the ideas of teaching and training and towards the concept of learning.'

The authors of one textbook on management development (Woodall and Winstanley, 1998) assert that

> 'The last 20 years have witnessed a transition from management *training* to management *learning*.'

Honey (1998), in introducing a 'declaration on learning', a statement agreed upon by what he termed 'some of the UK's leading authorities on learning in organizations', states that

> 'Few can seriously doubt that learning has come of age.'

According to that 'declaration', learning is 'the central issue for the 21st century' – an assertion that seems highly questionable in the context of issues such as the HIV/AIDS crisis, global warming, poor country indebtedness, and the political and military security problems arising from new forms of terrorism.

The above examples, and a host of others that could be mentioned, illustrate that the discursive shift from education and training to learning is generally taken to be significant, that it is a substantive change in conceptualization rather than one merely of style. Central and fundamental to that new conceptualization, the purported new model or paradigm, are two key concepts: the *learning process* and the *learner*.

The *learning process* is treated as if it were a naturally occurring phenomenon and amenable to empirical analysis. This process purportedly results in (i.e. causes) learning outcomes, which were traditionally referred to as knowledge, skills and attitudes, but are often now collectively referred to as 'competencies' or 'capabilities'. According to this new conceptualization, this new paradigm, the learning process itself may be considered in *abstracted* terms, free of context and of content. Such abstracted representations of the process are depicted in various models, the most famous probably being the Kolb experiential learning cycle (Kolb, 1984), which itself is often presented in a modified form that arguably distorts Kolb's original presentation. Whatever the model presented, the assumption is that by understanding better this (purported) generalized process of learning, we may apply that understanding to improve the effectiveness and efficiency of the accomplishment of the process.

The second key concept, 'the *learner*', locates the learning process within individual persons, monadic entities, capable of actively engaging in and managing their learning, rather than being merely passive in respect of the learning process. They are ascribed the identity of 'learner' where this term is taken as a nominal, i.e. a do-*er* of learning, rather than as adjectival (e.g. as in 'learner driver'). Learners, as particular types of persons, may engage in the learning process as an *activity*, one in which they may engage more effectively by 'learning how to learn'. This emphasis upon the individual learner is central to what we might regard as the strongest form of discourse following the learning turn, what we might term 'learnerism' or the 'learnerist paradigm'.

Proponents of learnerism present learning as unquestionably, self-evidently good, both enjoyable and rewarding (Honey, 1998). So, they argue, there is a need to encourage everyone to become active and lifelong learners. For example, David Blunkett, who was the UK Secretary of State for Education and Employment in 1998, wrote in his foreword to the government consultation paper on lifelong learning:

> 'To realize our ambition, we must develop and sustain a regard for learning at whatever age. For many people this will mean overcoming past experiences which have put them off learning.'
>
> (Department for Education and Employment, 1998a)

According to learnerism, only the individual learner should determine what they should learn, decide how to learn, and judge the effectiveness and value of learning, based on personal experience and personal preferences. However, according to advocates of learnerism, there is a problem for many people: their capacity and motivation to learn has been stultified because learning has become associated too much with formal education and training. This contrasts, they argue, with the 'natural' condition of humans, one in which learning spontaneously occurs as naturally as breathing. So, according to Senge (1990):

> '[d]eep down, we are all learners. No one has to teach an infant to learn. In fact, no one has to teach infants anything. They are intrinsically inquisitive, masterful learners who learn to walk, speak, and pretty much run their households all on their own.'[1]

The vice-chancellor of one UK university expressed a similar view, asserting that

> '[s]tudents are not empty vessels to be filled with facts, but active, enquiring human beings whose natural curiosity we must harvest. More importantly, we need to redefine our jobs. We academics are not here to teach students, but to show them how to learn.'
>
> (Schwartz, 2002)

Richard Reeves, who was Director of Futures at the Industrial Society, in his column for the *Guardian* newspaper on 20 February 2001, wrote that

> 'The only skill we really need is the ability to learn. And we do that best on the job, not in class. [...]
>
> Today, ... we cannot move for teachers of one sort or another – personal trainers, mentors, gurus, consultants. [...] Yet real learning remains a deeply personal experience, and an everyday activity. [...] We learn best from doing, rather than listening.'

In practice, there tends to be a blending together of the different forms of the discourse of learning, the 'weak' form where the term 'learning' is used as a single term to cover education, training and development, and the 'strong' form of learnerism. So we may often find a statement expressing a 'learnerist' view within a text which appears to adopt a more cautious and considered approach. Even many closely-argued academic texts are not immune to generalized statements about the 'naturalness' of learning. Policy and policy-advocacy documents, such as the UK government's consultation document on lifelong learning (Department for Education and Employment, 1998a) or the report of the National Committee of Inquiry into Higher Education (1997) combine both polemic and reasoned argument. Unless we are alert to these different uses we may fall prey to rhetoric masquerading as rational discourse.

■ The learning paradigm as rational discourse: conceptual analysis of learning

The many meanings of learning

As such views are presented as *rational* discourse, we may treat them as amenable to critical examination on the basis of the conceptual soundness of the key ideas and of the empirical grounds for accepting the claims made. On both counts, the learning paradigm may be shown to be flawed. Both of the key concepts referred to above, learning as a process and the individual as the locus for learning (the learner), will be shown to be highly problematic.

In textbook discussions of learning, the question is often posed: what is learning? This question is typically answered with a definition that is some variation on the notion of learning as a more-or-less permanent change of behaviour resulting from experience, with a reference to texts by Borger and Seaborne (1966) or Bass and Vaughan (1966). These definitional approaches tend to make the crucial assumption that the term 'learning' refers to, or denotes, a singular phenomenon. Thus, following presentation of a number of examples of what they refer to as 'learning', Borger and Seaborne (1966: 12, emphasis added) ask:

'What is it... that makes us use the same word "learning" in every case? What is *the common feature*?

Even Kolb, who provides a slightly different approach, presents a singular definitional denotation (1984: 38):

'Learning is *the process* whereby knowledge is created through the transformation of experience.'

Other writers turn to various dictionaries to provide definitions. Yet we surely need to ask some searching questions before accepting such definitional approaches. Firstly, quite simply, we might ask why it is necessary to engage in such attempts to define such a commonly used term. Presumably it is because the term 'learning' is to be used as a key technical concept. This should alert us to the problems that arise, as the philosopher Gilbert Ryle (1954) pointed out, when we adopt as a *technical* concept a term that is commonly used as an *untechnical* concept, i.e. in everyday, mundane conversation. As a technical concept, such a term carries 'theoretical luggage', i.e. it has meaning only within a particular theoretical framework and this meaning may be significantly different from the ordinary untechnical meaning of the term.

Secondly, two further questions arise:

1 Does the term 'learning' have a single meaning?
2 Is the meaning of learning denotational, i.e. does it *refer* to some empirical or hypothetical reality?

If we consider the variety of forms of discourse in which the term 'learning' is used, serious doubts must arise with regard to the first question. Amongst those forms of discourse are everyday mundane interaction and conversation, where the term is used as an untechnical concept, and a variety of discourses where the term is used as a technical concept, for example:

- in the arena of education and training;
- in professional and academic psychology;
- in the management of employees within work organizations, including their selection and appraisal;
- in the management of such organizations themselves;
- in the political–economic arena (Holmes, 2000).

Rather than assume that these uses are synonymous and search for (or simply impose) a singular meaning, we should begin by allowing the possibility of *systematic ambiguity*, where the meaning may be stable *within* any particular form of discourse but may differ *between* different forms of discourse (Ibid.). We should heed Wittgenstein's warning about the 'bewitchment of our intelligence by means of language', and 'look and see' how the term 'learning' is used in different contexts (or 'language games') (Wittgenstein, 1953). In particular, we should note the difference between the *explanatory* use of the term in psychological discourse, and its *evaluative* use in educational and training discourse (Holmes, 2001a).

Uses of 'learning': explanation v. evaluation

The concept of learning has been central to the development of psychology as a scientific discipline over the past century. Indeed, for a period in the first half of the twentieth century, the behaviourist or conditioning theory approach to psychology was often referred to as 'learning theory'. The purpose of the concept is to try to explain why particular non-instinctual patterns of behaviour occur in animals and humans. According to these psychological accounts, behavioural patterns are the result of a learning *process*, and the hypothetico-deductive and empiricist protocols of natural science may be deployed to analyze and explain that process. The nature of that analysis and explanation differs between different 'schools of thought' or paradigms within psychology, the dominant ones being conditioning theory and cognitivism. The assumption is that *any and every* behavioural pattern may be explained by reference to some theory of learning, although, of course, the explanation may differ between different theories.

In the sense discussed above, learning is treated as *natural* and regarded as subject to discoverable natural laws. We should note, however, that on this basis we can make no distinction between learning that is deemed 'good', 'worthwhile', 'true' and so on from learning that is deemed 'bad', 'worthless', 'false'. These expressions are *normative*: they are used to make judgements and *evaluations*. They imply a different use of the term 'learning', a different conceptualization. Critically, such use and conceptualization are central to educational and training discourse, where learning is an *evaluative* concept. There cannot, therefore, be *a* (or *the*) learning process, for natural processes are of a logically different kind from processes by which normative judgements come about.

The assumptions within learnerism that the concept of learning has singular reference to a natural process and that learning is unequivocally good, gives rise to paradoxes which may be resolved when we distinguish between explanatory and evaluative conceptualizations of learning. One key question is whether or not it is possible to learn something that is factually wrong or practically ineffective (or worse). For example, can someone learn that arsenic is an effective treatment for tuberculosis or that the sun, stars and planets move around the stationary earth? Certainly we can say that people in the past have held such a view about the astronomical phenomena and that medical practitioners have used the highly poisonous arsenic to treat tuberculosis and various other diseases. The explanatory use of the concept of learning would have no problem with accepting that these are examples of learning. Yet if an applicant for a post as a NASA scientist expressed such a view about the sun and earth, or if a trainee doctor prescribed arsenic as an effective treatment, these views would not be accepted as indicating that valid learning had taken place. Any assertion that learning is good, worthwhile, to be valued, is of a different *logical type* from a statement that learning is natural; to conflate the two is to commit what philosophers term a category mistake (Ryle, 1949).

◼ A logical analysis of learning

Some may argue, in response, that the difference in use, and therefore of meaning, presents no insurmountable problem here and that both meanings can be allowed for as follows. The normative use of the term applies to judgements about what *should* be learned by an individual or set of individuals. Once such judgements are made, the explanatory theories of learning may then be drawn upon to devise some method by which the desired learning can be effectively achieved. Later, the effectiveness by which the learning is achieved forms part of the criteria for normative judgement, what is termed 'evaluation'. In this way, the insights gained through the (scientific) study of learning, conceived as a natural process, may be put to use in bringing about desirable learning.

Unfortunately for those who would make such an argument, this response rests on the assumption that the concept of learning as a natural process is of a logical type that not only allows for *post hoc* causal explanation but also permits the bringing about of specifiable *outcomes*. But what would we mean by such 'outcomes'? If we are talking of knowledge, skills and attitudes, or of competencies and capabilities, then we are clearly *not* referring to empirically observable phenomena. These terms are also examples of what can be both referred to as 'untechnical concepts' (when used in mundane discourse) and 'technical concepts' (when used in psychological and pedagogic discourses) (Ryle, 1954). As technical concepts, because of the 'theoretical luggage' they bring with them, their meaning can only be ascertained in relation to the theories in which they play a role. To proceed on the assumption that meaning remains stable across these different discourses is to risk intellectual confusion.

In scientific psychological discourse, the concept of learning outcomes would normally be associated with empirical criteria relating to *observable behaviour*. This may be relatively easy in the case of observation of animal behaviour in experimental settings; but this is highly problematic in respect of human behaviour. Whilst human beings certainly engage in some physical behaviours that may be considered in the same terms as animal behaviour for psychological experimentation, what we would normally regard as characteristically *human* behaviour cannot be understood solely in terms of what is observable. We must also take account of its *meaning*, to the person whose behaviour is under consideration *and to others* in the social context within which the behaviour is of significance. This has long been recognized within philosophy. Hamlyn (1953) draws upon Aristotle's distinction between *kinesis* (translated by Hamlyn as 'movement') and *energeia* (translated as 'activity'); whilst the former may, sometimes, be analyzed and explained solely in causal terms, the latter must always be understood in terms of the actor's reasons. Harré and Secord (1972) draw a threefold distinction: movements, actions and acts. A movement or set of movements has meaning only insofar as it is intended by an actor, and is taken by others, to form meaningful action in the performance of an act, as, for example, when holding up an arm may be an intentional action in hailing a taxi (or waving goodbye or making a bid at an auction). Thus the relationship between an action and an associated act is not one of cause and effect but of social convention. As any proper account of human behaviour cannot be limited to one of cause and effect, but must include actor intention within a normative order, the relationship between what are termed 'learning process' and 'learning outcome' becomes problematic.

Of course, the concepts of the learning process and of learning outcomes do have a certain face validity. We are all aware of things that we know and understand *now*, and things we can do *now*, but which we did not know or could not do at some *earlier point in life*. So we might say that the concept of the learning process surely refers to the process by which we came to know or be able to do those things, and that the concept of learning outcomes refers to the states that are the end results of that process. However, these conclusions do not necessarily follow. Wittgenstein (1953: 308) points out that

'[we] talk of processes and states and leave their nature undecided. Sometime perhaps we shall know more about them – we think. But that is just what commits us to a particular way of looking at the matter.'

The particular way of looking at the matter here is that expressions of the form 'P has learnt (to) X' (e.g. 'Jane has learned to swim') describe some state of affairs. However, as the linguistic philosophy tradition of Wittgenstein, Austin, Ryle and others variously showed, description is only one possible *logical* function of sentences whose *grammatical* form is an indicative statement. Ryle (1949), subjects to conceptual analysis the kinds of utterances that are concerned with a person's abilities and dispositions. These, he argues, are not *descriptions* about states of affairs that exist *within* the person, in some Cartesian non-material realm, but rather serve as semi-hypotheticals to license assertions about how we expect or anticipate how that person would behave under certain (possibly undetermined) circumstances. This analysis may certainly be applied to statements which would normally be categorized as statements of 'learning outcomes' (Holmes, 1998). *A fortiori*, in contexts where a statement that someone has 'achieved' certain 'learning outcomes', Austin's notion *verdictives* as a category of performative utterances may be considered (Austin, 1962). Verdictives are those utterances (and by extension, writings) that deliver a finding or judgement, and their perlocutionary effect may be to permit the individual concerned to receive certain benefits. So to state that P has achieved certain learning outcomes may serve to permit the award of a qualification, and/or entry to an occupation or position (Holmes, 2001b). An alternative way of putting this is that learning outcome expressions provide *warranting discourse* (Draper, 1988; Toulmin, 1958) in educational and related contexts (Holmes, 2001b).

The concept of the learning process can be examined in a similar fashion. In Ryle's (1949) analysis, an expression of the form 'P is learning X' is not a description of an activity being undertaken by P, i.e. 'to learn' is not a *task* verb. Rather, it is better viewed as an *achievement* or *'success'* verb, similar to words such as 'win', 'find', 'cure', 'prove' and so on. Saying that S is winning a race is not to describe some additional activity to that of running the race, but rather to say that they are running it in such a way that a certain outcome (that they will win) may be anticipated. Similarly, to say that P is learning X is to say that they are undertaking a certain activity or activities such that we may anticipate that the activities will result in a situation where we would say that they have learnt (Holmes, 1998). We have a range of task or activity terms relating to learning as an achievement word: 'study', 'read', 'practise', 'rehearse', 'have a go at', 'think about', 'watch and copy', and so on. We also have terms such as 'being taught', being shown', 'receiving instruction', etc. The displacement of such well-established terms by the use of the verb 'to learn' as an activity tends to lead to conceptual confusion.

The analysis above may be considered in empirical terms. If we ask what empirical evidence may be adduced to demonstrate that learning outcomes have been achieved, we find that there is *no* evidence apart from specific, situated observations of performance or behaviour. However, as noted above, human behaviour cannot be objectively observed but requires interpretation as performance-of-a-kind. Moreover, to say that someone has learnt implies that we expect or anticipate that, if called upon, the person would be able to perform in like manner in the future, i.e. in situations about which by definition we have not made empirical observations. Any evidence we currently have, which itself has been subject to interpretation, usually provides the grounds for warranting judgements expressed as statements that learning has occurred and warranting consequential decisions (e.g. award of qualifications, appointment to a job) (Holmes, 2002). The concept of the learning process presents particular problems in respect of empirical reference: there is nothing amenable to observation that we can say is evidence of such a *process*. That is, there is no empirical observation that we can make over a continuous period of time that would constitute observation of learning taking place. The analogy is sometimes made with breathing, to suggest that learning is natural: but clearly the analogy fails.

◼ Ideological aspects of the learning turn

It is clear that, despite the *logical* problems discussed above, the discourse of the learning turn has persuasive power. We shall, therefore, now turn to consideration of that discourse in terms of how it serves to produce and reproduce aspects of what is taken to be reality, i.e. as *ideological discourse*. Of course, all discourse may be viewed as ideological in terms of what Mannheim called the 'total conception of ideology' (Mannheim, 1936), i.e. whatever can be meaningfully said is always located within some system of ideas, a shared understanding of what is real, valid, true and so on. More strongly, whilst avoiding the simplistic notion of ideology as 'false consciousness', the term 'ideological' draws our attention to the *way* that discourse functions in promoting or undermining the different interests of different social groups. Recent developments in the theory of ideology have taken a *discursive* approach (Thompson, 1984; Dant, 1991; van Dijk, 1998), focusing on *how* language and other forms of symbolic representation construct and reproduce the social world. That is, a discursive approach enables the analysis of ideology not merely in abstract terms ('ideas') but in terms of the empirical form it takes in texts, speech and other symbolic forms.

In this part of the paper we shall adopt such a discursive approach to examine in particular how learning has become constructed as an 'object of knowledge' within the discourse of education and training. Firstly, we shall examine how discursive processes produce a particular *meaning* of the term 'learning', especially in relation to related terms such as 'education' and 'training'. Such meanings carry normative force, indicating what sort of behaviour is permissible, appropriate, effective and so on; and, by implication, alternative behaviour is to be regarded as not permitted, inappropriate, ineffective, etc. Secondly, we shall examine how such processes set up and treat people as being certain kinds-of-persons, i.e. as having certain identities or subjectivities, with certain obligations, expected to behave in certain types of ways.

Interdiscursivity and exchange of meaning

How then might we attempt to examine ideological character of the learning turn within the discourse of education and training? To put it another way, how has learning as an *'object of knowledge'* been constructed by discursive processes? To understand this we might fruitfully compare it with the case of the rise of the competence movement in the early 1990s, which appeared to be 'irresistible' despite considerable criticism of the validity of the claims made for the competence approach (Holmes, 1995). An explanation can be found, arguably, in terms of the concepts of interdiscursivity or intertextuality, i.e. that our understanding of any particular discourse relies upon the understandings we already have from other forms of discourses, i.e. 'bodies of already formulated meanings' (Shotter, 1993). In the case of the discourse of competence, we can identity such 'bodies of already formulated meanings', in four areas (Holmes, 1995):

1 political intervention by government;
2 the administrative processes adopted by state (and quasi-state) agencies in translating policy into programmatic activity;
3 employment practices within organizations;
4 the processes and practices within educational institutions and agencies.

The 'discursive convergence' based on the key term 'competence' may, it is suggested here, be seen to have widened to give rise to the new discourse of learning (Holmes, 2001b). We might add, to the discourse domains indicated above, that of academic discourse on education and training, particularly where based in humanistic and andragogical perspectives.

We should note that the *rhetorical* presentation of the case for the learning turn often relies upon claims about both its liberatory/emancipatory and its pragmatic potential. Didactic modes of education and training are, it is claimed, characterized by exclusiveness, authoritarianism and oppressiveness. In contrast, the 'new paradigm' of the learning turn is said to be inclusive and 'democratic', as having empowering potential. Instead of being the passive recipients of what others have decided should be learned and how, learners would be set free to determine for themselves what and how they learn. Personal experience is privileged over the knowledge presented by others, and the naturally-occurring learning process, unimpeded by the distorting influence of authoritarian imposition, would ensure that the outcomes meet with the 'real world' needs of learners. The fast-moving nature of life in the 21st century world makes such a move imperative, it is argued, as 'old-world' knowledge rapidly becomes redundant: learning will need to be a lifelong process, and the individual learner will be at the centre. We should note, in particular, that a number of discursive themes are at work here: 'naturalness', 'individualism', 'empowerment', 'inclusiveness', 'democratic'. These terms have strong positive connotations in contemporary Western (particularly Anglophone) society.

We may examine how certain meanings are constructed within texts on learning by considering how certain terms, individual words and phrases, are exchanged with or replaced by others, either as equivalents or as negations (Dant, 1991). Here is one example, taken from the beginning of the document which launched the RSA's Campaign for Learning:

> 'Our purpose is to enable every person to develop their human potential as fully as possible by means of lifelong learning. This is because in the 21st century those individuals who do not practise lifelong learning will not find work [...] Learning pays. In a world which increasingly rewards learning, it provides economic, social and personal benefits which are, in principle, available to all.'
>
> (Ball, 1996)

Note the use of the phrase 'to enable every person to develop their human potential', carrying the unstated implication that the alternative (to agreement with the Campaign) is to *prevent* people from developing their potential. Note also how 'learning' and 'lifelong learning' are treated as equivalent, such that individuals can (and, by implication, ought to) *practise* lifelong learning.

The author of the text goes on to discuss what he means by the word 'learning', which (Ibid.: 2)

> 'is not intended to be synonymous with conventional education and training. Far from that. [...] Learning includes the products of both education and training, the processes of both formal and informal learning, and the various types of learning: skills, knowledge, understanding, experience, attitude, values. Most importantly, it shifts the emphasis from the activities of the teacher or trainer towards the development of the student.'

'Learning' is thus not equivalent to 'conventional education and training', which is thereby marginalized. We may note that the term 'conventional' is itself not explicated. We thus have the setting up the equivalence:

education and training = conventional education and training and so the negation:

learning ≠ education and training

The final sentence in the selected text sets up the equivalence

emphasis in education and training = emphasis on the activities of the teacher or trainer

By examining the actual texts that present learning discourse in order to iden-tify the manner in which such equivalences and negations are set up, we might thereby identify *how* such discourse achieves its effects.

The key term 'experience' may be subject to such discourse analysis: the term has central place in the discourse of the learning turn. We may thus note, in the above quotation, how the word is included in the list of 'various types of learning', so presenting experience as equivalent to those others listed as a 'type of learning'. More generally, the discourse of the learning paradigm, and particularly learnerism, sets up an equivalence between '*learning from or through experience*' and '*experiential learning*' as a *type* of learning. Often such references to experience are supported by citation of the work of Kolb (1984), whose model of the 'experiential learning cycle' is presented as a *fac-tual* description of 'how people learn'. However, examination of such texts, including Kolb's, shows that the term 'experience' appears to be used in *two different ways*. Kolb opens his first chapter with a quotation from Dewey about 'inner experience' as 'a realm of purely personal events' (Dewey, 1958). The next reference to experience is on the second page (Kolb, 1984: 2; empha-sis added):

'this learning process must be reimbued with the texture and feeling of human *expe-riences* shared and interpreted through dialogues with one another.'

Then, in chapter 2 which has the title 'The process of experiential learning', Kolb presents the 'Lewinian Experiential Model', through which learning is conceived as a four-stage cycle in which (Ibid.: 21, emphasis in original)

'Immediate concrete experience is the basis for observation and reflection. [...] its empha-sis [is] on *here-and-now concrete experience* to validate and test abstract concepts.'

Further on, he states that (Ibid.: 27: emphasis added)

'Knowledge is continuously derived and tested out in the *experiences* of the learner.'

The early use of the term 'experience' refers to what is diffuse and generalized, whereas the later use refers to something focused and specific. In the earlier usage, 'experience' is a non-count noun, whilst the later usage is as a count noun ('an experience', 'experiences'). Generally, later re-presentations of the Kolb model use the latter sense: a person has *an* experience, on which they

235

reflect, etc. Experience in a generalized sense is thereby treated as equivalent to the *set of separate, discrete experiences*. Moreover, such separate experiences are treated as having independent existence, such that they can be 'observed' and 'reflected on'. 'Learning from experience' as a continuous state of being is thereby elided with 'learning from experiences' as separate, discrete events that happen. Whilst proponents of learnerism may hold such a view of 'experience'/ 'experiences' equivalence, they do not do so: the equivalence is produced as a discursive effect.

Subjectivities and identities

A further aspect of the discourse of learning that we may consider is that of the way that certain identities or subjectivities are 'interpellated' (Althusser, 1971), that is, set up and evoked by the discourse. The main identity is that of the 'learner', represented as inherently, i.e. naturally, capable of engaging in what is regarded as the activity of learning. Critically, this subjectivity is instantiated solely in terms of 'the learning process': the person is separated from any social relationships and social structures. Issues of class, gender, ethnicity and so on are, in effect, by their absence from the discourse, treated as irrelevant. Because 'individuals who do not practise lifelong learning will not find work', as Ball puts it (quoted above), and because the benefits from learning are open to all who engage in learning, the identity of learner carries moral force. If you do not accept the need to engage in the learning process, then any failure to reap the benefit is your own fault; and by rhetorical implication, if you fail to gain the personal, social and economic benefits, that is because you failed to learn. In many ways, the social Darwinist rhetoric of the late 19th century may be seen as having a latter-day reflection in the discourse of the learning turn.

A second identity constructed by the learning discourse is that of the teacher or trainer, a type of person who is now seen as a key participant in what are now condemned as the outmoded, oppressive practices of education/training. Redemption from such condemnation may be gained by a change of subjectivity to that of 'facilitating' learning. Through various discursive practices, teachers are encouraged to demonstrate that they are embracing this new identity and rejecting the old one. In many universities, in the UK and elsewhere, course or module descriptions require the presentation of 'learning outcomes' and 'learning strategy', and assessment details are to be presented in a form that relates to the 'learning outcomes', often enumerated as if they referred to discrete entities. Anyone who becomes a new teacher in a university will now normally be required to undergo some form of initial programme, usually carrying a title with the phrase 'learning and teaching in higher education'. In the UK, such a programme will now be accredited by the Higher Education Academy, formerly by the Institute for Learning and Teaching in Higher

Education. In order to successfully complete and pass such a programme, which is often a condition for continued employment within teaching at the particular university, the new teacher will be assessed by a 'portfolio' in which they are required to 'reflect on' their attempts to 'facilitate learning'. A new generation of university teachers is being socialized through such programmes into a system in which the notion of the learning process is central. Within this system, it is assumed that if the new teachers are successful in becoming good 'facilitators of learning', and if the students (now 'learners') play their part by engaging in active learning, then higher education will be successful. Other matters previously considered important are thus marginalized, matters such as the provision of appropriate resources, student access to finance, social and educational conditions experienced prior to university entrance, and the inequitable field of post-graduation employment opportunity.

Beyond the learning paradigm

The considerations present above, albeit sketchily, indicate a need to move beyond the individualistic, psychologistic representations of the phenomena addressed by notions of learning, education and training. Greater recognition is required that these phenomena are social in character and due recognition must be given to their situated nature. Approaches to situated learning theory, particularly the legitimate peripheral participation approach of Lave and Wenger (1991) are gaining in recognition: however, there is a tendency to present such an approach as a *corrective supplement* to conventional presentations. Their contribution is thus limited to the supposed need to *include* 'social factors'. This is not sufficient to address the problems with the learning paradigm as discussed above.

Instead of considering learning as a phenomenon in its own right, albeit 'taking place' in social contexts, we need to examine the social processes by which the discourse of learning constructs identity and reproduces social practices (Holmes, 2001b). This requires us to recognize that learning as a concept in education and training does not refer to an empirical phenomenon and so cannot be understood through empirical analysis. Rather, we need to examine how various social processes are intimately connected with the trajectories of individual human beings through the kinds-of-persons that are afforded in contemporary and emerging society, and with the social practices that are salient in the particular social contexts for such kinds-of-persons. By such examination we may avoid the corruption of the emancipatory potential of the discourse of learning.

A key first step we must take is to take greater care over the language we use. Whenever we are inclined or tempted to use the words 'learn', learning', 'learner', etc., and phrases including such words, we should ask ourselves whether we do indeed mean those words and phrases. Do we really mean 'learning outcomes', or should we say '*intended* (or *required*) 'learning outcomes'? The latter expression is both logically preferable (outcomes cannot come before the event producing them, i.e. the training or educational programme) and raises the issue of *who* intends or requires such outcomes. Similarly, why should we refer to people as 'learners' in a generalized manner (as opposed to using the term in specific combinations, as in 'learner-driver')? Why not 'participants' (on a training programme) and 'students'? As for 'learning facilitator', 'manager of learning', and so on, how exactly are such terms an improvement over more traditional terms? I am not suggesting necessarily that such terms be eradicated completely, but that they should be used with caution and only after careful thought. Of course, the term 'human resource development' is itself one that is being debated on a similar basis.

More importantly, the conceptualization of learning needs (perhaps, urgent) attention from *within* the fields of HRD, training and education, rather than the theorization of learning being imported from dominant traditions within psychology. Newer approaches within psychology (see, for example, Smith *et al.*, 1995; Gergen, 1999; Harré and van Langenhove, 1999), particularly those taking a discourse or similar approach (Shotter, 1993; Harré and Gillet, 1994), offer different and potentially fruitful ways to reconsider how we might understand what is going on in those essentially *social* situations in which we are engaged as educational and training practitioners. Social situations are inescapably ones in which there is the ever-present possibility of differences and contestation between the people engaged, including contestation over what is right, proper, valid and so on. Questions thus arise over not only *how* such differences and contestation might be avoided or resolved, but also *whether* this is possible. Such questions go directly to issues of power, issues that have already been raised within critical perspectives (e.g. Vince, 1996; Raab, 1997; Reynolds, 1998). The key point that arises from the arguments presented in this chapter is that such issues are intrinsic to an evaluative conceptualization of learning, but may be masked by the failure to differentiate such a conceptualization from the explanatory conceptualization that is inappropriate to education and training contexts. The discourse of learning may yet have emancipatory potential, but only if it is deployed in a more critical manner than hitherto.

Notes

1 Senge is quite wrong. Human infants learn to talk, walk, feed themselves *with the help of other humans*. The fate of feral children, abandoned in infancy and raised by wild animals, clearly demonstrates this simple fact, one that can seen in the everyday interactions between parents and their infant children, in 'baby talk', holding them upright to 'pretend walk' and so on.

Chapter 12

Going beyond a critical turn: hypocrisies and contradictions

Kiran Trehan, Clare Rigg and Jim Stewart

■ Introduction

Critical HRD occupies some interesting educational territory. Given the rapid pace of development and innovation in education and in the practice of HRD, coupled with alternative approaches to learning, a re-evaluation of critical HRD might be expected to be a prominent feature within discussions of the future practice of HRD.

However, whilst there has been a growing demand in the academic literature of the past few years for management educators to engage more critically with their subject than has been the tradition in business schools, the case has been argued for strengthening the critical perspectives in contributory disciplines within management (Reynolds, 1999; Alvesson and Willmot, 1996), and for a revision of management more generally (French and Grey, 1996). Yet, while examples of critical pedagogies are accumulating, they seldom exhibit corresponding changes in HRD practices. Where critical HRD does depart from mainstream practices, alternatives are typically based on humanistic student-centred aspirations for social equality, rather than on an analysis of HRD in terms of power, politics, social dynamics and emotions.

The intention of this chapter is firstly to review the aspirations and threats of critical HRD and secondly to explore what going beyond a critical turn means for theory and practice. In doing so we hope to illuminate the quietly spoken aspects of critical HRD as a backdrop for unveiling the hypocrisies and contradictions of engaging in critical HRD.

■ What is critical HRD?

Critical HRD is a multi-perspectival construct. A growing body of theoretical knowledge is emerging that purports to illuminate the importance of critical HRD. McGuire *et al.* (2005) argue that the field within which critical HRD exists remains segmented. Whilst alternative approaches, models and theories offer interesting perspective on the different components of HRD, the theoretical base still highlights difficulties for academics and practitioners in attempting to define boundaries and delineate practices. The disputed, untidy and overlapping fields of HRD and critical HRD have, it seems, had few definite or agreed foundations. However, if HRD practitioners are to make a significant contribution to the success of their organizations, in whatever way that success might be defined, they will need to understand and respond to these disorientating changes in the contemporary condition. Paradoxically, some of these changes may actually lead to greater freedom to interpret the role/purpose of critical HR educators/developers and increase their potential to influence the strategic direction of organizations. Rigg and Trehan (2005) argue that critical approaches to HRD engage participants in a process of drawing from critical perspectives to make connections between their learning and work experience. Critical HRD is of increasing importance to the area of business and development, given its focus on how the comparatively abstract ideas of critical approaches can be mobilized and applied in the process of understanding and changing interpersonal and institutional practice.

In the Introduction we argued that a key rationale for encouraging HRD managers to be critically reflective lies in the realization of how powerful managers now are in the world, yet how poorly traditional HRD education has prepared them for considering questions of power and responsibility. Alvesson and Willmott argue (1992) that the practice of management has a dominant effect on the lives of an organization's employees, its customers and wider society.

Clearly, given the rationales advanced for critical HRD, the hopes of its proponents have been concerned with transforming society and making it more democratic or emancipatory. Key to this has been that through education individuals become conscious of the oppression of or constrains on their lives and take action to change that for the better. It is clear that critical HRD is qualitatively different from the concept of HRD. HRD focuses on the immediate, presenting details of a task or problem while critical HRD involves an analysis of power and control and an examination of the taken-for-granteds within which the issues are situated. The potential for critical HRD derives from the tensions, contradictions, emotions and power dynamics that inevitably exist in managers' lives. Critical HRD as a pedagogical approach emerges when these dynamics are treated centrally as a site of learning about managing and organizing. McLaughlin and Thorpe (1993: 25) argue:

'At the level of their own expertise, managers undertaking critical reflection can come to know themselves and their organization much better. In particular they can become aware of the primacy of politics, both macro and micro, and the influence of power on decision making and non-decision making, not to mention the "mobilization of bias".'

Thus critical approaches to HRD claim to offer innovative and challenging perspectives, which unveil functionalist and performative approaches that fail to address the wider social, political, emotional and psychodynamic context in which HRD is organized.

Exploring critical HRD

Critical HRD has emerged as a field that goes beyond ideas of traditional HRD education. Burgoyne and Reynolds (1997) see, as central to it, an emphasis on understanding the whole person as mediated through experience, thus paying attention to a more connectedness to daily personal and professional life. Also, by avoiding the passivity thought to be associated with more conventional HRD methods, critical approaches offer more opportunity for development than seemed possible in focusing exclusively on the acquisitions of knowledge and skills.

In this sense, a basis of critical HRD has been that it is no longer acceptable that HRD educators allow practitioners to maintain the illusion that their choices and action are without political consequences. Porter *et al.* (1989: 71) suggest that the purpose of critical thinking is to develop in managers 'habits of critical thinking... that prepare them for responsible citizenship and personally and socially rewarding lives and careers'.

McGuire *et al.* (2005) critically challenge some assumptions to HRD and argue that HRD has emerged as a complex heterogenous field serving many constituencies with diverse purpose. This multiplicity of purposes has led to questioning about whether critical HRD is concerned with developing such resources for the benefit of employees or for the benefit of organizations, or both. In addressing these issues it is important to consider: what discourse is being applied, how it is perceived and what its purpose is, i.e. control, domination, exploitation, empowerment or oppression.

From the discussion presented, we would argue that critical HRD is not simply about raising consciousness. Learning is not simply an individual process but, as Vince (2003: 559) argues, 'HRD has found it difficult to change itself and has largely ignored the wider politics of organizing in which HRD exists and can have an impact'. Similarly, critical HRD practice could draw from radical feminist pedagogy and address questions such as: 'How does discourse function? Where is it to be found? How does it get produced and regulated, and what are its social effects?' (Gore, 1993: 62). Gore's focus is on practices within institutions and disciplines of critical and feminist pedagogy. Those issues are then situated in social theoretical discussions about power and knowledge. This would mean critical HRD would need to acknowledge that learning is embedded in historical, social and material contexts.

Jarvis (1987: 227) believes

> 'Learning can never be value free; it must either work towards supporting the status quo or undermining it and replacing it with something which represents a better form of society.'

However, we must recognize the caution advocated by Luke (1986: 283) who asserts that the dynamics of power and authority underpinning pedagogical relations are not easily dislodged by theoretical shifts from 'transmission to emancipatory or patriarchal to feminist pedagogy models, or from enlightenment concepts of undifferentiated subjectivity to post-modern difference'.

■ Complexities, contradictions and hypocrisies in critical HRD

The problem of researching the relevance, appropriateness and impact of critical HRD has attracted considerable attention. Much of the evidence points to the inadequacies of the policy, procedures and approaches and methods traditionally employed in HRD education and research. The view that appears to be emerging is that traditional HRD approaches encourage a narrow instrumental approach to learning that places the emphasis on the reproduction of what is presented at the expense of critical thinking, deep understanding and independent activity. Critical HRD is now being advanced as a corrective to the instrumentalist, humanistic and performative values that have preoccupied this vital area of study.

However, much of this response has been dominated by the advocacy of theoretical debate. Little attention is accorded to the more fundamental underpinning processes. Other voices also challenge the optimism of critical learning programmes, particularly along the interface with managers' work role. Reynolds (1998) articulates four possible hazards. The first is for managers to resist engagement in critical processes, because to do so would be to question their profession and challenge their status quo. Reed and Anthony (1992: 607) suggest managers would find the approach 'irrelevant, unreal and impractical'. Jackall (1988) implies that within the management education domain, managers found it counter cultural to the pressures to conform to organizational ideologies. Secondly, Reynolds suggests that, relevant or not, students might find the language of much critical theory impenetrable.

The third hazard Reynolds outlines is the potential for managers to merely assimilate critical ideas into their existing perspective, without really unpicking the underlying assumptions and ideologies. The fourth danger relates to the potential adverse psychological and social consequences for individuals engaging in critical learning. As Reynolds (1998: 16) cautions:

> 'It can prove unsettling, mentally or emotionally and a source of disruption at home or at work... it carries the risk to employment and even – if we include stress related illness – to life itself.'

It would appear from these ideas that critical approaches do not necessarily create more liberating or empowering arenas of learning. It could be argued that critical approaches within HRD simply reflect and produce a more sophisticated exercising of control, whether intentionally or by default (Trehan, 2004). HRD practitioners are asked to believe they have a greater measure of control over their learning and, whilst they may seemingly have greater control over operational processes, both within education establishment and in organizations, the nature of the underlying power, political and emotional relationships remain significantly unaffected. Gore (1993) argues that critical discourses are presented as liberating because they challenge dominant discourse, not because they have proved liberatory for the individual, the group or the organization.

■ Going beyond a critical turn

Going beyond a critical turn involves the deconstruction of a discourse that exposes the power, politics and emotional dynamics structured into it, recognizing that the discourse of a particular field of knowledge does not describe the world in that field but instead inscribes or 'writes' the world of this field. Identifying who the 'authors' are in a particular discourse points to those with 'authority', i.e. the power to define the knowable and the permissible, often, but not always, academics. In other words, power and knowledge are inseparable. This perspective on power that recognizes its inseparability from knowledge leads to new ways of seeing issues of power in organizations. The underlying politics and ethics of critical HRD, constructed from the discourses of humanism, economics, HRM and the wider managerialist discourse, have increasingly become foregrounded for the management education and HRD practitioner. These discourses shape the whole body of knowledge in critical HRD, actually constituting them as fields. Professional practices are constructed through these discourses, rather than received in tablets of stone, and are therefore open to the possibility of change. Issues of power and influence in the HRD professional, and by definition for the management educator/developer, have been acknowledged as important and explored in the HRM literature, in particular by Legge (1995), Guest (1989) and Townley (1994). Corresponding changes in HRD are still limited. Where HRD does depart from mainstream practices, alternatives are typically based on humanistic student-centred aspirations for social equality rather than on an analysis of HRD in terms of institutional power, politics and social dynamics.

Townley's (1994) analysis, making use of the critical perspective on power, breaks out of the rather stale and action-inhibiting analysis of power in organizations provided by much of the critical HRD literature. Townley makes use of a non-economistic, non-commodity conception of power/knowledge provided by Foucault that focuses on the 'how?' of power rather than the 'who?' the 'where?' the 'how much?' This analysis points towards new practices that enable rather than inhibit action. This Foucauldian critique of critical HRD practices suggests a critically sustainable, politically and ethically aware model for practitioners. A model that involves individual informed experimental action, i.e. praxis, to first understand, challenge and then rewrite existing mechanisms of power/knowledge formation and asymmetry. Whether explicitly acknowledged, or not, the experience of work is located in, and constituted by, power relations. To be relevant, therefore (we) must provide people with a framework for understanding power (Townley 1994: 1).

Working in the organizational context involves making the decision of whether to work within the dominant power/knowledge formation or whether to consciously privilege new and/or previously subjugated discourses and the voices of those hitherto ignored or shut out of the debate. To choose either is an inescapably political act; hence it can be argued that organizations are major sites of political activity, whether this is the uncritical support of the status quo or critically conscious emancipatory action, i.e. praxis (e.g. interventions genuinely aimed at increasing empowerment and emancipation). By encouraging awareness of how power operates, practitioners need not be peddling a particular political standpoint over another but facilitating the development of an awareness of the mechanisms of power, thus giving people the opportunity to decide for themselves. Some critics of the Foucauldian conception of power read it as an all-pervasive and oppressive disciplinary power that as such provides little basis for emancipatory action. Townley argues that to the contrary, Foucault's focus on the 'how?' of power rather than the 'who?' or 'why?' is significant in its implications for the politics of the workplace: 'The focus is practice and its effects not power and its source' (Townley, 1994: 18). Exploring the implications of this view of power could be very fruitful for critical HRD professionals, managers and anyone else involved in an organization development context. To understand power within the HRD practice, we have to understand the mechanics of power relations within institutions.

Reconceptualizing power as a relational activity means power cannot be portrayed as external, something which operates on something or someone. It is integral to that relation. Power is positive and creative, not just negative or repressive. As Foucault (1997: 194) argues, 'We must cease once and for all to describe the effects of power in negative terms; it excludes, it represses, it censors, it abstracts, it masks, it conceals. In fact power produces, it produces reality; it produces domains of objects and rituals of truth.'

Within critical HRD, understanding power as a relational activity means we need to recognize that power operates in areas which may be obscured by traditional theories. As Fraser (1989: 126) argues, 'power is as present in the most apparently trivial details and relations of everyday life'. This is further reinforced by Foucault (1991) who points out the identification of the nature of power, how it operates as a microphysics, and how it is experienced in practice is the foundation of a political agenda which 'allows for the questioning of the mode of existence and the functioning of discourse in the name of political practice' (1991: 68). For Foucault (1983) power exists with three distinct qualities: origins (why?), nature (what?) and manifestations (how?). The implication of his work is that we broaden analysis from the 'what?' and 'why?' of power to the 'how?'. 'How not in the sense of how does it manifest itself? But by what means is it exercised and what happens when individuals exert power over others' (Foucault, 1983: 217).

Thus a Foucauldian analysis involves an ascending analysis of power; this means to delineate the way power is exercised, concretely and in detail. It is a study of how mechanisms of power affect everyday lives. In short, power must be analyzed as a micro-process of social life, within critical HRD practices.

Foucault offers a way of analyzing the control of practices by introducing the idea of governmentality. The power relations of the workplace continue to condition people into accepting discipline by others and to develop a type of self-discipline that can be understood through the concept of 'governmentality' (Foucault, 1979). If something is to be controlled, governed or managed, it must first be known. Governmentality is the necessary process that precedes administration and control, the process by which a domain becomes knowable and thereby 'governable'. This process involves formulating that which is to be known in some particular conceptual way, developing measures by which fit can be quantified, values assigned and coded, and the provision of a method of representation that facilitates decision-making and the application of value judgements. Once this system of knowledge is in place, a complex and qualitative group of variables can be reduced to a single measure of performity. Examples of the techniques of governmentality in organizations include accounting procedures, by which the whole complex performance of a business unit can be communicated to head office by the means of a single financial figure. Within critical HRD particularly, human asset accounting and value added is the obvious example. Governmentality, in organizations, is mostly exercised unconsciously by the governed (employees) through the action of 'being one's own policeman', managing one's own practices. This understanding of 'self-control' is an important aspect of the concept of governmentality.

> 'His, (Foucault's) approach is to deconstruct practices and examine in detail how they work... focused on the processes of normalisation whereby practices are sanctioned not by an external authority or an appeal to collective sentiments, but by mundane acts of self-authorisation which sustain in the practitioner as a compliant identity, a self-policing individual.'
>
> (Usher *et al.*, 1997: 56)

■ Concluding reflections

In the debates presented above we have reviewed and discussed the various perspectives on critical HRD and the challenges it presents in relation to future practice. A number of conclusions can be distilled from the discussion.

Firstly, in the field of management education and management learning critiques of the values, the purpose and approaches to management education and development have become well developed in recent years. At the same time critical HRD has been another emerging area of academic debate and practitioner focus. Yet, whilst there are many potential areas of overlap between HRD, HRM and management learning, they have been evolving as parallel discourses, with little attention accorded to exploiting their interconnections.

Secondly, the exploration of critical HRD from within the critical paradigm has highlighted that overcoming the functionalist representation of HRD cannot be achieved unless the field of HRD applies a critical perspective to content as well as to method or process. This means encompassing the following as outlined by Reynolds (1999):

■ questioning the assumptions and taken-for-granteds embodied in both theory and professional practice;
■ foregrounding the process of power and ideology subsumed within the social fabric of institutional structures, procedures and practices;
■ confronting spurious claims of rationality and objectivity, and revealing the sectional interests which can be concealed by them;
■ working towards an emancipatory ideal – the realization of a more just society based on fairness and democracy.

Thirdly, the theoretical debates presented have sought to emphasize the distinctive nature of critical HRD and to argue for its place in the professional activity of HRD education and practice. Critical HRD, whether in educational institution or in organizations, can support people in an examination of the social and political processes within the workplace. Critical practice is about moral issues and requires ethical consideration because these are fundamentals upon which any organizational reality rests. It is also important for education and organizational practice to counter current preoccupations with instrumentalism and introduce methodologies which focus their attention to the moral, political and cultural aspects of HRD.

For HRD educators and HRD practitioners, adopting critical approaches is a choice and responsibility. As Kemmis (1985: 148) argues:

'in reflection we choose, implicitly or explicitly, what to take for granted and what to treat as problematic in the relationships between our thoughts and action and the social order we inhabit. In reflection, we have a choice about whether to think and act in conformity and the patterns of communication, decision making and action in our society, or whether we will intervene at this historical moment on behalf of more rational communication, more just decision making and more fulfilling human and social action.'

In going beyond a critical turn it is important to illuminate the relevance of power, emotions and politics to the study of HRD. It is even more crucial to examine beyond critical debate the impact of critical HRD on practice. By examining and researching the inseparability of power and emotions between academic disciplines, and between HRD practitioners, inserting and using the techniques of deconstruction, storytelling and narratives into the dominant and subjugated discourses that occur in the processes of organizational activity, HRD practitioners could gain far greater insights into the invisible workings of managing and organizing than is provided by other analyses of organizational workings. This could provide us with a powerful tool for understanding and influencing future re-authoring of HRD practice in the workplace.

The professional education system of the Chartered Institute of Personnel and Development (CIPD) plays a major role in the UK, and increasingly in other countries, in defining the accepted discourse of the profession; the rather disparate bag of practices that have almost by default become the responsibility of the profession could be questioned and subjected to critical examination through this system. The overall ethical stance of practitioners is also rarely discussed, being a kind of invisible acceptance of the managerialist, efficiency meta-narrative drives everything. The concept of habitus (Bourdieu and Wacquant, 1992: 120) applies to the way that practices 'become at home with themselves' (Usher *et al.*, 1997: 59). The habitual practices that are so comfortably a part of an uncritical HRD role are the personnel habitus. As Brubaker puts it, 'The habitus determines the manner in which problems are posed, explanations constructed, and instruments employed' (Brubaker, 1993: 213). If HRD practitioners are going to expand their view of what is possible from within an HRD role and change their practices to reflect this, then a major hurdle that needs to be explored is their own self-imposed limits on the role of the HRD profession and this may be reinforced within the educational and academic arena.

Another consideration to reviewing the role of an HRD practitioner is the way in which they and their role can be inscribed and objectified, defined in a limiting way, by others in the organization. Lyotard provides the concept of 'the differend' to explain the difficulties in gaining acceptance for new ideas that fall outside of the accepted discourse. The 'differend' is the name Lyotard uses to describe the shutting out of one player from a 'language game'. The concept of a 'language game' is derived from Wittgenstein. This shutting out phenomenon occurs where there are no agreed rules for the introduction of something new to the game. This could be a new rule, a new idea, principle or grievance. The differend is the impossibility of giving expression to an injustice, as it is rendered invisible. This has implications for HRD practitioners trying to introduce new concepts and values to an organization.

In addition to these conclusions, the following implications emerge. Firstly, whilst critical approaches to HRD may be appealing in theory, they are also fraught with difficulties and problematic consequences. However, in arguing for a more critical perspective in HRD, we would concur with Reed and Anthony, who call teachers to account, insisting on their responsibility to 'recover their institutional and pedagogical nerve' (1992: 610), in supporting managers in critical learning within their working environment, notwithstanding the complexities and conflicts of interests which may surface. Similarly Reynolds argues the function of management education should not be to help managers fit unquestioningly into the roles traditionally expected of them, but to assist them in engaging with the social and moral issues inherent within existing management practice and to become more conscious of the ideological forces which constrain their actions (1999: 182).

Secondly, the issues and dilemmas that have been highlighted are those that teachers and practitioners might identify for discussion even if they cannot be neatly or easily resolved. Equally there is a role for tutors in supporting discussions of these issues when they are initiated by students. Where critical HRD in some form is practised, there is value in an open examination of what it entails. Within this context the importance of being a critically reflective practitioner becomes clear. As Burgoyne and Reynolds (1997: 2) argue, the critically reflective practitioners play an important role as:

'they are aware that with every practical action they take they are fixing (temporally) their belief and acting their current best working theory, but they realize that this may also be open to challenge and improvement.'

Many of the issues we have explored in this chapter are complex and pose as many questions as they provide answers. The aim of the chapter is not to offer a prescription, but to stress the importance of actively exploring and working with the complexities and contradictions within critical HRD. In this respect, therefore, the issues unveiled within the chapter are likely to generate additional uncertainties in the design and process of critical HRD. However, it is important that our own hesitancies and anxieties about working with these differences (power, conflict, authority and emotion) do not impede such a process because, as educators and practitioners, we encounter these ambiguities in the workplace every day.

Activities for Part Four

1 (a) Drawing on the chapters in this part evaluate the case for adopting a critical approach in HRD practice.

  (b) Present the results to colleagues for debate and discussion.

  (c) Review your original case and produce a revised version.

2 (a) Produce a statement describing your personal understanding of the concept of learning.

  (b) Review the arguments presented in Chapter 11 by Leonard Holmes.

  (c) Critique your statement in the light of those arguments and revise as desired.

  (d) Identify the implications of the revised statement for HRD practice.

3 (a) Identify the main themes of this book.

  (b) Using these themes, re-evaluate your understanding of critical HRD produced in the Activities at the end of Part One.

  (c) Produce a revised new personal understanding and associated rationale.

  (d) Present the results of (c) to colleagues and identify the implications for future professional practice.

References and further reading

Abrahamson, L. (2001) 'Gender based dilemmas in organizations', *Journal of Workplace Learning*, 7/8: 298–307.

Acker, J. (1990) 'Hierarchies, jobs, bodies: A theory of gendered organizations', *Gender and Society*, 4: 139–58.

Acker, J. (1998) 'The future of gender and organizations: Connections and boundaries', *Gender, Work and Organization*, 5(4): 195–206.

Ackerman, F. and Belton, V. (1994) 'Managing corporate knowledge experiences with SODA and VISA', *British Journal of Management*, 5: 163–76.

Adkins, L. (2002) *Revisions: Gender and Sexuality in Late Modernity*, Buckingham: Open University.

Adkins, L. (2004) 'Reflexivity: Freedom of habit or gender?', *Sociological Review*, 5(2): 191–210.

Althusser, L. (1971) 'Ideology and ideological state apparatuses', in Althusser, L. *Lenin and Philosophy*, London: NLB, 127–86.

Alvesson, M. (1990) 'Organisation: From substance to image', Organisation Studies, 11: 373–94.

Alvesson, M. and Deetz, S. (1999) 'Critical theory and postmodernism: Approaches to organizational studies', in Clegg, S. (ed.), *Organization Theory and Method*, London: Sage.

Alvesson, M. and Deetz, S. (2000) *Doing Critical Management Research*, London: Sage.

Alvesson, M. and Karreman, D. (2000a) 'Taking the linguistic turn in organizational research: Challenges, responses, consequences', *Journal of Applied Behavioural Science*, 36(2): 136–58.

Alvesson, M. and Karreman, D. (2000b) 'Varieties of discourse: On the study of organizations through discourse analysis', *Human Relations*, 53(9): 1125–1150.

Alvesson, M. and Skoldberg (2000) *Reflexive Methodology*, London: Sage.

Alvesson, M. and Willmott, H. (eds) (1992) *Critical Management Studies*, London: Sage.

Alvesson, M. and Willmott, H. (1992) 'On the idea of emancipation in management and organisation studies', *Academy of Management Review*, 17(3): 432–64.

Alvesson, M. and Willmott, H. (1996) *Making Sense of Management*, London: Sage.

Alvesson, M. and Willmott, H. (2000) *Doing Critical Management Research*, London: Sage.

AMBA (the Association for MBAs) at www.mbaworld.com

Andreski, S. (1972) *Social Sciences as Sorcery*, London: Deutsch.

Andrews, K. M. and Delahaye, B. L. (2000) 'Influences on knowledge processes in organizational learning: The psycho-social filter', *Journal of Management Studies* 37(6): 797–810.

Anthony, P. D. (1986) *The Foundation of Management*, London: Tavistock.

Apple, M. W. (1979) *Ideology and Curriculum*, London, Boston and Henley: Routledge and Kegan Paul.

Aragon, S. and Hatcher, T. (2001) 'Ethics and integrity in HRD: Case studies in research and practice', in S. Aragon and T. Hatcher (eds), *Advances in Developing Human Resources*, 3(1).

Ardichvili, A., Page, V. and Wentling, T. (2003) 'Motivation and barriers to participation in virtual knowledge-sharing communities of practice', *Journal of Knowledge Management*, 7(1): 64–77.

Armitage, A., Bryant, R., Dunhill, R., Hammersley, M., Hayes, D., Hudson, D. and Lawes, S. (1999) *Teaching and Training in Post-Compulsory Education*, Buckingham and Philadelphia: Open University Press.

Armstrong, S. (2005) 'Postgraduate management education in the UK: lessons from or lessons for the US model', *Academy of Management Learning and Education*, 4(2): 229–35.

Astley, W. G. and Zammuto, R. F. (1992) 'Organisation science, managers and language games', *Organisation Science*, 3(4): 443–60.

Austin, J. L. (1962) *How to Do Things with Words*, London: Oxford University Press.

Bach, S. and Sisson, K. (2000) *Personnel Management: A Comprehensive Guide to Theory and Practice*, Oxford: Blackwell.

Bakhtin, M. M. (1986) *Speech Genres and Other Late Essays* (trans. by V.W. McGee), Austin: University of Texas Press.

Bakhtin, M. M. (2002) *The Dialogic Imagination*, 14th edition, first published, 1981, Emerson, C. and Holquist, M. (eds) translated by Holquist, M., Austin: University of Texas Press.

Ball, C. (1996) 'A learning society: A vision and plan to change the learning culture of the United Kingdom', in RSA *For Life*, London: Royal Society of Arts, 1–4.

Barker, J. (1992) *Paradigms: The Business of Discovering the Future*, New York: HarperBusiness.

Barnett, R. (2000) 'Working knowledge', in Garrick, J. and Rhodes, C. (eds) *Research and Knowledge at Work*, London and New York: Routledge.

Barr, G. and Tagg, J. (1995) 'From teaching to learning – A new paradigm for undergraduate education', *Change*, 13–25.

Bartky, S. (1997) 'Foucault, femininity and the modernization of patriarchal power', in Conboy, K., Medina, N., Stanbury, S. (eds) *Writing on the Body*, New York: Columbia University Press.

Bass, B. and Vaughn, J. (1966) *Training in Industry: The Management of Learning*, London: Wadsworth Publishing.

Bates, R. and Hsin-Chih, C. (2004) 'Human resource development value orientations: A construct validity study', *Human Resource Development International*, 7: 3.

Bates, R., Hsin-Chih, C. and Hatcher, T. (2002) 'Value priorities of HRD scholars and practitioners', *International Journal of Training and Development*, 6: 4.

Bates, R., Hatcher, T., Holton, E. and Chalfonsky, N. (2001) 'Redefining human resource development: An integration of the learning, performance and spirituality or work perspectives', Proceedings of the annual AHRD conference, Tulsa, Feb–March.

Bateson, G. (1972) *Steps to an Ecology of Mind. Collected Essays in Anthropology, Psychiatry, Evolution and Epistemology*, San Francisco, Scranton, London, Toronto: Chandler.

Bateson, P. and Martin, P. (2000) *Design for a Life: How Behaviour Develops*, London: Vintage.

Beech, N. and Bockbank, A. (1999) 'Power, knowledge and psychodynamics in mentoring', *Management Learning*, 30(1): 7–27.

Beech, N., MacIntosh, R., MacLean, D., Shepherd, J. and Stokes, J. (2002) 'Exploring constraints on the development of knowledge: On the need for conflict', *Management Learning* 33(4): 459–75.

Bennis, W. G. and O'Toole, J. (2005) 'How business schools lost their way'. *Harvard Business Review*, May, 96–104.

Berger P. L. and Luckmann, T. (1966) *The Social Construction of Reality*, New York: Doubleday.

Bernstein B. (1990) *The Structuring of Pedagogic Discourse, Vol IV, Class, Codes and Control*, London: Routledge.

Best, S. (1998) 'Murray Bookchin's theory of social ecology', *Organization and Environment*, 11(3): 334–48.

Bierema, L. L. (2001) 'Women work and learning', in *New Directions for Adult and Continuing Education*, 92: 51–62.

Bierema, L. L. (2005) 'Women's networks: A career development intervention or impediment', *Human Resource Development International*, 8(2): 207–24.

Bierema, L.L. and Cseh, M. (2003) 'Evaluating AHRD research using a feminist research framework', *Human Resource Development Quarterly*, 14(1) Spring: 5–26.

Billett, S. (2001) *Learning in the Workplace: Strategies for Effective Practice*, Crows Nest, Australia: Allen and Unwin.

Billig, M. (2000) 'Towards a critique of the critical', *Discourse and Society* 11(3) July: 291–92.

Blake, R. (1995) 'Memories of HRD', *Training and Development*, March, 49(3): 22–8.

Boje, D. M. (1996) 'Management education as a panoptic cage', in French, R. and Grey, C. (eds) *Rethinking Management Education*, London, Thousand Oaks, New Delhi: Sage.

Bookchin, M. (1971) *Post-Scarcity Anarchism*, Berkeley: Ramparts Press.

Bookchin, M. (1990) *Remaking Society: Pathways to a Green Future*, Boston: South End Press.

Bookchin, M. (1991) *The Ecology of Freedom: The Emergence and Dissolution of Hierarchy* (Rev. edn), Montreal: Black Rose.

Booth, A. and Snower, D. J. (eds) *The Skills Gap and Economic Activity*, Cambridge: CUP.

Bordo, S. (1997) 'The body and the reproduction of femininity', in Conboy, K., Medina, N., Stanbury, S. (eds) *Writing on the Body*, New York: Columbia University Press.

Borger, R. and Seaborne, A. (1966) *The Psychology of Learning*, Harmondsworth, Middlesex: Penguin Books.

Boud, D. and Garrick, J. (eds) (1999) *Understanding Learning at Work*, London: Routledge.

Bourdieu P. (1977) *Reproduction in Education, Society and Culture*, London: Sage.

Bourdieu, P. and Wacquant, L. (1992) *An Invitation to Reflexive Sociology*, Chicago: Chicago University Press.

Bowie, N. E. and Duska, R. F. (1990) *Business Ethics*, 2nd edition, Englewood Cliffs: Prentice Hall, Inc.

Boxall, P. and Purcell, J. (2003) *Strategy and Human Resource Management*, Palgrave.

Boyer, E. L. (1997) *Scholarship Reconsidered – Priorities of the Professoriate*, San Francisco: Jossey-Bass.

Braidotti, R. (1989) 'Bodies without organs', *Differences*, 1: 147–62.

Braidotti, R. (1996) 'Embodiment and sexual difference in contemporary feminist theory', in Eagleton, M. *Feminist Literary Theory, A Reader*, Oxford: Blackwell.

Brewis, J. (2000) 'When a body meets a body: Experiencing the female body in and out of work', in McKie, L. and Watson, L. (eds) *Organized Bodies*, Basingstoke: Macmillan.

Britton, D. (2000) 'The epistemology of the gendered organization', *Gender and Society*, 14(3): 418–34.

Broadfoot, K., Deetz, S. and Anderson, D. (2004) Multi-levelled, multi-method approaches in organizational discourse, in Grant, D., Hardy, C., Oswick, C. and Putnam, L. (eds) *The Handbook of Organizational Discourse*, 193–211, London: Sage.

Brookfield, S. D. (1987) *Developing Critical Thinkers*, Buckingham: Open University Press.

Brookfield, S. D. (1994) 'Tales from the dark side: A phenomenology of adult critical reflection', *International Journal of Lifelong Education*, 13(3): 203–16.

Brookfield, S. D. (2005) *The Power of Critical Theory for Adult Learning and Teaching*, Maidenhead and New York: Open University Press.

Brown, A. (1999) *The Darwin Wars: The Scientific Battle for the Soul of Man*, London: Simon and Schuster.

Brown, D., Caldwell, R., White, K., Atkinson, H., Tansley, T., Goodge, P., Emmott, M. (2004) *Business Partnering: A New Direction for HR*, London: CIPD.

Brown, J. S. and Duguid, P. (1991) 'Organizational learning and communities-of-practice: Toward a unified view of working, learning and innovation', *Organization Science* 2(1): 40–57.

Brown, J. S. and Duguid, P. (2001) 'Knowledge and organization: A social practice perspective', *Organization Science* 12(2): 198–213.

Brown, R. (1996) 'What is scholarship?', *British Academy of Management Conference*.

Brown, R. (2006) 'The language of Management Studies: Poetical ways of saying', *Management Decision special issue on Poetry, Organisation, Emotions, Management and Enterprise (POEME)* 4(4): 464–73.

Brubaker, R. (1993) 'Rethinking classical theory', *Theory and Society*, 14: 745–75.

Buber, M. (2000) *I and Thou*, trans. by Ronald Gregor Smith, 1st Scribner Classics edn. New York, NY: Scribner.

Buchholz, R.A. (1993) *Principles of Environmental Management: The Greening of Business*, Englewood Cliffs, NJ: Prentice Hall.

Bunning, C. (1992) 'Turning experience into learning' *Journal of European Industrial Training*, 16(6): 7–12.

Burgoyne, J. (1994) 'Stakeholder analysis', in C. Cassell and G. Symon (eds), *Qualitative Methods in Organisational and Occupational Psychology*. London: Sage.

Burgoyne, J. and Jackson, B. (1997) 'The arena thesis: Management development as a pluralistic meeting point', in Burgoyne, J. and Reynolds, M. (eds) *Management Learning: Integrating Perspectives in Theory and Practice*, London, Thousand Oaks, New Delhi: Sage.

Burgoyne, J. and Reynolds, M. (eds) (1997) *Management Learning, Integrating Perspectives in Theory and Practice*, London: Sage.

Burrell G (2001) 'Critical dialogues on organization', *ephemera* 1(1): 11–29.

Butler, J. (1990) *Gender Trouble*, New York: Routledge.

Butler, J. (1993) *Bodies that Matter*, New York: Routledge.

Butler, J. (1995) 'Contingent foundations', in Benhabib, S., Butler, J., Cornell, N., Fraser, N. (eds) *Feminist Contentions: A Philosophical Exchange*, New York: Routledge.

Calás, M. and Smircich, L. (1999) 'Past postmodernism? Tentative reflections and directions', *Academy of Management Review*, 24(4): 649–71.

Capra, F. and Flattau, M. (1996) *Elegant Solutions: The Power of Systems Thinking*, San Francisco: New Leaders Press.

Carr, W. and Kemmis, S. (1986) *Becoming Critical: Education Knowledge and Action Research*, London: Falmer Press.

Carson, L. (2001) 'Gender relations in higher education: Exploring lecturers' perceptions of student evaluations of teaching', *Research Papers in Education*, 4(1): 337–58.

Cavanaugh, J. and Prasad, A. (1996) 'Critical theory and management education: Some strategies for the critical classroom', in R. French and C. Grey (eds) *Rethinking Management Education*, London: Sage.

Chalofsky, N. (2003) 'An emerging construct for meaningful work', *Human Resource Development International*, 6(1): 69–84.

Chia R. (1997) 'Process philosophy and management learning, cultivating "foresight" in management', in Burgoyne, J. and Reynolds, M. (eds) *Management Learning*, London: Sage.

Chouliaraki, L. and Fairclough, N. (1999) *Discourse In Late Modernity, Rethinking Critical Discourse Analysis*, Edinburgh: Edinburgh University Press.

Ciborra, C. U. and Patriotta, G. (1998) 'Groupware and teamwork in R and D: Limits to learning and innovation', *R and D Management*, 28(1): 43–52.

CIPD (2003) HR Survey Report, *Where we are and where we are going*, www.cipd.co.uk/subjects/hrpract/hrtrends/hrsurvey.htm?IsSrchRes=1

CIPD (2004) *CIPD Professional Standards*, London: Chartered Institute of Personnel and Development. www.cipd.co.uk/mandq/standards/professionalstandardsfullversion.htm?IsSrchRes=1

Clark, T. (2004) 'Controversies and continuities in management studies: Essays in honour of Karen Legge', *Journal of Management Studies*, 41(3): 367–76.

Clegg, S. R. (1999) 'Professional education, refletive practice and feminism', *International Journal of Inclusive Education*, 3(2): 167–79.

Clegg, S. R. and Hardy, C. (eds) (1999) *Studying Organizations*, London: Sage.

Clegg, S. R. and Palmer, G. (1996) 'Introduction: Producing management knowledge', in Clegg, S. R. and Palmer, G. (eds) *The Politics of Management Knowledge*, London, Thousand Oaks, New Delhi: Sage.

Clutterbuck, M. (2000) 'How to select a business school partner', *People Management*, 7 December, 40–42.

Collins, J. and Porras, J. (1994) *Built to Last*, New York: Harper.

Collins, M. (1995) 'Critical commentaries on the role of the adult educator: From self-directed learning to postmodernist sensibilities', in Welton, M. R. (ed.) *In Defense of the Lifeworld: Critical Perspectives on Adult Learning*, Albany: State University of New York Press.

Collins, P. H. (1991) *Black Feminist Thought*, New York: Routledge.

Constable, J. and McCormick, R. (1987) *The Making of British Managers*, London: British Institute of Management Confederation of British Industry.

Contu, A. and Willmott, H. (2003) 'Re-embedding situatedness: The importance of power relations in learning theory', *Organization Science*, 14(3): 283–96.

Cornelius, N. and Gagnon, S. (1999) 'From ethics "by proxy" to ethics in action: New approaches to understanding HRM and ethics', *Business Ethics: A European Review*, 8(4): 225–35.

Covey, S. (1989) *The Seven Habits of Highly Effective Managers: Restoring the Character Ethic*, New York: Simon and Schuster.

Cunliffe, A. (2002) 'Reflexive dialogical practice in management learning', *Management Learning*, 33(1): 33–61.

Currie, G. and Knights, D. (2003) 'Reflecting on a critical pedagogy in MBA education', *Management Learning*, 34(1): London, Thousand Oaks, New Delhi: Sage.

Czarniawska, B. (1998) *A Narrative Approach to Organization Studies*, London: Sage.

Dalal, F. (1998) *Taking the Group Seriously*, London: Jessica Kingsley.

Dalal, F. (2002) *Race, Colour and the Processes of Racialization*, Hove: Brunner-Routledge.

Dant, T. (1991) *Knowledge, Ideology and Discourse*, London: Routledge.

Davenport, T. O. (1999) *Human Capital: What It Is and Why People Invest it*, San Francisco: Jossey-Bass Publishers.

Davies, P. (1997) *Current Issues in Business Ethics*, London: Routledge.

Davis, H. and Scase, R. (2000) *Managing Creativity: The Dynamics of Work and Organisation*, Buckingham: Open University Press.

De Fellippi, R. J. (2001) 'Introduction: Project-based learning, reflective practices and learning outcomes', *Management Learning*, 32(1): 5–10.

De Rond, M. (1996) 'Business ethics, where do we stand? Towards a new inquiry', *Management Decision*, 34: 58.

Dean, P. J. (1997) 'Examining the profession and the practice of business ethics', *Journal of Business Ethics*, 16: 1637–50.

Deem, R. (2003) 'Gender, organizational cultures and the practices of manager-academics in UK universities', *Gender Work and Organization*, 10(2): 239–59.

Deetz S. (1996) 'Describing differences in approaches to organizational science: Rethinking Burrell and Morgan and their legacy', *Organization Science*, 7: 191–207.

Dehler, G.E., Welsh, M.A. and Lewis, M.W. (2001) 'Critical pedagogy in the "new paradigm",' *Management Learning*, 32(4): 493–511, London: Sage.

Denzin, N.K. (1994) 'The art and politics of interpretation', in Denzin, N. and Lincoln, Y. (eds) *Handbook of Qualitative Research*, Thousand Oaks: Sage.

Department for Education and Employment (DfEE) (1998a) *The Learning Age*, London: The Stationery Office.

Department for Education and Employment (1998b) *Research Report* No 6, London.

Department of Trade and Industry (DTI) (1991) *Managing into the 90s*, October, 37–44, London: HMSO.

Des Jardins, J.R. (2001) *Environmental Ethics: An Introduction to Environmental Philosophy*, 3rd edn, Belmont, CA: Wadsworth/Thomson Learning.

Devall, B. and Sessions, G. (1985) *Deep Ecology: Living as if Nature Mattered*, Layton, UT: Gibbs-Smith.

Dewey, J. (1958) *Experience and Nature*, New York: Dover Publications.

Dirkx, J. M. (1996) 'Human resource development and adult education: Fostering the educative workplace', in R. Rowden (ed) *Workplace Learning: Debating Five Critical Questions of Theory and Practice*, San Francisco: Jossey-Bass.

Dirkx, J. M. (2005) 'Fostering a "firm persuasion" in workplace leaning: Helping workers discover work that is good for them and the world', in Elliott, C. and Turnbull, S. (eds) *Critical Thinking in Human Resource Development*, Routledge: London.

Dobson, A. (1998) *Justice and the Environment: Conceptions of Environmental Sustainability and Dimensions of Social Justice*, Oxford, UK: Oxford University Press.

Domagalski, T. A. (1999) 'Emotion in organizations: Main currents', *Human Relations*, 52(6): 833–52.

Donaldson, J. (1992) *Business Ethics: A European Casebook*, London: Academic Press Limited.

Dopson, S. (2001) 'Applying an Eliasian approach to organizational analysis', *Organization* 8(3): 515–35.

Douglas, D. (2004) 'Ethical challenges of an increasingly diverse workforce: The paradox of change', *Human Resource Development International*, 7: 2.

Draper, S. (1988) 'What's going on in everyday explanation?', in Antaki, A. *Analysing Everyday Explanation: A Casebook of Methods*, 15–31, London: Sage.

Driver, M. (2002) 'Learning and leadership in organizations: Toward complementary communities of practice', *Management Learning*, 33(1): 99–126.

Duffy, M. K., Ganster, D. C. and Pagon, M. (2002) 'Social undermining in the workplace', *Academy of Management Journal*, 45(2): 331–51.

du Gay, P. and Salaman, G. (1996) 'The conduct of management and the management of conduct: Contemporary managerial discourse and the constitution of the "competent" manager', *Journal of Management Studies*, 33(3): 263–82.

Easterby-Smith, M.P.V. and Cunliffe, A. (2004) 'From reflection to practical reflexivity: Experiential learning as lived experience', in Reynolds, P.M. and Vince, R. (eds) *Organizing Reflection*, 30–46, Aldershot: Ashgate Publishing.

Eco, U. (2000) 'Ethics are born in the presence of the other', in Eco, U. and Martini, C.M., *Belief or Non Belief: A Confrontation*, New York: Arcade Publishing, Inc.

Eden, C. (1988) 'Cognitive mapping', *European Journal of Operational Research*, 36: 1–13.

Eden, C. and Jones, S. (1984) 'Using repertory grid for problem construction', *Journal of Operational Research Society*, 35: 779–90.

Eden, C., Sims, D. and Jones, S. (1983) *Messing About in Problems; An Informal, Structured Approach to their Identification and Management*, Oxford: Pergamon Press.

Edwards, D. and Potter, J. (1992) *Discursive Psychology*, London: Sage.

Edwards, R. and Usher, R. (2000) 'Research on work, research at work: Postmodern perspectives', in Garrick, J. and Rhodes, C. (eds) *Research and Knowledge at Work*, London and New York: Routledge.

EEF/CIPD Report (2004) *Maximizing employee potential and business performance: The role of high performance working*, www.cipd.co.uk/subjects/corpstrtgy/general/mxempot.htm?IsSrchRes=1

Elias, N. (1974) 'Foreword: Towards a theory of communities', in C. Bell and H. Newby (eds) *Community Studies: An Introduction to the Sociology of the Local Community*, London: Allen and Unwin.

Elias, N. (1978) *What Is Sociology?* (first published in German 1970, translated by S. Mennell and G. Morrissey), New York: Columbia University Press.

Elias, N. (1987) *Involvement and Detachment*, Oxford: Blackwell.

Elias, N. (1991a) *The Society of Individuals* (first published in German 1987, translated by E. Jephcott), New York: Continuum.

Elias, N. (1991b) *The Symbol Theory*, London: Sage.

Elias, N. (2000) *The Civilizing Process* (revised edition, first published in German 1939, translated by E. Jephcott), Oxford: Blackwell.

Elias, N. and Scotson, J. S. (1994) *The Established and the Outsiders* (first published 1965), London: Sage.

Elkjaer, B. (1999) 'In search of a social learning theory', in M. Easterby-Smith, J. Burgoyne and L. Araujo (eds) *Organizational Learning and the Learning Organization: Developments in Theory and Practice*, London: Sage.

Ellinger, A,D., Ellinger, A.E., Yang, B., Howton, S. (2002) 'The relationship between the learning organization concept and firms' financial performance: An empirical assessment', *Human Resource Development Quarterly*, 13(1): 5–21.

Elliott C. (1998) 'HRD in the United Kingdom – A review of the literature', Proceedings of the AHRD Conference, 536–43.

Elliott, C. and Turnbull, S. (2002a) Proceedings of the annual AHRD conference, Hawaii, Feb–March.

Elliott, C. and Turnbull, S. (2000b) Book proposal, personal email.

Elliott, C. and Turnbull, S. (2003) 'Reconciling autonomy and community: The paradoxical role of HRD', *Human Resource Development International*, 6(4): 457–74.

Elliott, C. and Turnbull, S. (2005) 'Critical thinking in human resource development: An introduction', *Critical Thinking in Human Resource Development*, London: Routledge.

Ellis, C. and Bochner, A. (2000) 'Autoethnography, personal narrative, reflexivity: Researcher as subject', in N. K. Denzin and S. Lincoln (eds) *Handbook of Qualitative Research* (2nd edn), 733–86, Thousand Oaks, CA: Sage.

Ely, M., Vinz R., Downing M., Anzul M. (1999), *On Writing Qualitative Research: Living by Words*, Falmer Press: London.

Engestrom, Y (2001) 'Expansive learning at work: Toward an activity, theoretical reconceptualization', *Journal of Education and Work*, 14(1): 133–56.

Evans, P.A. (1999) 'A duality perspective', *Organization*, 6(2): 325–38.

Fairclough, N. (1992) *Discourse and Social Change*, Cambridge: Polity Press.

Fairclough, N. (1995) *Critical Discourse Analysis: Papers in the Critical Study of Language*, London: Longman.

Fairclough, N. (2001) *Language and Power*, 2nd edn, London: Pearson Education.

Fairclough, N. (2003) 'Emancipatory potential of action learning: A critical analysis', *Journal of Organizational Change Management*, 16(6): 619–32.

Feldman D. (2005) 'The food's no good and they don't give us enough: Reflections on Mintzberg's critique of MBA education', *American Academy Learning and Education*, 217–21.

Fenwick, T. (2003) 'Emancipatory potential of action research: A critical analysis', *Journal of Organizational Change Management*, 16(6): 619–32.

Fenwick, T. (2005a) 'Conceptions of critical HRD', *Human Resource Development International*, 8(2): 225–38.

Fenwick, T. (2005b) 'Ethical dilemmas of critical management education; Within classrooms and beyond', *Management Learning*, 36(1): 31–48, London, Thousand Oaks, New Delhi: Sage.

Field, J. (2000) *Lifelong Learning and the New Educational Order*, Stoke on Trent: Trentham Books.

Fineman, S. (2000) *Emotion in Organizations* (2nd edn), London: Sage.

Fineman, S. (2003) 'Emotionalizing organizational learning', in M. Easterby-Smith and M. A. Lyles (eds) *The Blackwell Handbook of Organizatinal Learning and Knowledge Management*, Oxford: Blackwell.

Fisher, C. (2005) 'HRD attitudes: Or the roles and ethical stances of human resource developers', *Human Resource Development International*, 8: 2.

Fletcher, S. (1991), *NVQs Standards and Competence*, Kogan Page: London.

Fondas, N. (1997) 'Feminization unveiled: Management qualities in contemporary writings', *Academy of Management Review*, 22(1), 257–82.

Foot, P. (2001) *Natural Goodness*, Oxford: Oxford University Press.

Forester, J. (1989) *Planning in the Face of Power*, Berkeley, CA: University of California Press.

Foucault, M. (1979) *Discipline and Punish: The Birth of the Prison*, Harmondsworth: Penguin.

Foucault, M. (1983) 'The subject of power', in Drefus, H.L. and Rainbow, P. (eds) *Beyond Structuralism and Hermeneutics*, 2nd edn, Chicago IL: University of Chicago press.

Foucault, M. (1991) 'Politics and the study of discourse', in Burchell, G., Gordon, C. and Miller, P. (eds) *The Foucault Effect: Studies in Govermentality*, London: Harvester Wheatsheaf.

Foucault, M. (1997) *Discipline and Punish: The Birth of the Prison*, London: Allen Lane.

Fournier (2002) 'Fleshing out gender: Crafting gender identity on women's bodies', *Body and Society*, 8(2), 55–77.

Fournier, V. and Grey, C. (2000) 'At the critical moment: Conditions and prospects for critical management studies', *Human Relations*, 53(1): 7–32.

Fox, S. (1997) 'From management education and development to the study of management learning', in Burgoyne, J. and Reynolds, M. (eds) *Management Learning: Integrating Perspectives in Theory and Practice*, London, Sage.

Fox, S. (2000) 'Communities of practice, Foucault and actor-network theory', *Journal of Management Studies*, 37(6): 853–67.

Francis, H. (2003), 'HRM and the beginnings of organizational change', *Journal of Organizational Change Management*, 16(3): 309–28.

Francis, H. and D'Annunzio-Green, N. (2004) 'A discourse perspective on change and management learning', Fifth International Conference on HRD Research and Practice Across Europe, 27–28 May.

Francis, H. and Keegan, A. (2005a) 'Slippery slope', *People Management*, 30 June, 26–31.

Francis, H. and Keegan, A. (2005b) 'Thinking critically about the thinking performer', CIPD Standards Conference, June, Keele University.

Francis, H. and Keegan, A. (forthcoming) 'The changing face of HR: In search of balance', *Human Resource Management Journal*.

Francis, H. and Sinclair, J. (2003) 'A processual analysis of HRM-based change', *Organization*, 10(4): 685–706.

Fraser, N. (1989), *Unruly Practices: Power Discourse and Gender in Contemporary Social Theory*, Minneapolis MN: University of Minnesota Press.

Freire, Paulo (1972) *Pedagogy of the Oppressed*, Middlesex: Penguin.

French, R. and Grey, C. (1996) (eds) *Rethinking Management Education*, London, Thousand Oaks, New Delhi: Sage.

Fuller, A., Hodkinson, H., Hodkinson, P. and Unwin, L. (2005) 'Learning as peripheral participation in communities of practice: A reassessment of key concepts in workplace learning', *British Educational Research Journal* 31(1): 49–68.

Fulop, L. (2002) 'Practicing what you preach: Critical management studies and its teaching', *Organization*, 9(3), Sage.

Fulop, L. and Rifkin, W. D. (2004) 'Management knowledge and learning', in Linstead, S., Fulop, L. and Lilley, S. (eds) *Management and Organization : A Critical Text*, Basingstoke and New York: Palgrave Macmillan.

Garavan, T., Costine, P. and Heraty, N. (1995) 'The emergence of strategic human resource development', *Journal of European Industrial Training*, 19(10).

Garavan, T., Gunnigle, P. and Morley, M. (2000) 'Contemporary HRD research: A tri-archy of theoretical perspectives and their prescriptions for HRD', *Journal of European Industrial Training*, 24(1,2,3,4): 65–93.

Garavan, T., Heraty, N. and Barnicle, B. (1999) 'Human resource development literature: Current issues, priorities and dilemmas', *Journal of European Industrial Training*, 23(4/5) 169–79.

Garavan, T., McGuire, D. and O'Donnell, D. (2004) 'Exploring human resource development: A levels of analysis approach', *Human Resource Development Review*, 3(4): 417–41.

Garavan, T., Morley, M., Gunnigle, P. and Collins, E. (2001) 'Human capital accumulation: The role of human resource development', *Journal of European Industrial Training*.

Garrick, J. (1998) *Informal Learning in the Workplace: Unmasking Human Resource Development*, Routledge.

Garrick, J. and Clegg, S. (2001) 'Stressed-out knowledge workers in performative times: A postmodern take on project-based learning', *Management Learning*, 32(1): 199–34, London: Sage.

Garrick, J. and Rhodes, C. (2000) *Research and Knowledge at Work*, Routledge, London.

Gergen, K. (1998) *Realities and Relationships, Soundings in Social Construction*, Harvard University Press: Cambridge.

Gergen, K. (1999) *An Invitation to Social Constructionism*, London: Sage.

Gherardi, S. (1995) *Gender Symbolism and Organisational Culture*, Routledge, London.

Gherardi, S. (1999) 'Learning as problem-driven or learning in the face of mystery?', *Organization Studies*, 20(1): 101–24.

Gherardi, S. and Nicolini, D. (2002) 'Learning the trade: A culture of safety in practice', *Organization* 9(2): 191–223.

Gherardi, S. and Poggio, B. (2001) 'Creating and recreating gender order in organisations', *Journal of World Business*, 36(3): 245–59.

Gibb, A. A. (1996) 'Entrepreneurship and small business management: Can we afford to ignore them in the 21st century business school?' *British Journal of Management*, 7: 309–21.

Gibbons, M., Limoges, C., Nowotny, H., Schartzman, S., Scott, P. and Trow, M. (1994) *The New Production of Knowledge: The Dynamics of Science and Research in Contemporary Societies*, London: Sage.

Gill, R. (1995) 'Relativism, reflexivity and politics: Interrogating discourse analysis from a feminist perspective', in Wilkinson, S. and Kitzinger, C., *Feminism and Discourse*, London: Sage.

Giroux, H.A. (1992) *Ideology, Culture and the Process of Schooling*, Philadelphia, PA: Temple University Press.

Gold, J. Holman, D. and Thorpe, R. (2002) 'The role of argument analysis and story telling in facilitating critical thinking', *Management Learning*, 33(3): 371–88.

Gore, J. (1993) *The Struggle for Pedagogies: Critical and Feminist Discourses as Regimes of Truth*, New York: Routledge.

Gorringe, T. (1999) *Fair Shares: Ethics and the Global Economy*, London: Thames and Hudson.

Gramsci, A. (1971) *Selections from the Prison Notebooks*. London: Lawrence and Wishart.

Grant, D. and Shields, J. (2002) 'In search of the subject: Researching employee reactions to human resource management', *The Journal of Industrial Relations*, 44(3): 313–34.

Grant, D., Keenoy, T. and Oswick, C. (eds) (1998) *Discourse and Organization*, London: Sage.

Grant, D., Hardy, C., Oswick, C. and Putnam, L. (2005) 'Introduction – organizational discourse: exploring the field' in Grant, D., Hardy, C., Oswick, C. and Putnam, L. (eds) *The Handbook of Organizational Discourse*, 1–36, London: Sage.

Grey, C. and French, R. (1996) 'Rethinking management education: An introduction' in French, R. and Grey, C. (eds) *Rethinking Management Education*, London, Thousand Oaks, New Delhi: Sage.

Grey, C., Knights, D. and Wilmott, H. (1996) 'Is a critical pedagogy of management possible?', in French, R. and Grey, C. (eds) *Rethinking Management Education*, London, Thousand Oaks, New Delhi: Sage.

Griffin, D., Shaw, P. and Stacey, R. (1998) 'Speaking of complexity in management: Theory and practice', *Journal of Organisation*, 5(3): 315–39.

Grosz, E. (1994) *Volatile Bodies: Toward a Corporeal Feminism*, Bloomington: Indiana University Press.

Grugulis, I. (2003) 'Putting skills to work: Learning and employment at the start of the century', *Human Resources Management Journal*, 13(2): 3–12.

Guba, E. and Lincoln, Y. (1994) 'Competing paradigms in qualitative research', in N. K. Denzin and Y. S. Lincoln (eds) *Handbook of Qualitative Research*, Thousand Oaks, CA: Sage.

Guest, D. (1989) 'Human resource management: Its implications for industrial relations', in J. Storey (ed) *New perspectives on Human Resource Management*, London: Routledge.

Habermas, J. (1987) *The Theory of Communicative Action: Lifeworld and System*, Boston: Beacon Press.

Halford, S. and Leonard, P. (1999) 'New identities, professionalism, managerialism and the construction of the self', in Exworthy, M. and Halford, S. (eds) *Professionals and New Managerialism in the Public Sector*, Buckingham: Oxford University Press.

Hall, B. (2001), 'I wish this were a poem of practices of participatory research', in Reason, P., and Bradbury, H. (eds) *Handbook of Action Research*, 171–9, London: Sage.

Hamilton, P. M. (2001) 'Rhetoric and employment relations', *British Journal of Industrial Relations*, 39, September, 433–49.

Hamlyn, D. (1953) 'Behaviour', *Philosophy*, XXVIII, 132–45.

Handy C. (1987) *The Making of Managers*, London: NEDO.

Hanscombe, L. and Cervero, R.M. (2003) 'The impact of gendered power relations on HRD', *Human Resource Development International*, 6(4): 509–25.

Hardy, C. and Clegg, S. R. (1996) 'Some dare call it power', in Clegg, S. R., Hardy, C. and Nord, W. R. *Handbook of organisational studies*, 622–41, London: Sage.

Harley, B. and Hardy, C. (2004) 'Firing blanks? An analysis of discursive struggle in HRM', *Journal of Management Studies*, 41(3): 377–400.

Harré, R. and Gillet, G. (1994) *The Discursive Mind*, London: Sage.

Harré, R. and Secord, P. (1972) *The Explanation of Social Behaviour*, Oxford: Blackwell.

Harré, R. and Stearns, P. (eds) (1995) *Discursive Psychology in Practice*, London: Sage.

Harré, R. and van Langenhove, L. (eds) (1999) *Positioning Theory*, Oxford: Blackwell.

Harrison, R. (1998) *Employee Development*, London: CIPD.

Harrisson, D., Laplante, N. and St-Cyr, L. (2001) 'Cooperation and resistance in work innovation networks', *Human Relations* 54(2): 215–55.

Hatcher, T. (2002) *Ethics and HRD: A New Approach to Leading Responsible Organisations*, Cambridge, MA: Persens Publishing.

Hatcher, T. (2003) 'Worldviews that enhance and inhibit HRD's social responsibility', in M. Lee (ed) *HRD in a Complex World*, 42–56, London: Routledge.

Hatcher, T. (2004a) 'Economics, human potential and the Stockholm syndrome: A call for the liberation of HRD through ecocentric theory', 5th International Human Resource Development Conference on HRD Research and Practice, 27–29 May, Limerick, Ireland.

Hatcher, T. (2004b) 'A rationale for HRD-ethics and its inclusion as a theoretical foundation', Academy of Human Resource Development International Research Conference, Feb/Mar, Austin, TX.

Hatcher, T. (2004c) 'HRD and democracy: An idea whose time has come', 5th International Human Resource Development Conference on HRD Research and Practice, 27–29 May, Limerick, Ireland.

Hatcher, T. and Lee, M. (2003) 'HRD and the democratic ideal: The conflict of democratic values in undemocratic work systems', in J. Winterton, *Proceedings of 3rd European HRD Conference*, Toulouse.

Hatcher, T. and Lee, M. (2005) 'HRD and the democratic ideal: The conflict of democratic values in undemocratic work systems', in Elliott, C. and Turnbull, S., *Critical Thinking in Human Resource Development*, Routledge: London.

Hatcher, T. and Reio, T. (2003) 'Politics, power, and HRD: Toward an ecocentric view', Academy of Human Resource Development International Research Conference, Minneapolis, MN, Feb/Mar, 631–36.

Heyes J. (2000) 'Workplace industrial relations and training', in Rainbird, H. (ed.), *Training in the Workplace, Critical Perspectives on Learning at Work*, Basingstoke: Macmillan.

Hickling, A. (1994) 'The environment as radical politics: Can third world education rise to the challenge?', *International Review of Education*, 40, 19–36.

Hiltrop J. (1996) 'The impact of human resource management on organizational performance: Theory and research', *European Management Journal*, 14(5), 628–36.

Hirsch, W. and Strebler, M. (1994), 'Defining managerial skills and competences', in Mumford, A. (ed) *Gower Handbook of Management Development*, Gower.

Hirshhorn, L. (1988) *The Workplace Within*, London: MIT Press.

Hodges, D. C. (1998) 'Participation as dis-identification with/in a community of practice', *Mind, Culture and Activity*, 5(4): 272–90.

Hodkinson, H. and Hodkinson, P. (2004) 'The significance of individuals' dispositions in workplace learning: A case study of two teachers', *Journal of Education and Work*, 17(2): 167–82.

Hoggett, P. (1992) *Partisans in an Uncertain World: The Psychoanalysis of Engagement*, London: Free Association Books.

Holden, R. J. and Hamblett, J. (1998) 'Learning lessons from non work-related learning', *Journal of Workplace Learning*, 10(5), MCB University Press.

Holmberg, J. and Sanderbrook, R. (1992) 'Sustainable development: What is to be done?', in J. Holmberg (ed) *Policies for a Small Planet*, 19–38, London: Earthscan.

Holmes, L. (1995) 'HRM and the irresistable rise of the discourse of competence', *Personnel Review*, 24: 34–49.

Holmes, L. (1998) 'Learning as a "confidence trick": Exorcising the ghost in the machine', presented at Emergent Themes in Management: Connecting Learning and Critique conference, University of Leeds.

Holmes, L. (2000) 'What can performance tell us about learning? Explicating a troubled concept', *European Journal of Work and Organizational Psychology*, 9: 253–66.

Holmes, L. (2001a) 'Decontaminating the concepts of "learning" and "competence": Education and modalities of emergent identity', presented at Second International Conference on Critical Management Studies, Manchester.

Holmes, L. (2001b) 'Towards a relational perspective on higher-level learning and skill: graduate employability and managerial competence', unpublished PhD thesis, Institute of Education, University of London.

Holmes, L. (2002) 'Emergent identity, education and distributed assessment: an ethnomethodological exploration', presented at Ethnomethodology: A Critical Celebration conference, Essex University, Colchester.

Holt, N. L (2003) 'Representation, legitimation and autoethnography: An autoenthographic writing story', *International Journal of Qualitative Methods*, 2 (1), Article 2. Retrieved from www.ualberta.ca/iiqm/backissues/2_1final/html/holt.html

Honey, P. (1998) 'The debate starts here', *People Management*, 28–9.

hooks, bell (1993) 'bell hooks speaking about Paulo Freire – the man, his work' in P. McLaren and P. Leonard, *Paulo Freire: A Critical Encounter*, New York: Routledge.

Hope Hailey, V., Farndale, E. and Truss, C. (2005) 'The HR department's role in organisational performance', *Human Resource Management Journal*, 15(3), 49–66.

Hosking, M. (1999) Social construction as process: Some new possibilities for research and development, *Concepts and Transformation*, 4(2) 117–32.

Howson, A. Inglis, D. (2001) 'The body in sociology: Tension inside and outside sociological thought', *The Sociological Review*, 49(3): 297–317.

Hughes, C. (2000) 'Painting new (feminist) pictures of HRD (and) identifying research issues for political change', *Management Learning*, 31(1): 51–66.

Hughes, C. (2005) 'Deconstructing the human in human resource development', in Elliott, C. and Turnbull, S. *Critical Thinking in Human Resource Development*, Routledge: London.

Humphreys, M. and Brown, A. D. (2002) 'Narratives of organizational identity and identification: A case study of hegemony and resistance', *Organization Studies*, 23(3): 421–47.

Iles, P. and Salaman, G. (1995) 'Recruitment, selection and assessment', in Storey, J. (eds) *Human Resource Management: A Critical Text*, London, Sage.

Irigaray, L. (1985) *This Sex Which Is Not One*, translation by G. Gill, Ithaca: Cornell University Press.

Irigaray, L. (1995) 'The question of the other', *Yale French Studies*, 20(87), 7–19.

Jackall, R. (1988) *The Moral Mazes: The World of Corporate Managers*, Oxford: OUP.

Jackson, S. (1997) 'Crossing borders and changing pedagogies: From Giroux and Freire to feminist theories of education', *Gender and Education*, 9(4).

Jackson, S. (1999) 'Feminist sociology and sociological feminism: Recovering the social in feminist thought', *Sociological Research Online*, 4(3): 1–17.

Jackson, S. and Scott, S. (2001) 'Putting the body's feet on the ground: Towards a sociological reconceptualisation of gendered and sexual embodiment', in Backett-Milburn, D., McKie, L. (eds) *Constructing Gendered Bodies*, Basingstoke: Palgrave Macmillan.

Jacob, M. (1994) 'Toward a methodological critique of sustainable development', *Journal of Developing Areas*, 28: 237–51.

Jacques, L. S. (1999) 'Saving the "subject" in HRM: Suggesting an interdependent relationship between theorist and practitioner', *Organization*, 6(2): 265–76.

Jarvis, P. (1987) *Adult Learning in the Social Context*, London: Croom Helm.

Jessup, G. (1991) *Outcomes: NVQs and the Emerging Model of Education and Training*, London: Falmer Press.

Johnson, M. (2005) *The New Rules of Engagement, Life Work Balance and Employee Commitment*, CIPD: London.

Kaler, J. (1999) 'What's the good of ethical theory?', *Business Ethics: A European Review*, 8(4), 206–13.

Keegan, A. and Boselie, P. (2003) 'Guess Who's Coming to Dinner? The Impact of Dissensus Inspired Analysis on Developments in the Field of Human Resource Management', Third International Conference, Dutch HRM Network, University of Twente.

Keegan, A. and Boselie, P. (forthcoming) 'The lack of impact of dissensus inspired analysis on developments in the field of HRM', *Journal of Management Studies*.

Keegan, A. and Turner, J. R. (2001) 'Quantity vs quality in project-based learning practices', *Management Learning*, 32(1): 77–98.

Keenoy, K. and Oswick, C. (2004) 'Organizing textscapes', *Organization Studies*, 25(1): 135–42.

Keenoy, T. (1997) 'Review article: HRMism and the languages of re-presentation', *Journal of Management Studies*, 34(5): 825–41.

Keenoy, T. (1999) HRM as hologram: A polemic, *Journal of Management Studies*, 36(1): 1–23.

Keep, E. and Mayhew, K. (1996) 'UK training policy – assumptions and reality', in Kelemen, M. (2000) 'Too much or too little ambiguity: The language of total quality management', *Journal of Management Studies*, 37(4): 484–97.

Kemmis, S. (1985) 'Action research and the politics of reflection', in Boud, D. *et al.* (eds) *Reflection: Turning Experience into Learning*, London: Kogan Page.

Kemmis, S. (1993) 'Action research and social movement: A challenge for policy research', *Education Policy Analysis Archives*, 1(1): retrieved 12 May 1998 from http://olam.ed.asu.edu/epaa

Kemmis, S. and McTaggart, R. (2000) 'Participatory action research', in Denzin, N. and Lincoln, Y. (eds) *Handbook of Qualitative Research*, 2nd edn, London: Sage.

Kennedy, P. and Mason, A. (1993) *The Company MBA*, London: Harbridge House.

Kersten, A. (2001) 'Organizing for powerlessness: A critical perspective on psychodynamics and dysfunctionality', *Journal of Organizational Change Management*, 14(5): 452–67.

Kessels, J. (2002) Proceedings of the annual European conference on HRD Research and Practice, Edinburgh, January.

Kirkwood, G. (1991) 'Fallacy: The community educator should be a non-directive facilitator', in O'Hagan, B. (ed) *The Charnwood Papers: Fallacies in Community Education*, Education Now.

Knights, D. and Morgan, G. (1991) 'Strategic discourse and subjectivity: Towards a critical analysis of corporate strategy in organisations', *Organisation Studies*, 12(3): 251–73.

Knights, D. and Wilmott, H. (2000) *The Reengineering Revolution*, London: Sage.

Kolb, D. (1976) *The Learning Style Inventory*, Boston: McBerg and Co.

Kolb, D. (1984) *Experiential Learning*, Englewood Cliffs, New Jersey: Prentice Hall.

Korcynski, M. (2003) 'Communities of coping: Collective emotional labour in service work', *Organization*, 10(1): 55–79.

Kuchinke, K.P. (1998) 'Moving beyond the dualism of learning versus performance as root metaphors for HRD: A response to Barry and Pace', *Human Resource Development Quarterly*, 9(4): 377–84.

Kuchinke, K. P. (2001) 'HRD university education: An international research agenda', *Human Resource Development International*, 4(2), London, Boston and Henley: Routledge.

Kuchinke, K. P. (2002) Proceedings of the annual AHRD conference, Feb–March, Hawaii.

Kuchinke, K. P. (2005) 'The self at work: Theories about persons, the meaning of work, and their implications for HRD' in Elliott, C. and Turnbull, S. *Critical Thinking in Human Resource Development*, London: Routledge.

Kuhn, T. (1962) *The Structure of Scientific Revolutions*, Chicago: University of Chicago Press.

Landen, M. (2002) 'Emotion management: Dabbling in mystery – white witchcraft or black art?', *Human Resource Development International*, 5(4): 507–21.

Lather, P. (1991) *Getting Smart*, Routledge: New York.

Lave, J. (1988) *Cognition in Practice: Mind, Mathematics and Culture in Everyday Life*, Cambridge: Cambridge University Press.

Lave, J. and Wenger, E. (1991) *Situated Learning: Legitimate Peripheral Participation*, Cambridge: Cambridge University Press.

Lave, J., Murtaugh, M. and de la Rocha, O. (1984) 'The dialectic of arithmetic in grocery shopping', in B. Roggoff and J. Lave (eds) *Everyday Cognition: Its Development in Social Context*, London: Harvard University Press.

Lee, M. M. (1997), 'The developmental approach: a critical reconsideration', in Burgoyne, J. and Reynolds, M. (eds) *Management Learning: Integrating Perspectives in Theory and Practice*, 199–215, London: Sage.

Lee, M. M. (1998) 'HRDI: A journal to define', *Human Resource Development International*, 1(1): 1–6.

Lee, M. M. (1999) 'The lie of power: Empowerment as impotence', *Human Relations*, 52(2): 225–62.

Lee, M. M. (2003) 'The complex roots of HRD', in M. M. Lee (ed) *HRD in a Complex World*, 7–24, London: Routledge.

Lee, M. M. (2004) 'A refusal to define HRD', in M. M. Lee, J. Stewart and J. Woodall (eds) *New Frontiers in Human Resource Development*, London: Routledge.

Lee, M. M. (2005) 'Critiquing codes of ethics', in Elliott, C. and Turnbull, S. (eds) *Critical Thinking in Human Resource Development*, London: Routledge.

Lee, M. M. and Hatcher, T. (2003), 'HRD and the democratic ideal: The conflict of democratic values in undemocratic work systems', in Winterton, J. (ed) *International, Comparative and Cross-Cultural Dimensions of HRD*, Toulouse.

Legge, K. (1995) *Human Resource Management: Rhetoric and Reality*, London: Macmillan.

Leopold, A. (1966) *A Sand County Almanac*, New York: Ballantine.

Lyotard, J. E. (1984) *The Postmodern Condition*, Manchester: Manchester University Press.

Macfarlane, B. and Lomas, L. (1995) 'Client-based management education: Values and quality', *Management Development Review*, 8(1): 32–6.

Machiavelli, N. (1961) *The Prince*, Harmondsworth: Penguin.

Mackaness, W. and Clarke, I.M. (2001) 'Management intuition: An interpretative account of structure and content using cognitive maps', *Journal of Management Studies*, 38(2): 147–72.

Mangham, I. and Silver, M. (1986) *Management Training: Context and Practice*, ESRC.

Mannheim, K. (1936) *Ideology and Utopia*, London: Routledge and Kegan Paul.

Marsick, V. (1990) 'Action learning and reflection in the workplace', in J. Mezirow (ed) *Fostering Critical Reflection in Adulthood. A Guide to Transformative and Emancipatory Learning*, San Francisco: Jossey Bass.

Marsick, V. and O'Neil, J. (1999) 'The many faces of action learning', *Management Learning*, 30(2): 159–76.

Marsick, V. and Watkins, K. (1990) *Informal and Incidental Learning in the Workplace*, London and New York: Routledge.

Mason, J. (1994) 'Linking qualitative and quantitative data analysis', in Bryman, A. and Burgess, R. G. (eds) *Analysing Qualitative Data*, 89–110, London: Routledge.

Mastenbroek, W. F. G. (1991) 'Organizations as parties in a system: A concept and its practical relevance', *Research in the Sociology of Organizations*, 9: 49–78.

Mastenbroek, W. F. G. (1993) *Conflict Management and Organization Development*, Chichester: John Wiley and Sons.

Mauch, J. E. and Birch, J. W. (1983) *Guide to the Successful Thesis and Dissertation: A Handbook for Students and Faculty*, New York: Marcel Dekker.

McCarthy, A., Garavan, T. and O'Toole, T. (2003) 'HRD: Working at the boundaries and interfaces of organisations', *Journal of European Industrial Training*, 27(2/3/4): 58–72.

McDowell, L. (1997) *Capital Culture: Gender at Work in the City*, Oxford: Blackwell.

McGill, I. and Beaty, L. (1992) *Action Learning: A Practitioner's Guide*, London: Kogan Page.

McGill, I. and Beaty, L. (1996) *Action Learning*, London: Kogan Page.

McGivern, J. and Thompson, J. (2000) 'Teaching management through reflective practice', in Golding, D. and Currie, D. (eds) *Thinking About Management – A Reflective Practice Approach*, London, Boston and Henley: Routledge.

McGoldrick, J., Stewart, J. and Watson, S. (2002) 'Researching HRD: Philosophy, process and practice', in McGoldrick, J. *et al.*, *Understanding HRD: A Research-based Approach*, London: Routledge.

McGuire, D., Donnell, D. and Cross, C. (2005) 'Critically challenging some assumptions in HRD', *International Journal of Training and Development*, 10:1.

McLagan, P. (1989) *Models for HRD Practice*, Alexandria VA: ASTD.

McLaughlin, H. and Thorpe, R. (1993) 'Action learning – a paradigm in emergence: The problems facing a challenge to traditional management education and development', *British Journal of Management*, 4: 19–27.

McLean, G. (1998) 'HRD: A three-legged stool, an octopus or a centipede', *Human Resource Development International*, 1(4): 375–7.

McLean, G. (1999) 'Get out the drill, glue and more legs', *Human Resource Development International*, 2(1): 6–7.

McLean, G. (2001) 'Ethical dilemmas and the many hats of HRD', *Human Resource Development Quarterly*, 12: 219–21.

McNay, L. (1992) *Foucault and Feminism*, Cambridge: Polity Press.

McNay, L. (2000) *Gender and Agency: Reconfiguring the Subject in Feminist and Social Theory*, Cambridge: Polity.

Meldrum, M., and Atkinson, S. (1998) 'Meta-abilities and the implementation of strategy: Knowing what to do is simply not enough', *Journal of Management Development*, 17(8).

Mennell, S. (1992) *Norbert Elias: An Introduction* (first published 1989), Dublin: University College Dublin Press.

Metcalfe, B. (2003a) 'Exiling the feminine? Re-imagining Luce Irigaray in the philosophy of organization', Paper presented in philosophy of organization stream, Critical Management Studies Conference, Lancaster University, July.

Metcalfe, B. (2003b) 'Writing though the body: Autobiography, femininity and organization', Paper presented in Literature stream, Critical Management Studies Conference, Lancaster University, July.

Metcalfe, B. and Rees, C. (2005) 'Theorising advances in international HRD', *Human Resource Development International*, 8(4).

Midgley, M. (1996) *The Ethical Primate: Humans, Freedom and Morality*, London: Routledge.

Miles, B. M. and Huberman, A. M. (1994) *Qualitative Data Analysis : An Expanded Source book*, London: Sage.

Mingers, J. (2000) 'What is it to be critical? Teaching a critical approach to management to management undergraduates', *Management Learning*, 31(2), June, London, Thousand Oaks, New Delhi: Sage.

Mintzberg, H. (1973) *The Nature of Managerial Work*. London: Harper and Row.

Mintzberg, H. (2004) *Managers not MBAs: A Hard Look at the Soft Practice of Managing and Management Development*, San Francisco: Berrett-Koehler Publishers.

Mirza, H. (1997) *Black British Feminism: A Reader*, London: Routledge.

Moore, S. and Patterson, S. (2005) 'HRD as Strategic Partner', Paper Presented at the Academy of Human Resource Development International Research Conference, Colorado, February.

Morgan, G. (1986) *Images of Organization*, London: Sage.

Morgan, G. (1997) *Images of Organizations*, London: Sage.

Morgan, G. and Sturdy, A. (2000) *Beyond Organizational Change Structure, Discourse and Power in UK Financial Services*, Macmillan: Basingstoke.

Mumby, D. K. (1996) 'Feminism, postmodernism, and organization communication studies', *Management Communication Quarterly*, 9(3): 259–96.

Mumby, D.K. (2004). 'Discourse, power and ideology: unpacking the critical approach', in Grant, D., Hardy, C., Oswick, C. and Putnam, L. (eds) *The Handbook of Organizational Discourse*, 237–58, London: Sage.

Mumby, D.K. and Clair, R.P. (1997) 'Organizational discourse', in Van Dijk, T. (ed) *Discourse as Social Interaction, A Multidisciplinary Introduction*, London: Sage.

Mutch, A. (2002) 'Applying the ideas of Bernstein in the context of in-company management education', *Management Learning*, 33(2): 181–96, London: Sage.

Naess, A. (1973) 'The shallow and the deep: Long-range ecology movement', *Inquiry*, 16: 95–100.

Nason, J. (2000) 'Treading treacle at parties and parapets; excursions into management ideology', in Golding, D. and Currie, D. (eds) *Thinking About Management – A Reflective Practice Approach*, London: Routledge.

National Committee of Inquiry into Higher Education (1997) *Higher Education in the Learning Society*, London.

Newton, T. J. (1996) 'Resocialising the subject? A re-reading of Grey's "Career as a project of the self..."', *Sociology*, 30(1): 137–44.

Newton, T. J. (2001) 'Organization: The relevance and The limitations of Elias', *Organization* 8(3): 467–95.

Nord, W. (2005) 'When Henry Mintzberg writes, people react', *Academy of Management Learning and Education*, 4(2): 213–14.

Nord, W. R. and Jermier, J. M. (1992) 'Critical social science for managers? Promising and perverse possibilities', in Alvesson, M. and Wilmott, H. (eds) *Critical Management Studies*, London: Sage.

Obholzer, A. and Roberts, V. Z. (1994) *The Unconscious at Work*, London: Routledge.

O'Donnell, D. and Garavan, T. (1997) 'Viewpoint: Linking training policy and practice to organizational goals', *Journal of European Industrial Training*, 21(9).

O'Donnell, D., Mcguire, D. and Cross, C. (2007, forthcoming) 'Critically challenging some assumptions in HRD', *International Journal of Training and Development*, 10(1).

Oswick, C., Keenoy, T. and Grant, D. (1997) 'Managerial discourses: Words speak louder than actions?', *Journal of Applied Management Studies*, 6(1): 1–8.

Oswick, C., Keenoy, T. and Grant, D. (2000) 'Discourse, organizations and organizing: Concepts, objects and subjects', *Human Relations*, 9: 115–24.

Owenby P. H. (2002) 'Organizational learning communities and the dark side of the learning organization', *New Directions for Adult and Continuing Education*, 95 (Fall): 51–60.

Owen-Pugh, V. A. (2005) 'Complexity and process in communities of practice: An Eliasian critique of learning as social engagement', Leicester: CLMS, University of Leicester, mimeo.

Pálsson, G. (1994) 'Enskilment at sea', *Man (N.S.)*, 29(4): 901–27.

Pedler, M. (1991) *Action Learning in Practice*, 2nd edn, Brookfield, VT: Gower.

Pedler, M. (1992) 'Biography work for organisation learning: strategy or destiny', *Management Education and Development*, 23(3): 258–70.

Perriton, L. (2004) 'A reflection of what exactly?' in M. Reynolds and R.Vince (eds) *Organising Reflection*, Aldershot: Ashgate.

Perriton, L. (2005a) 'Sense and sensibility? A reflection on virtue and "emotional" HRD interventions', in Elliott, C. and Turnbull, S. (eds) *Critical Thinking in Human Resource Development*, London: Routledge.

Perriton, L. (2005b) 'The moral limits of self-development', in Elliott, C. and Turnbull, S., *Critical Thinking in Human Resource Development*, Routledge: London.

Perriton, L. and Reynolds, M. (2004) 'Critical management education: From pedagogy of possibility to pedagogy of refusal?', *Management Learning*, 35(1), London, Thousand Oaks, New Delhi: Sage.

Pettigrew, A. (1979) 'On studying organisational cultures', *Administrative Science Quarterly*, 24: 570–81.

Pfeffer, J. (1994) 'Producing sustainable competitive advantage through the effective management of people', *Academy of Management Executive*, 9(1): 55–69.

Pfeffer, J. and Fong, C.T. (2002) 'The end of business schools? Less success than meets the eye', *Academy of Management, Learning and Education*, 1(1): 78–95.

Phillips, N. and Hardy, C. (2002) *Discourse Analysis: Investigating Processes of Social Construction*, London: Sage.

Pidd, M. (2003) *Tools for Thinking; Modelling in Management Science*, 2nd edn, Chichester: Wiley.

Poell, R. and Wasti, A. (2005) 'Towards further development of HRD as an academic discipline: Comparing HRD Research published in HRD and mainstream Journals', Proceedings of 6th International Conference on HRD Research and Practice Across Europe, Leeds: Leeds Metropolitan University.

Porter, J.L., Muller, H.J. and Rehder, R.R. (1989) The making of managers: An American perspective, *Journal of General Management*, 14(4), 62–76.

Porter, W. and McKibben, L. E. (1988) *Management Education and Development: Drift or Thrust into the 21st Century*, New York: Basic Books.

Post, J. E., Lawrence, A. T. and Weber, J. (2002) *Business and Society: Corporate Strategy, Public Policy, Ethics*, 10th edn, Boston: McGraw-Hill Irwin.

Praechter, C. (2003) 'Masculinities and femininities as communities of practice', *Women's Studies International Forum*, 26(1): 69–77.

Prichard, C., Jones, D. and Stablein, R. (2004) 'Doing research in organizational discourse: the importance of researcher context', in Grant, D., Hardy, C., Oswick, C. and Putnam, L. (eds) *The Handbook of Organizational Discourse*, 213–35, London: Sage.

Prince, C. and Stewart, J. (2000) 'The dynamics of the corporate education market and the role of business schools', *The Journal Management Development*, 19(3): 207–19.

Purcell, J., Kinnie, N., Hutchinson, S., Rayton, B. and Swart, J. (2003) *Understanding the People and Performance Link: Unlocking the Black Box, Research Report*, London: Chartered Institute of Personnel and Development.

Purser, R. (1994) 'Shallow versus deep organizational development and environmental sustainability', *Journal of Organizational Change Management*, 7(4): 223–45.

Purser, R.E., Park, C. and Montuori, A. (1995) 'Limits to anthropocentrism: Toward an ecocentric organization paradigm', *Academy of Management Review*, 20(4): 1053–89.

Raab, N. (1997) 'Becoming an expert in not knowing: Reframing teachers as consultants', *Management Learning*, 28: 161–75.

Rainbird, H. and Munro, A. (2003) 'Workplace learning and the employment relationship in the public sector', *Human Resource Management Journal*, 13(2): 30–44.

Ramazanoğlu, C. and Holland, J. (2002) *Feminist Methodology*, London: Sage.

Reason P. (1997) *Political, Epistemological, Ecological and Spiritual Dimensions of Participation*, Centre for Action Research in Professional Practice, University of Bath.

Reason P. and Rowan J. (eds) (1981) *Human Inquiry: A Sourcebook of New Paradigm Research*, London: John Wiley.

Reed, M. and Anthony, P. (1992) 'Professionalizing management and managing professionalization', *Journal of Management Studies*, 23: 537–53.

Regan, T. (1983) *The Case for Animal Rights*, London: Routledge.

Revans, R. (1971) *Developing Effective Managers*, New York: Appleton Century Crofts.

Reynolds, M. (1998) 'Reflection and critical reflection in management learning', *Management Learning*, 29(2): 183–200.

Reynolds, M. (1999) 'Grasping the nettle: possibilities and pitfalls of a critical management pedagogy', *British Journal of Management*, 9: 171–84.

Reynolds, M. and Trehan, K. (2003) 'Learning from difference,' *Management Learning*, 34(2): 163–80.

Reynolds, M. and Vince, R. (2004) 'Organizing reflection: an introduction' in M. Reynolds and R. Vince (eds) *Organizing Reflection*, Aldershot: Ashgate Publishing.

Rich, A. (2001) *Arts of the Possible*, New York: W. W. Norton.

Richardson, L. (1992) *Writing Strategies: Reaching Diverse Audiences*, Sage: London.

Richardson, L. (2000) *Writing: A Method of Inquiry*, in Denzin, N., and Lincoln, Y., *Handbook of Qualitative Research*, 923–49, London: Sage.

Rifkin, J. (2000) *The Age of Access: The New Culture of Hypercapitalism, Where All of Life is a Paid-for Experience*, New York: Jeremy P. Tarcher/Putnam.

Rigg, C. (2005) 'Becoming critical: Can critical management learning develop critical managers?' in C. Elliott and S. Turnbull (eds) *Critical Thinking in Human Resource Development*, 37–52, London: Routledge.

Rigg, C. and Trehan, K. (1999) 'Not critical enough? Black women raise challenges for critical management learning', *Gender and Education* 11(3): 265–80.

Rigg, C. and Trehan, K. (2003) 'Reflections on working with critical action learning', Paper presented at CMS 3, Lancaster.

Rigg, C. and Trehan, K. (2004) 'Reflections on working with critical action learning', *Action Learning: Research and Practice*, 1(2), September: 151–67.

Rigg, C. Stewart, J. and Trehan, K. (2007) *Critical Human Resource Development: Beyond Orthodoxy*, Harlow: Pearson.

Roberts, J. (1996) 'Management education and the limits of technical rationality', in French, R. and Grey, C. (eds) *Rethinking Management Education*, London, Thousand Oaks, New Delhi: Sage.

Rorty, R. (ed) (1967) *The Linguistic Turn: Recent Essays in Philosophical Method*, Chicago: University of Chicago Press.

Rosenthal, P., Hill S. and Peccei, R. (1996) 'Checking out service: Evaluating excellence, HRM and TQM in retailing', in Mabey, C., Salaman, G. and Storey, J. (eds) *Strategic Human Resource Management, A Reader*, 170–81, London: Sage.

RSA (1996) *For Life*, London: The Royal Society for the Encouragement of Arts, Manufacture and Commerce.

Ruona W. E. A. (2000) 'Should we define the profession of HRD? Views of leading scholars', in K. P. Kuckinke (ed) *AHRD 2000 Conference Proceedings*, 1: 188–95, Raleigh-Durham, NC: AHRD.

Ruona W. E. A. (2002) 'Town forum', Proceedings of the annual AHRD conference, Hawaii, Feb–March.

Ruona, W. E. A. (2005) 'Experiences and social realities of individuals: A philosophical and methodological imperative for a critical and effective HRD profession', in Elliott, C. and Turnbull, S., *Critical Thinking in Human Resource Development*, London: Routledge.

Russ-Eft, D. (2000) 'That old fungible feeling: Defining human resource development', *Advances in Developing Human Resources*, 7: 49–55.

Russ-Eft, D. (2003) 'Corporate ethics: A learning and performance problem for leaders?', *Human Resource Development Quarterly*, 14(1): 1–4.

Russ-Eft, D., and Hatcher, T. (2003) 'The issue of international values and beliefs: The debate for a global HRD code of ethics, *Advances in Developing Human Resources – The Future of HRD*, 5(3): 296–307.

Russel, T. (1988) 'Autoethnography: Journeys of the self', published in *Haussite*, Script section, January 2001. Retrieved from www.haussite.net/site.html

Ryle, G. (1949) *The Concept of Mind*, London: Hutchinson.

Ryle, G. (1954) *Dilemmas*, Cambridge: Cambridge University Press.

Salama, A. (1992) 'The use of an organisation's biography as a research method for investigating organisational development', *Management Education and Development*, 23(3): 225–33.

Sambrook, S. (1998) 'Models and concepts of human resource development: academic and practitioner perspectives', (unpublished) Doctoral thesis, Nottingham Business School, The Nottingham Trent University.

Sambrook, S. (2000) 'Talking of HRD', *Human Resource Development International*, 3(2): 159–78.

Sambrook, S. (2001) 'HRD as emergent and negotiated evolution', *Human Resource Development Quarterly*, 12(2): 169–93.

Sambrook, S. (2002) 'Writing the research story', in McGoldrick, J., Stewart, J. and Watson, S. (eds) *Understanding Human Resource Development*, 226–54, London: Routledge.

Sambrook, S, (2004) 'A "critical" time for HRD?', *Journal of European Industrial Training*, 28(8/9): 611–24, Emerald Literati Awards for Excellence, Outstanding Paper.

Sambrook, S. and Stewart, J. (2002) 'Reflections and discussion', in Tjepkema, S., Stewart, J., Sambrook, S., Mulder, M., Horst, H. and Scheerens, J. (eds) *HRD and Learning Organizations in Europe*, 178–87, London: Routledge.

Sambrook, S. and Stewart, J. (2005) 'A critical review of researching human resource development', in Elliott, C. and Turnbull, S. (eds) *Critical Thinking in Human Resource Management*, 67–84, New York: Routledge.

Schein, E. (1992) *Process Consultation in Action*, vol. 1, Reading, MA: Addison-Wesley.

Schön D. (1987) *Educating the Reflective Practitioner*, San Fransisco: Jossey-Bass.

Schön, D. (1983) *The Reflective Practitioner*, New York: Basic Books.

Schwartz, S. (2002) 'Show them how to learn', The *Guardian*, 29 October.

Senge, P. (1990) *The Fifth Discipline: The Art of Practice of the Learning Organization*, New York: Doubleday.

Sessions, G. (1985) 'Ecological consciousness and paradigm change', in M. Tobias (ed) *Deep Ecology: An Anthology*, 60–91, San Diego: Avant Books.

Shaw, P. (2002) *Changing Conversations in Organizations: A Complexity Approach to Change*, London: Routledge.

Shor, I. (1992) *Empowering Education: Critical Teaching for Social Change*, Chicago: University of Chicago Press.

Short, D. and Callahan, J. (2005) 'Would I work for a global corporation? And other ethical questions for HRD', *Human Resource Development International*, 8: 1.

Short, D. C. and Yorks, L. (2002) 'Analyzing training from an emotions perspective', *Advances in Developing Human Resources*, 4(1): 80–96.

Shotter, J. (1993) *Conversational Realities: Constructing Life Through Language*, London: Sage.

Shotter, J. (1995) 'The manager as practical author: A rhetorical-responsive, social constructionist approach to social-organisational problem', in D. M. Hosking, H.P. Dachler and K.J. Gergen (eds) *Management and Organisation: Relational Alternatives to Individualism*, 125–47, Aldershot: Avesbury.

Shotter, J. and Gergen, K. (eds) (1989) *Texts of Identity*, London: Sage.

Simpson, B. N. (1995) 'A university: An organisation for learning ... but a learning organisation?', Master of Science dissertation, Manchester Metropolitan University.

Simpson, B. N. and Thorpe, R. (1996) 'Are universities learning organisations?', British Academy of Management Conference, Aston Business School.

Simpson, P. and Lenoir, D. (2003) 'Win some, lose some: Women's status in the field of human resources in the 1990s', *Women in Management Review*, 18(4): 191–8.

Sinclair, A. (2005) 'Body and management pedagogy', *Gender, Work and Organization*, 12(1): 89–104.

Singer, P. (1975) *Animal Liberation*, New York: Review Press.

Sisson, K. and Storey, J. (2000) *The Realities of Human Resource Management*, Buckingham: OUP.

Skolimowski, H. (1994) *The Participatory Mind*, London: Penguin.

Slotte, V., Tynjälä, P. and Hytönen, T, (2004) 'How do HRD practitioners describe learning at work?', *Human Resource Development International*, 7(4): 481–99.

Smith, C. (2000) 'Notes from the field: Gender issues in the management curriculum: A survey of student experiences', *Gender Work and Organization*, 7(3): 158–67.

Smith, J., Harré, R. and van Langenhove, L. (eds) (1995) *Rethinking Psychology*, London: Sage.

Snell, R. (2001) 'Moral foundations of the learning organization', *Human Relations*, 54(3): 319–42.

Sorell, T. (1998) 'Beyond the fringe? The strange state of business ethics', in Parker, M. (ed) *Ethics and Organisations*, London: Sage.

Srikantia, P. and Bilimoria, D. (1997) 'Isomorphism in organization and management theory', *Organization and Environment*, 10(4): 384–406.

Stacey R. (1996), *Complexity and Creativity in Organisations*, Sage: London.

Stacey, R. (2001) *Complex Responsive Processes in Organisations: Learning and Knowledge Creation*, London: Routledge.

Stacey, R. (2003) *Strategic Management and Organisational Dynamics: The Challenge of Complexity* (4th edn), Harlow, Essex: Pearson Education.

Stacey, R., Griffin, D. and Shaw, P. (1998) *Speaking of Complexity in Management Theory and Practice*, Complexity and Management Centre, University of Hertfordshire.

Stanley, L. (2000) 'From self-made women to women's made selves? Audit selves, simulation and surveillance in the rise of public woman', in Coslett, T., Lury, C., Summerfield, P. (eds), *Feminism and Autobiography, Texts, Theories and Methods*, London: Routledge.

Stewart, J. (1991) *Managing Change through Training and Development*, London: Kogan Page.

Stewart, J. (1996) *Managing Change Through Training and Development*, 2nd edn, London: Kogan Page.

Stewart, J. (1998) 'Intervention and assessment: The ethics of HRD', *HRD International*, 1(1).

Stewart, J. (1999) *Employee Development Practice*, London: FT Pitman Publishing.

Stewart, J. (2003a) 'The ethics of HRD', in M. Lee (ed) *HRD in a Complex World*, 83–99, London: Routledge.

Stewart, J. (2003b) 'The ethics of PI: A polemical overview', in Hatcher, T. (ed) Special Section on Ethics, *Performance Improvement Quarterly*, 16(2), 90–104.

Stewart, J. (2005) 'The current state and status of HRD research', *The Learning Organization*, 12(1): 90–5.

Stewart, J. and McGoldrick, J. (1996) *HRD: Perspectives, Strategies and Practice*, London: Pitman Publishing.

Stewart, J., McGoldrick, J. and Watson, S. (2002) 'Postscript: The future for HRD research', in Stewart, J., with McGoldrick, J. and Watson, S. (eds) *Understanding Human Resource Development. A Research-based Approach*, London: Routledge.

Steyaert, C. and Bouwen, R.(1994) 'Group methods of organizational analysis' in C. Cannell and G. Symon (eds) *Qualitative Research in Organisations*, 123–46, London: Sage.

Stokvis, R. (2000) 'Globalization, commercialization and individualization: Conflicts and changes in elite athletics', *Culture, Sport and Society*, 3(1): 22–34.

Storey, J. (ed.) (2001) *Human Resource Management: A Critical Text* (2nd edition), Thomson Learning.

Storey, J., Edwards, P. and Sisson, K. (1997) *Managers and their Making*, London: Sage.

Swan, E. (2005) 'On bodies, rhinestones and pleasures: Women teaching managers', *Management Learning*, 36(3): 317–33.

Swann, J., Scarbrough, H. and Robertson, M. (2002) 'The construction of "communities of practice" in the management of innovation', *Management Learning*, 33(4): 477–96.

Swanson, R. A. (1992) 'Human resource development: Performance is key', *Human Resource Development Quarterly*, 6(2): 205–13.

Swanson, R. A. (1995) 'HRD: Performance is the key', *Human Resource Development Quarterly*, 6: 207–13.

Swanson, R. A. (1999a) 'HRD theory, real or imagined?', *Human Resource Development International*, 2(1): 2–5.

Swanson, R. A. (1999b) 'Foundations of performance improvement and implications for practice', in R. J. Torraco (ed) *Performance Improvement Theory and Practice*, 1–25, Baton Rouge, LA: The Academy of Human Resource Development.

Swanson, R. A. (2001) 'Human resource development and its underlying theory', *Human Resource Development International*, 4(3), September, London, Boston and Henley: Routledge.

Swanson, R. A. (2002) 'Theoretical assumptions underlying the performance paradigm of human resource development', *Human Resource Development International*, 5(2): 199–215.

Swanson, R. A. and Holton, E. F. (2001) *Foundations of Human Resource Development*, San Francisco: Berrett-Koehler.

Swart, J., Kinnie, N. and Purcell, J. (2003) *People and Performance in Knowledge-Intensive Firms*, London: Chartered Institute of Personnel and Development.

Taylor, C. (1964) *The Explanation of Behaviour*, London: Routledge and Kegan Paul.

Thomas, A. B. and Anthony, P. D. (1996) 'Can management education be educational?', in French, R. and Grey, C. (eds) *Rethinking Management Education*, London, Thousand Oaks, New Delhi: Sage.

Thomas, P. (2003) 'The recontextualization of management: A discourse-based approach to analysing the development of management thinking', *Journal of Management Studies*, 40(4): 775–801.

Thompson, J. (1984) *Studies in the Theory of Ideology*, Cambridge: Polity Press.

Thompson, P. and McHugh, D. (1995) *Work Organizations: A Critical Introduction*, Basingstoke: Macmillan.

Thomson, A., Mabey, C., Storey, J., Gray, C. and Iles, P. (2001) *Changing Patterns of Management Development*, Oxford: Blackwell.

Thorpe, R. (1992) 'Alternative theory of management education', *Journal of European Industrial Training*, 14(2).

Thorpe, R. and Cornelissen, J. (2003) 'Practical authorship in practice: Visual media and the social construction of meaning', in D. Holman and R. Thorpe (eds) *Management and Language*, London: Sage.

Thorpe, R. and Holman, D. (eds) (2002) *Management and Language*, London: Sage.

Tietze, S. Cohen, L. and Musson, G. (2003) *Understanding Organizations Through Language*, London: Sage.

Torraco (1999) (ed) 'Performance improvement: Theory and practice', *Advances in Developing Human Resources*, 1, Academy of Human Resource Development, San Francisco, CA: Berrett-Kohler.

Toulmin, S. (1958) *The Uses of Argument*, Cambridge University Press.

Townley, B. (1994) *Reframing Human Resource Management, Power Ethics and the Subject at Work*, London: Sage.

Trehan, K. (2004) 'Who is not sleeping with whom? What's not being talked about in HRD?, *Journal of European Industrial Training*, 28(1): 23–38.

Trehan, K. (2005) 'Exploring the relationship between critical HRD and psychodynamic approaches to leadership development', Proceedings of 6th International Conference on HRD Research and Practice Across Europe, Leeds: Leeds Metropolitan University.

Trehan, K. and Rigg, C. (2002) 'Propositions for incorporating a pedagogy of complexity, emotion and power in HRD education', Chapter 14 in Lee, M. (ed) *HRD in a Complex World*, London: Routledge.

Trehan, K. and Rigg, C. (2005) 'Beware the unbottled genie: Unspoken aspects of critical self-reflection', in Elliott, C. and Turnbull, S. (eds) *Critical Thinking in Human Resource Development*, London, New York: Routledge.

Trehan, K., Rigg, C. Stewart, J. (2002) 'A critical turn in HRD'. Call for papers for the Critical Management Studies 3 Conference, www.cms3.org

Trehan, K., Rigg, C. and Stewart, J. (2004) Special issue on Critical Human Resource Development, *Journal of European Industrial Training*, 28(8/9).

Trehan, K., Rigg, C. and Stewart, J. (2006) Special issue on A Critical Turn in HRD, *International Journal of Training and Development*, 10(1), (March).

Trethaway, A. (1999) 'Disciplined bodies: Women's embodied identities at work', *Organisation Studies*, 20(3): 423–50.

Turnbull, S. (2002) Proceedings of the annual AHRD conference, Hawaii, Feb–March.

Turnbull, S. and Elliott, C. (2005) 'Pedagogies of HRD: The socio-political implications', in Elliott, C. and Turnbull, S. (eds) *Critical Thinking in Human Resource Development*, 189–201, London, New York: Routledge.

Tyson, L. D. (2005) 'On managers not MBAs', *Academy of Management Learning and Education*, 4(2), 235–37.

Ulrich, D. (1997) *Human Resource Champions: The Next Agenda for Adding Value and Delivering Results*, Harvard Business School Press.

Ulrich, D. and Beatty, D. (2001) 'From partners to players: Extending the HR playing field', *Human Resource Management*, 40(4): 293–307.

Ulrich, D. and Brockbank, W. (2005) 'Changing roles for HR professionals', *People Management*, 16 June, 24–8.

Usher, R. S., Bryant, I. and Johnson, R. A. (1997) *Adult Education and the Postmodern Challenge: Beyond the Limits*, London: Routledge.

Valentin, C. (2005) 'What's critical about qualitative methodology? An exploration of theory and method in critical HRD research', Proceedings of 6th International Conference on HRD Research and Practice Across Europe.

van Dijk, T. (1998) *Ideology: A Multidisciplinary Approach*, London: Sage.

van Dijk, T. and Teun, A. (eds) (1997) *Discourse as Structure and Process*, Vol. 1, London: Sage.

van Iterson, A., Mastenbroek, W., Newton, T. and Smith, D. (2002) *The Civilized Organization: Norbert Elias and the Future of Organization Studies*, Amsterdam: John Benjamins.

van Vree, W. (1999) *Meetings, Manners and Civilization: The Development of Modern Meeting Behaviour* (translated by Kathleen Bell), London: Leicester University Press.

Vince, R. (1996) 'Experiential management education as the practice of change', in R. French and C. Grey (eds) *Rethinking Management Education*, London: Sage.

Vince, R. (1999) *Managing Change: Reflecting on Equality and Management Learning*, Bristol: Policy Press.

Vince, R. (2001) 'Power and emotion in organizational learning', *Human Relations*, 54(10): 1325–51.

Vince, R. (2003) 'The future practice of HRD', *Human Resource Development International*, 6(4): 559–64.

Vince, R. (2005) 'Ideas for critical practitioners', in C. Elliott and S. Turnbull (eds) *Critical Thinking in Human Resource Development*, 26–36, London, New York: Routledge.

Walton, J. (1999) *Strategic Human Resource Development*, Harlow: Pearson Education Limited.

Walton, J. (2002) 'Town forum', Proceedings of the annual AHRD conference, Hawaii, Feb–March.

Walton. J. (2003) 'How shall a thing be called? An argumentation on the efficacy of the term HRD', *Human Resource Development Review*, 2(3): 310–26.

Wasko, M. M. and Faraj, S. (2000) '"It is what one does": Why people participate and help others in electronic communities of practice', *Journal of Strategic Information Systems*, 9: 155–73.

Watson T. (1994) *In Search of Management: Culture, Chaos and Control in Managerial Work*, London: Routledge.

Watson, T. (1995) 'Rhetoric, discourse and argument in organizational sensemaking: A reflexive tale', *Organization Studies*, 16(5): 805–21.

Watson, T. (1998) 'Ethical codes and moral communities: The Gunlaw temptation, the Simon solution and the David dilemma', in Parker, M. (ed) *Ethics and Organisations*, London: Sage.

Watson, T. (1999) 'Beyond Managism: Negotiated narratives and critical management education in practice', paper presented to the First International Conference on Critical Management Studies, University of Manchester, July 14–16.

Watson T. (2002) *Organising and Managing Work*, Harlow: Pearson Education.

Watson, T. (2004) 'HRM and critical social science analysis', *Journal of Management Studies*, 41(3): 447–67.

Weedon, C. (1999) *Feminism, Theory and the Politics of Difference*, London: Routledge.

Weick, K. E. (1995) *Sensemaking in Organisations*, Thousand Oaks, CA: Sage.

Weil S. (1998) 'From Dearing and systemic control to post Dearing and systemic inquiry: Re-creating universities for beyond the stable state?', *Systems Research*, January 1998.

Weil S. (1999) 'Rhetorics and realities in public service organisations', *Systemic Practice and Action Research*, 11(1).

Weiler, K. (1995) 'Freire and a feminist pedagogy of difference', in J. Holland and M. Blair with S. Sheldan, *Debates and Issues in Feminist Research and Pedagogy*, Milton Keynes: Open University Press.

Weinberger, L.A. (1998) 'Commonly held theories of human resource development', *Human Resource Development International* 1(1).

Weiner, G. (1994) *Feminisms in Education*, Milton Keynes: Open University Press.

Weinstein, K. (1995) *Action Learning: A Journey in Discovery and Development*, London: Harper Collins.

Welch, P. (1994) 'Is a feminist pedagogy possible?', in S. Davies, C. Lubelska and J. Quinn (eds) *Changing the Subject: Women in Higher Education*, London: Taylor and Francis.

Welton, M. R. (1995) 'The critical turn in adult education theory', in Welton, M. R. (ed) *In Defense of the Lifeworld: Critical Perspectives on Adult Learning*, Albany: State University of New York Press.

Wenger, E. (1998) *Communities of Practice: Learning, Meaning and Identity*, Cambridge: Cambridge University Press.

Wenger, E. (2000) 'Communities of practice and social learning systems', *Organization*, 7(2): 225–46.

Wenger, E. and Snyder, W. M. (2000) 'Communities of practice: The organizational frontier', *Harvard Business*.

Wenger, E., McDermott, R. and Snyder, W. M. (2002) *Cultivating Communities of Practice*, Boston: Harvard Business School Press.

Wheatley, M. J. (1992) *Leadership and the New Science*, San Francisco: Berret-Koehler.

Whitehead, S. (1998) 'Disrupted selves: Resistance and identity work in the managerial arena', *Gender and Education*, 10(2): 199–215.

Whitehead, S.M. (2002) *Men and Masculinities*, Oxford: Polity Press.

Whittington, R. (1992) 'Putting Giddens into action: Social systems and managerial agency', *Journal of Management Studies*, 29(6): 693–712.

Wildermeersch, D. and Vandenabeele J. (1998) 'Learning for sustainable development: Examining lifeworld transformation for farmers', in Wildermeersch, D., Finger, M. and Jansen, T. (eds) *Adult Education and Social Responsibility*, New York: Peter Lang.

Willmott, H. (1994) 'Management education. Provocations to a debate', *Management Learning*, 25(1): 105–36.

Willmott, H. (1997) 'Critical management learning', in Burgoyne, J. and Reynolds, M. (eds) *Management Learning: Integrating Perspectives in Theory and Practice*, London, Thousand Oaks, New Delhi: Sage.

Wittgenstein, L. (1953) *Philosophical Investigations*, Oxford: Blackwell.

Wolf, N. (1990), *The Beauty Myth*, London: Chatto and Windus.

Woodall, J. (1996) 'Managing culture change: Can it ever be ethical?', *Personnel Review*, 25, 26–41.

Woodall, J. and Douglas, D. (2000) 'Winning hearts and minds: Ethical issues in human resource development', in Winstanley, D. and Woodall, J. (eds) *Ethical Issues in Contemporary Human Resource Management*, Basingstoke: Macmillan Business.

Woodall, J. and Winstanley, D. (1998) *Management Development: Strategy and Practice*, Oxford: Blackwell.

World Commission on Environment and Development (1987) *Brundtland Report*, Geneva: UN.

Index